Finding the time to appreciate the bounty of our world can be tricky amid the demands of work, family and scrolling our phones.

Happily, E. Foley and B. Coates have curated a book of daily shots of knowledge that will lift your spirits and expand your mind in just a few minutes a day. You can start at any time of the year and in 365 joyfully random, utterly fascinating entries, you'll learn what the Japanese mean by 'kuchisabishii' and how the Victorians communicated through flowers; you'll start to grasp quantum computing and discover the secret history of the bobble hat. There are tales of footballing bees and Viking mice, the beginning of the thesaurus and the end of the library of Alexandria.

Filled with words you didn't know you needed and wisdom you'll never forget, *A Year of Living Curiously* is a brilliant almanac of curious treasure.

A Year of
Living Curiously

also by E. Foley & B. Coates

Homework for Grown-ups
Advanced Homework for Grown-ups
Homework for Grown-ups Quiz Book
Shakespeare for Grown-ups
What Would Boudicca Do?
You Goddess!

A Year of Living Curiously

365 Things Really Worth Knowing

E. Foley & B. Coates

faber

First published in the UK and the USA in 2024
by Faber & Faber Limited
The Bindery, 51 Hatton Garden
London EC1N 8HN

Typeset by Faber & Faber Limited
Printed and bound by CPI Group (UK) Ltd, Croydon, CR0 4YY

A CIP record for this book
is available from the British Library

ISBN 978–0–571–38448–8

Printed and bound in the UK on FSC® certified paper in line with our continuing
commitment to ethical business practices, sustainability and the environment.
For further information see faber.co.uk/environmental-policy

2 4 6 8 10 9 7 5 3 1

Contents

Remember to look up at the stars and
not down at your feet. Try to make sense of what
you see and wonder about what makes
the universe exist. Be curious.

Stephen Hawking

'Curiouser and curiouser!' cried Alice
(she was so much surprised, that for the moment
she quite forgot how to speak good English);
'now I'm opening out like the largest telescope
that ever was!'

Lewis Carroll,
Alice's Adventures in Wonderland

Introduction

We live in the most extraordinary world: we're surrounded by miraculous nature; we're well versed in embracing mind-boggling technology; we have millennia of art, culture and history behind us . . . and yet. Every day it feels harder and harder to cut through the cacophony of noise and appreciate this bounty. Why is it that instead of diving into the wonder around us, most of us lose a frightening number of hours down negative internet wormholes devouring stuff that doesn't matter and doesn't make us feel good? We believe it's time to pause and remind ourselves of what is worth knowing, and *A Year of Living Curiously* will show you the way. A proven antidote to the adverse effects of too much screen time is the tried-and-tested old technology of the book. As two editors, we find there is very little that some time with a good book can't solve, and here we bring you some of the knowledge that has stood out for us over our years of reading and working on all manner of subjects.

Our guiding principle is the belief in the joy of a nip of wonder for every day of the year: in 365 bitesize pieces we will bring you fascinating cultural and historical events that influence our world today, themes of current social concern, mind-blowing scientific and technological facts and some surprising curiosities that might be fun to throw into conversation with your friends or colleagues. Recent studies have demonstrated the beneficial psychological and physical effects of the sensation of being inspired, but finding the time to contemplate the majesty of a lofty mountaintop can be tricky amid the demands of work, commuting, family, taking the cat to the vet and finding PE kit. We've designed this guide to give you a shot of something interesting in two minutes a day; we guarantee you'll end the year feeling that you are intellectually richer, that your horizons have been broadened, and that the journey has put a smile on your face. Our book is a celebration of our world in all its glory – and our hope is that you will come away from it with your spirits lifted and your mind expanded.

For each day of the year we've crafted an entry on a subject worth knowing about. Taking you from the elements that make up your body on 1 January to global New Year's traditions on 31 December, *A Year of Living Curiously* celebrates knowledge for its own sake. Each month has a guiding flavour or atmosphere: January is positive and affirming, February has a thread of romance, March focuses on nature, and so on. Along the way we'll help you discover the thirteenth Olympian goddess, what cryptocurrency actually is, and the secrets of how great white sharks breed. We'll show you the mysteries of antimatter, investigate the origin of the hashtag, marvel at Charles Dickens's talent for character names and introduce you to the vile trials of Renaissance art's most extraordinary woman. Ever wondered what would really happen if you found yourself in a black hole? Or how floriography can explain what someone *really* means when they send you a bunch of irises? Or how the Chinese zodiac system works? Perhaps these aren't the burning questions that have kept you tossing and turning at night, but once you've found out the answers in *A Year of Living Curiously* you will open up to all manner of inquisitiveness. And, as the saying goes, a mind that opens to a new idea never returns to its original size.

E. Foley & B. Coates, 2024

January

1 JANUARY

What Are You Made Of?

Of the ninety-eight naturally occurring elements in the periodic table we have about sixty of them in our bodies, although we are largely made up of the big four: oxygen, carbon, hydrogen and nitrogen. The rest occur in trace amounts. And get this: most of the elements in our bodies were formed in stars over the course of billions of years and multiple star lifetimes. So yes, we really are made of stardust.

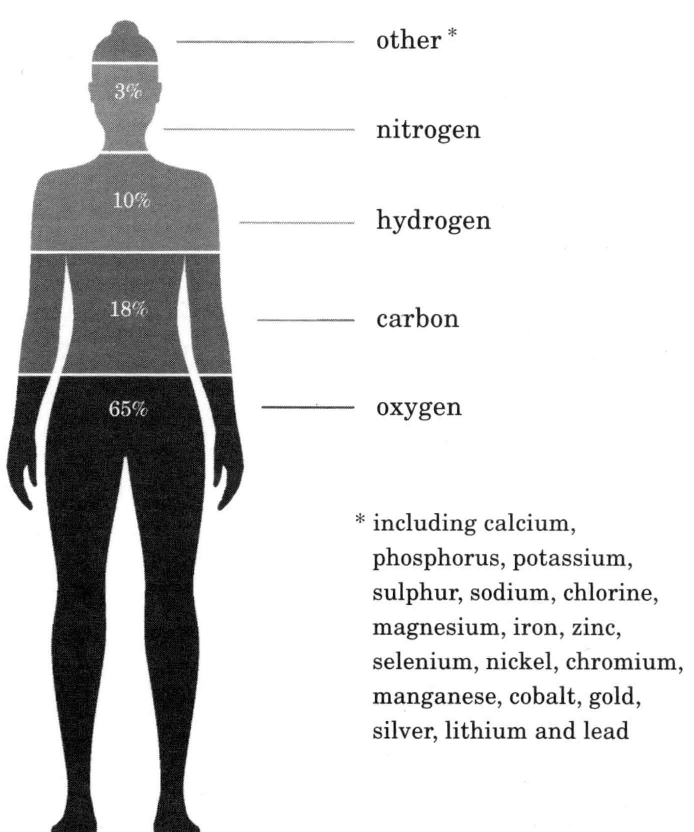

2 JANUARY

Science Faction

Pioneering Russian-American sci-fi writer and professor of biochemistry Isaac Asimov was born in 1919 or 1920 (it's complicated) and celebrated his birthday on 2 January. A true polymath, and proud owner of some exceptional sideburns, Asimov is famous for inventing the term 'robotics' in one of his stories way back in 1941. As well as making for spine-tingling reading, sci-fi is often spookily prescient about technological advances. Here are a few to note.

- In a 1964 essay, Asimov predicted that by the early twenty-first century we'd have video calling, flat-screen TVs, automated coffee machines, self-driving cars, lab-grown meat and disappointing robots. Spot on, Prof A!
- *The World Set Free*, published in 1914 by H. G. Wells, featured an atomic bomb, thirty-one years before the USA detonated the first one. H. G. also predicted automatic sliding doors in 1899.
- *Fahrenheit 451* by Ray Bradbury predicted earbud earphones, which he described as 'little seashells' in a character's ears, in 1953.
- *From the Earth to the Moon* by Jules Verne imagined a spaceship powered by light, like NASA's extraordinary developments around solar sails, way back in 1865.
- *Brave New World* by Aldous Huxley depicted a version of antidepressants in 1932, well before they came on the market in the 1950s.
- *Nineteen Eighty-Four* by George Orwell prophesied the wide- spread use of state-controlled video security cameras in 1949.
- *Snow Crash* by Neal Stephenson described the online 'metaverse' in 1992, envisioning a virtual-reality-based digital world, which characters would explore using avatars.

3 JANUARY

The Anatomy of a Coffee Machine

Legend has it that coffee's origins lie in Ethiopia, where many hundreds of years ago a goatherd named Kaldi noticed that his flock became very peppy after eating the berries from a certain wild plant. Nowadays, billions of us start the day with a caffeine kick – but what's actually going on inside the machine that delivers your daily black nectar?

To make your morning espresso your barista will grind coffee beans then tamp them down into a circular portafilter, which is latched on to the coffee machine. At the press of a button pressurised hot water from the boiler and water reservoir at the back of the machine is pushed through the portafilter, and beautiful smooth espresso drips out into the cup waiting on the drip tray below, with a foamy layer of delicious crema on top. You only get crema on coffee from espresso machines as it's the pressure from the machine that interacts with the carbon dioxide in the grounds to create the dense foam.

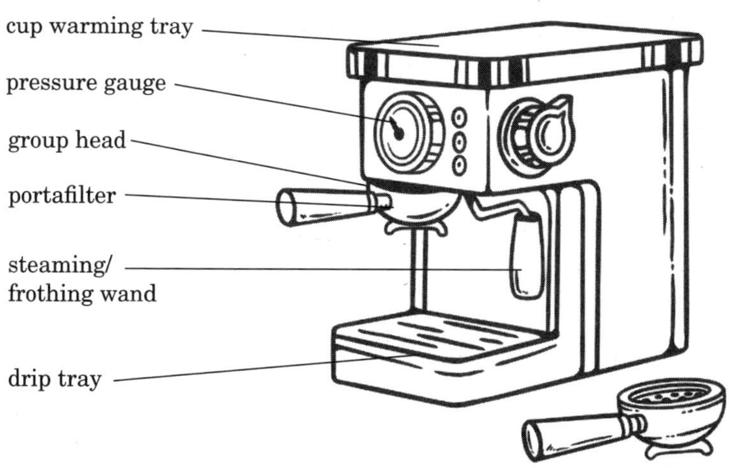

How good your coffee will be depends on the alchemy of the bean quality, their roast, how freshly they've been ground, the acidity and temperature of the water and how much time the grounds are given to infuse. A magical mixture of chemistry and physics produces a delicious cup!

BEANS FOR YOUR BEANS

The 'puck' of used coffee grounds in a portafilter is thrown away after one go, but used grounds make great fertiliser for your garden because they are rich in nitrogen, which plants love.

4 JANUARY

A Visionary Invention

Louis Braille (1809–52) was just three when he lost his sight in an accident whilst playing with his father's tools. He was sent to the Royal Institution for Blind Children in Paris, and it was there that his life changed: he learned to read using a system of writing formed of embossed dots, which had been developed years earlier by a literacy campaigner and former soldier called Charles Barbier.

Fanciful biographers claim that Barbier invented his blueprint of dots punched through paper for Napoleon's army so they could read communications at night without using lamps that might alert the enemy. In fact, Barbier always intended his method to help the blind. In 1824, aged just fifteen, Louis adapted and simplified Barbier's codes for letters and punctuation, and even musical notation, and developed the Braille system we still use today.

EXPAND YOUR VODKABULARY

Japanese braille is called 'tenji', meaning 'dot characters', and it's used on drinks cans so that visually impaired customers can tell whether they are selecting a soft drink or an alcoholic one.

5 JANUARY

The Secret to a Healthy Diet

Eat food. Not too much. Mostly plants.
That, more or less, is the short answer to the supposedly incredibly complicated and confusing question of what we humans should eat in order to be maximally healthy.

Michael Pollan,
In Defense of Food: An Eater's Manifesto

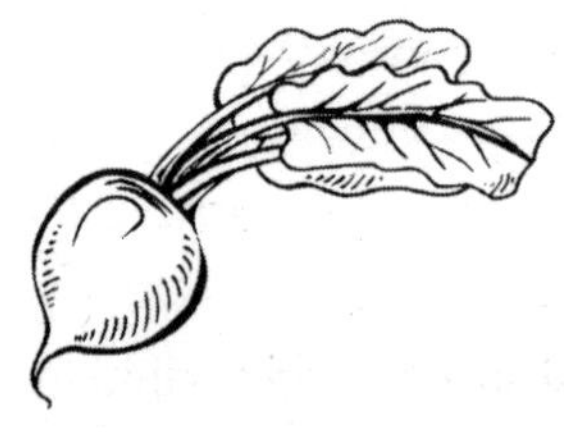

6 JANUARY

Why Are the Himalayas Getting Taller?

Feel like you're standing still, stuck in one place? Rest assured you aren't. The continents on the surface of the earth are constantly moving, albeit very slowly. As far back as the sixteenth century, cartographers noticed that Africa and South America seem to make a neat jigsaw together despite being thousands of miles apart. But it wasn't until 6 January 1912 that German scientist Alfred Wegener first comprehensively outlined the theory of continental drift – and it was only fully accepted outside Europe in the 1960s, long after his death. Alfred's theory said that our continents were once fused together in one land mass he called Urkontinent (now known as Pangaea) before fragmenting and drifting apart 200 million or so years ago. A very special lizard helped prove Alfred right when his research revealed that fossils of the Mesosaurus are only found in southern Africa and South America. As there's no way a weedy freshwater lizard of this type could have made the marathon swim across the Atlantic Ocean, the discovery backed up Alfred's theory that Africa and South America had once been joined.

Underneath the land masses we can see, there are seven massive pieces of the earth's crust that move about on the liquid mantle beneath. These are called the primary tectonic plates, and they are still moving a few centimetres each year. Because of this, the Himalayas grow over a centimetre taller every year as the Indian and Eurasian plates push together; scientists predict that in around 5 million years Africa may split into two continents along the Great Rift Valley, and Africa and Asia will separate when the Red Sea becomes an ocean.

7 JANUARY

The Mysteries of the Bobble Hat

Bobble hats are thought to have a pompom on the top from the days when they were worn by sailors who would often bump their heads on the low ceilings aboard ship. Some people think they originally appeared on woolly hats in the Viking era: a thousand-year-old statuette of the Norse god Freyr depicts him with a pompom on his headgear.

8 JANUARY

Is Everything Getting Worse?

It can sometimes be hard to stay positive, particularly in the dark and cold winter months. But there are reasons to be cheerful if you take the long view:

- 100 years ago child mortality was around 12% in the UK and 28.4% in India. In the OECD's most recent official figures from 2021, this had dropped to 0.4% in the UK and 2.5% in India.
- 100 years ago Our World in Data states that 17% of people lived in democracies but by 2022 measures this had risen to 51%.
- 100 years ago average life expectancy in the UK was around fifty-eight years. In 2023 it was over eighty-one.
- 100 years ago 31% of adults in the world were literate. By 2022 this had climbed to 87%.
- 100 years ago we had no antibiotics, so people frequently died from what we'd consider minor infections today.
- 100 years ago women still couldn't vote in many countries around the world, and they didn't have equal voting rights with men in the UK until 1928.
- 100 years ago there was no telly, internet or mobile phones, and people were expected to wear hats.
- And just ten years ago the percentage of people around the world living in extreme poverty was 12.4%, whereas in 2021 it was judged to be 8%; less of our power was produced by renewable energy sources, the Spix's macaw was heading for extinction, we used more plastic bags for our shopping, the hole in the ozone layer was worse and pandas were endangered and there weren't any otters in the Thames in London.

9 JANUARY

The Only Thing

'The only thing that will redeem mankind is cooperation.'

Bertrand Russell,
Human Society in Ethics and Politics

The largest foodbank network in the UK, the Trussell Trust, was founded in 1997 by Carol and Paddy Henderson, using a legacy left by Carol's mother, Betty Trussell. After Paddy narrowly escaped death in the Clapham Junction rail disaster in 1988, the couple decided to devote themselves to charity, initially working overseas. Their first project was set up to help homeless children who lived in the Central Railway Station in Sofia, Bulgaria. When they returned to the UK their story was picked up by a local paper and, in 2000 a woman from Salisbury called Paddy to explain that children were going hungry on their own doorstep too, and that the choice between heating and eating was a real dilemma for many British families. Paddy started the Salisbury Foodbank from his garden shed, and the model spread rapidly. Today the Trussell Trust has hundreds of foodbanks running more than 1,400 distribution centres with the help of 28,000 trained volunteers. To find your nearest go to www.trusselltrust.org.

10 JANUARY

Pamphlets and Patriots

Today the top five world superpowers are ranked as the USA, China, Russia, Germany and the UK. However, just 300 years ago, the USA wasn't even a country.

After the Italian explorer Christopher Columbus 'discovered' the Americas in 1492, various European nations determined to get their hands on these rich lands, with little consideration for the rights of the existing native population. By the mid-eighteenth century, Britain, France and Spain all ruled areas that make up part of today's USA. (Sweden, the Netherlands and Russia all had a pop at various points too.)

Britain had a substantial colonial presence, stretching from Maine to Georgia, and tensions had started to rise over the discomfort the colonists felt at being ruled and taxed from London without having their own representatives in Parliament. This led to the American Revolutionary War of 1775–83 between the Thirteen Colonies and the British.

In January 1776, the scholar Thomas Paine, who had moved from London to Philadelphia shortly before the war, published *Common Sense*, in which he argued there was a way to thrive without British government authority, adding fuel to the colonists' fire: 'We have it in our power to begin the world over again.' It's estimated that his forty-seven-page pamphlet sold over 120,000 copies in its first few months; it was so influential that he is credited with building support for the colonists' cause, culminating in their Declaration of Independence from the British Crown on 4 July 1776.

11 JANUARY

The Magical Islets of Langerhans

Diabetes was first recorded nearly five thousand years ago, when ancient Egyptian physician Hesy-Ra alluded to an illness that caused sufferers to lose weight rapidly and pee more than usual. The ancient Greek physician Galen later hypothesised that this was a disease of the kidneys, and Avicenna, one of the Islamic Golden Age's most prominent doctors, identified sugar in patients' urine as far back as 1025 CE.

By the 1920s, the link between the pancreas and diabetes had been established, but the only effective treatment was a strict low-carbohydrate, low-sugar diet, and even that only gave patients another year or so of life. Drs Frederick Banting and Charles Best of the University of Toronto moved things forward. Insulin, the hormone produced by the romantically named areas of the pancreas called the Islets of Langerhans, is the key to regulating blood sugar. In 1921 they isolated insulin and successfully treated dogs with it, and by early 1922 they were ready for their first human trial. On 11 January, a thirteen-year-old boy named Leonard Thompson, who was drifting in and out of a diabetic coma and not expected to survive, was injected successfully with insulin. A purer version given a few days later brought his blood sugar levels under control and he lived until the age of twenty-seven. Over 8.5 million people across the world with type 1 diabetes still rely on this treatment today.

12 JANUARY

Hello Sunshine!

See if you can find an opportunity to see the sky today. Even if it's chilly and grey you'll be doing yourself good by popping out for a stroll, a lunch-break wander or just a few deep breaths on your doorstep.

Here are some facts to help boost your enthusiasm for getting outside:

- Exposure to sunlight helps your body's natural circadian rhythm **(see 4 June)** stay in sync, leading to better sleep.
- Even on the cloudiest winter's day it is at least ten times brighter outside than in a typical room indoors.
- Sunlight is used by our bodies to make vitamin D, which keeps our bones healthy and supports the immune system.
- Our natural wake-up time is linked to sunrise: researchers have shown that, despite the fact that all of Germany is in the same time zone, people wake up on average thirty-six minutes earlier in the east of the country compared to the far west. This has been seen in US states on the same time zones too.

13 JANUARY

Cryptocurrency and Climate Change

In ye olden days currency was made up of coins and notes. Coins often had intrinsic value – a gold coin was literally worth its weight in gold and you could exchange it for what you needed because everyone loved gold. Notes usually had representative value – a ten-pound note was an IOU saying the bank would exchange it for gold of the same value, saving you from lugging all that metal around in your handbag. Don't try demanding gold from the cashier now, though: the currency we use today only has value because the government, and all of us, agree it has value. This is known as fiat money, from the Latin 'fiat', meaning 'Let it be done!'

In January 2009 the mysterious Satoshi Nakamoto launched Bitcoin, the world's most famous cryptocurrency. Cryptocurrency is different because it only exists digitally: instead of being kept safe in your jeans or a bank vault, it's secured using unbelievably complex cryptography or codes. New units of cryptocurrency are created by 'mining', which involves solving the kind of maths problems that would drive mere mortals to ruin. You'd think a purely online currency that doesn't involve digging minerals out of the earth would be more environmentally friendly, but sadly it's not that simple. Crypto-mining can only be done with highly sophisticated computers that use a lot of electricity. Estimates show that the annual power used by computers on the Bitcoin network is similar to the electricity consumption of Belgium or the Netherlands.

14 JANUARY

Whither the Wildebeest?

The annual great migration of the wildebeest of Tanzania and Kenya is a wonder of the natural world. Visible from space, it involves hundreds of thousands of wildebeest and other grazing animals including zebra, gazelle and other antelope. (Wildebeest, also known as gnus, are a kind of antelope.) The animals travel over 800 kilometres as they move to the best sources of food and water as the year unfolds, crossing the Masai Mara plains in Kenya, heading south into Tanzania's Serengeti and the edge of the Ngorongoro Crater, before circling up and around in a clockwise direction. But how do they know where to go?

Scientists researching the wildebeest believe that it's possible they find their way to rich pastures using the scent of rain. Others point to the 'swarm intelligence' shown by fish, birds and insects like bees and ants, who solve problems using a 'hive mind' system of decision-making that means they can move as a unit without constant confusion. AI developers are looking into how technology could be used to mimic this effect in human mass decision-making, which would make organising group holidays and work away-days a lot easier.

GOOD GNUS

In the 1960s there were about 200,000 wildebeest in the Serengeti, and thanks to conservation efforts there are now around 1.5 million. They are a crucial part of the rich ecosystem of the area.

15 JANUARY

Control Yourself

ascesis: extreme self-discipline.

'Veganuary and Dry January combined can make the start of the year an ascetic month.'

Ascetism is often practised as part of religious ritual. It focuses on avoiding the attractive distractions of sensory pleasure in order to concentrate on higher ideals. The Greek origin word 'askeo' means 'to train', and the idea of rigorous training and self-denial has been seen since ancient times to help with both physical fitness and mental and spiritual prowess.

16 JANUARY

The Voice that Changed a Nation

Civil rights leader Martin Luther King, who won the Nobel Peace Prize in 1964 for his endeavours to bring an end to racial segregation in the USA, was a legendary orator. MLK came from Baptist lineage – his father and his grandfather were both in the ministry, so he had strong examples of how to use his rich, emotionally intense voice to deliver game-changing speeches. His 'I Have a Dream' speech of 1963 is one of the most famous in the world.

Here are five of MLK's most powerful quotes:

'The time is always right to do what is right.'

'Darkness cannot drive out darkness; only light can do that. Hate cannot drive out hate; only love can do that.'

'Out of the mountain of despair, a stone of hope.'

'I have decided to stick with love. Hate is too great a burden to bear.'

'A man dies when he refuses to stand up for that which is right. A man dies when he refuses to stand up for justice. A man dies when he refuses to take a stand for that which is true.'

17 JANUARY

The Floating World

Elegant ladies pick their way through a wintry scene in this beautiful 1834 image, known as *The Gion Shrine in Snow*, by Utagawa Hiroshige. He was a master of the ukiyo-e style, which means 'pictures of the floating world'. The idea of floating had its origin in the Buddhist sense of life being transitory and fleeting, but over time came to be associated with the more buoyant hedonism and joie de vivre of the theatre and brothel neighbourhoods that sprang up all over Japan's largest cities during the Edo period (1603–1868). Incredibly stylish working women and Kabuki actors, previously relegated to lowly echelons of society, were celebrated in these hugely popular woodcuts, which could be reproduced in their inexpensive thousands, so for the first time in Japan the appetites of the general public were reflected in the world of art. Eat your heart out, *Hello!* magazine.

18 JANUARY

The Inconstant Moon

O, swear not by the moon, the inconstant moon,
That monthly changes in her circled orb,
Lest that thy love prove likewise variable.

William Shakespeare, *Romeo and Juliet*

As the earth and moon dance around the sun, so different parts of the moon's face are visible to us down below. This is not, as is popularly believed, because of the shadow of the earth moving across the moon's face but because the sun only lights up parts of the moon at different points in its orbit. When the earth casts its shadow over the moon we get the more dramatic lunar eclipse.

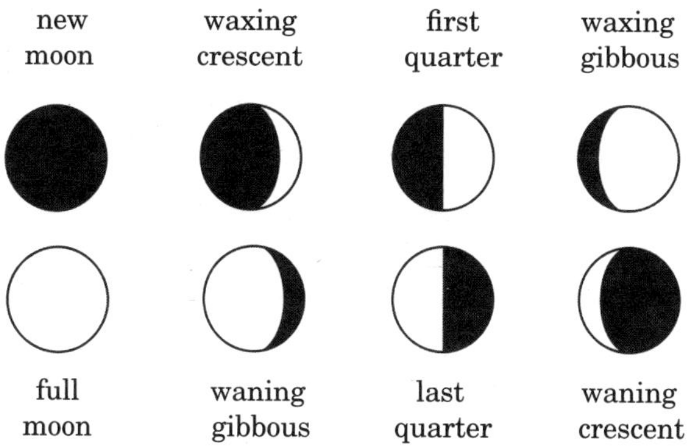

new moon — waxing crescent — first quarter — waxing gibbous

full moon — waning gibbous — last quarter — waning crescent

GOODBYE MOON

The moon is moving approximately 3.8cm away from us every year.

19 JANUARY

The Beginning

'The beginning is always today.'

Attributed to **Mary Shelley** (1797–1851), novelist and short story writer

Mary Shelley's mother was the pioneering feminist writer Mary Wollstonecraft, who died just after Mary was born. She was just eighteen when she had the idea for her famous novel *Frankenstein* on a stormy night in the Swiss Alps when Lord Byron challenged Mary and her husband, Percy Bysshe Shelley, to a ghost-story-telling competition. In 1826 she also published the first English dystopian novel, *The Last Man*, which centres on the sole survivor of a twenty-first-century pandemic.

20 JANUARY

The Singularity of Snowflakes

It takes a person with a heart of ice not to feel a thrill when snowflakes first begin to tumble from the sky. Snowflakes are formed when a droplet of water freezes around dust or pollen particles in the air to create an ice crystal that falls to the ground, gathering more water particles as it descends. Water always freezes as a hexagonal crystal but no two snowflakes can ever be the same because different atmospheric factors create infinitely various shapes as each flake descends to the earth in its own unique way. An international classification system shows that, broadly, snowflakes come in ninety separate shapes, from the extraordinary needle-shaped formation to the classic six-armed star.

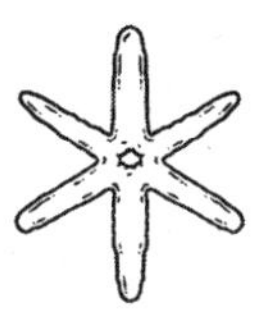

Simple Stars

Crossed Needles

Fernlike Stellar Dendrites

Stellar Dendrites

Sectored Plates

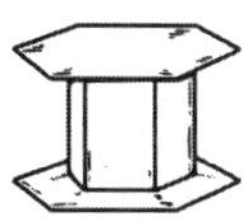

Capped Columns

Bullet Rosettes

Stellar Plates

21 JANUARY

Burst Your Bubble

Confirmation bias is the tendency we all have to seek out information that supports our views. It takes critical thinking to overcome this natural inclination and help us on the way to objectivity. Highly educated people are more prone to confirmation bias because they are good at finding back-up arguments. Here are a few methods for counteracting it and boosting your variety of outside influences, which can also enhance creativity and empathy:

- Actively look for evidence that challenges your point of view. Look at a wide variety of reputable news sources on the opposite side of the political spectrum, listen to people from different backgrounds, watch and read media you wouldn't usually be drawn to – but always make sure you are judging the factual accuracy of what you hear and see. Seen something in the media and want to check it's accurate? Visit the brilliant Full Fact website. Is the news making you sure things are terrible and only getting worse? Counteract that conviction by visiting the excellent Positive News website.
- Try new activities that take you out of your comfort zone, which in turn will bring you into contact with different people and broaden your knowledge and horizons.
- Hold on to the principle that everyone makes mistakes. You are not infallible and neither is anyone else. It's the room for error that makes life interesting.

22 JANUARY

The Great Race

Based on the lunar calendar, the Chinese zodiac involves a twelve-year cycle of animal forms, which are thought to influence the attributes of people born under each sign. The zodiac has a wonderful origin story. Legend has it that the Jade Emperor – the ruler of heaven – invited a host of animals to compete in a race to cross a river. Present and correct at the starting line were: a pig, a dog, a rooster, a monkey, a goat, a horse, a snake, a dragon, a rabbit, a tiger, an ox and a rat.

Rat and Ox went first, with wily Rat persuading the kindly Ox to let him hitch a lift in his ear, then dashing ahead. Next was valiant Tiger, who swam strongly despite being buffeted by currents, and timid Rabbit, who was flagging until he found a log to float across on. Rabbit was also secretly aided by magisterial Dragon, who, despite his ferocious persona, was in fact truly helpful – stopping halfway to help some villagers put out a fire, and giving Rabbit a little puff of air to push his log along. Horse and Snake were up next, with the sly Snake slithering round Horse's leg as they crossed the water, and then giving Horse a fright on the bank so he could grab sixth place. Goat, Monkey and Rooster built a raft and arrived together, impressing the Emperor with their team mindset. Dog and Pig were last: Dog kept getting distracted, and Pig stopped for a meal and a post-prandial lie-down. The story goes that Cat was supposed to be in the starting line-up too, but Rat had 'forgotten' to wake Cat up on the morning of the race.

23 JANUARY

What Is Happiness?

Well done. By now you'll have passed Blue Monday, the third Monday in January, which is commonly believed to be the most miserable day of the year. But what are the ingredients for avoiding sadness? Researchers at the Office for National Statistics say it's less meaningful to search for happiness, as that can be a short-lived response to specific circumstances, when what people really want is quality of life or 'well-being'.

The ONS defines well-being as a combination of our feelings about ten separate areas of our lives: personal well-being; relationships; health; what we do (including metrics such as the unemployment rate and how much we exercise, enjoy cultural activities or volunteer); where we live; personal finance; the economy; education and skills; governance; and environment. This is a useful framework for considering which areas of your life are being neglected and which are flourishing.

One of the keys to well-being is to spend less time worrying about 'pursuing' it and instead trying to live in the present, with integrity, counting your blessings.

WHO INVENTED BLUE MONDAY?

In 2005, psychologist Dr Cliff Arnall was asked by a TV company to create a formula to work out which day of the year people find most depressing. He came up with:

$$[W+(D-d)]\times TQ/M\times NA$$

W is weather, D is debt, d monthly salary, T time since Christmas, Q time since failure of New Year's resolutions, M low motivational level and NA the need to take action.

24 JANUARY

Do You Have Kuchisabishii?

口寂しい

At this time of year we often crave comfort food – pies and mash, hot chocolate, buttered crumpets – but do you also find that you just want to mindlessly graze more? That you're craving more food even after meals? If so you could have what the Japanese call 'kuchisabishii', or 'lonely mouth'. It refers to the feeling of wanting to eat out of boredom or for comfort, rather than to satisfy hunger. Ex-smokers also get it when they miss the feeling of a cigarette in their mouth. Kuchisabishii can often be a symptom of a deeper feeling of disconnection and longing, so the next time you feel a bit lonely, try picking up the phone to a friend instead of raiding the fridge.

25 JANUARY

Fabby Rabbie Burns

First held in 1801, five years after Scotland's greatest bard died, Burns Night is when Scots across the world come together to celebrate his life with music, song, food and drink. The running order can vary, but haggis is always eaten with neeps and tatties (mashed swede or turnips and potato), the Selkirk Grace is said before the meal and 'the great chieftain o' the pudding race', the haggis, is of course given its own salute. The Scottish diaspora will go to any lengths to get their sheep-offal delicacy. When, in 1989, the US banned imports of haggis due to the BSE ('mad cow') crisis, Americans attempted to make their own beef version, with dispiriting results. A brisk trade in illegal haggis sprung up at the Canadian border, until the ban was lifted in 2010 to the salivating delight of haggis enthusiasts.

THE SELKIRK GRACE

Some hae meat and canna eat
And some wad eat that want it:
But we hae meat and we can eat,
And sae the Lord be thankit.

26 JANUARY

Five Australian Icons

Australia Day is a public holiday that was originally set up to celebrate the settlement of the first European colony at Sydney Cove in 1788. Given the ensuing appropriation of land and centuries of oppression that the British brought to the Indigenous Australian population, it is also known by some as Invasion Day or Survival Day.

Here are five Aboriginal Australian icons
to celebrate instead:

FANNY COCHRANE SMITH (1834–1905)

RECORDING ARTIST

Fanny was recognised as the last Aboriginal Australian solely of Tasmanian descent, and was the first to be recorded: the phonographs of her songs kept her language from extinction; you can find her songs – full of defiance and joy – on the internet.

DAVID UNAIPON (1872–1967)

INVENTOR

Known as the Australian Leonardo da Vinci, Unaipon invented the modern mechanical sheep-shearer, and made early drawings for a helicopter design inspired by the shape of a boomerang.

PEARL GIBBS (1901–83)

ACTIVIST

Gibbs worked tirelessly to get the government to recognise Aboriginal people as citizens with the right to cast a vote. It was not until 1984 that Aboriginal Australians gained full and equal rights and obligations for all elections.

NEVILLE BONNER (1922–99)

POLITICIAN

Bonner was the first Indigenous member of Australia's Parliament, advocating for Aboriginal rights. He also set up a boomerang manufacturing business, snappily named Bonnerang.

BRONWYN BANCROFT (1958–PRESENT)

FASHION DESIGNER, ACTIVIST AND ARTIST

Bancroft was among the first Australians to take a show to Paris Fashion Week. A champion of Indigenous art, she has also illustrated over thirty children's books.

DEEP ROOTS DOWN UNDER

The Australian Aboriginal peoples have one of the oldest continuous cultures on earth: there is evidence that humans were living in Australia 65,000 years ago.

27 JANUARY

Let There Be Light!

On this day in 1880, American inventor Thomas Edison was granted the patent for his electric light bulb, the first suitable for use in ordinary people's homes. It was a game-changing moment for human civilisation, though its invention can't be credited to Edison alone; a series of pioneering inventors came before him.

Traditional incandescent light bulbs work on a straightforward technical principle: a current of electricity is run through a filament in a vacuum (created inside the bulb), which heats up and emits light. However, the physics behind what happens when you flick a light switch is mind-bogglingly complex, involving quantum mechanics, photon theory and black body spectrums. Even Einstein struggled to articulate it. So here instead are some fun light bulb facts:

- The human brain runs on about a fifth of the wattage of an average traditional light bulb.
- There are 10,000,000,000,000,000,000,000 atoms of tungsten in the average light bulb.
- There is a light bulb in a California fire station which has been burning since 1901.
- Brazilian football legend Pelé was named Edson (his parents dropping the 'i') because electricity had just arrived in his hometown when he was born.
- Electric Avenue in Brixton was so named because it was the first market street to be lit by incandescent bulbs.
- Only about 5% of the energy emitted from an incandescent bulb turns into light; the rest dissipates as heat.

28 JANUARY

Would Mr Darcy Make a Good Life Partner?

Pride and Prejudice by Jane Austen was first published on this day in the UK in 1813. Its readers immediately fell for the bumpy love story of Elizabeth Bennet and Mr Fitzwilliam Darcy, and for over two centuries the book has been finding and seducing new audiences; it still sells hundreds of thousands of copies a year.

Would Mr Darcy really make a good life partner?

CONS

- He's a terrible communicator who takes thirty-four chapters to confess his feelings for Elizabeth – feelings which have made him unspeakably cross.
- He is judgemental and rude. His words when he first lays eyes on his future wife are: 'She is tolerable; but not handsome enough to tempt me.'
- He is rich.

PROS

- He is rich.
- But Mr Darcy believes in ethics, not economics.
- He (eventually) tries to help Elizabeth's family, encouraging a good marriage for one, and forcing another's fiancé to stand by his promises.
- On balance, the key to Darcy's attractiveness lies in his ability to change and transform. The emotional trajectory Austen sends him on allows him to get over his pride and his prejudice and find lasting love.

29 JANUARY

Our Ice Age

There have been at least five major ice ages in world history, some lasting for tens of millions of years. During the last ice age in the British Isles, the whole of Ireland and Scotland, most of Wales and the north of England were covered in a 1-kilometre-thick sheet of ice. We are technically still in the middle of an ice age that began 2.6 million years ago, but since about eleven thousand years ago we've been in a warmer 'inter-glacial' stage.

30 JANUARY

Winter Rainbow

Thou Winter, thou art keen, intensely keen;
Thy cutting frowns experience bids me know,
For in thy weather days and days I've been,
As grinning north-winds horribly did blow,
And pepper'd round my head their hail and snow:
Throughout thy reign 'tis mine each year to prove thee;
And, spite of every storm I've beetled in,
With all thy insults, Winter, I do love thee,
Thou half enchantress, like to pictur'd Sin!
Though many frowns thy sparing smiles deform,
Yet when thy sunbeam shrinketh from its shroud,
And thy bright rainbow gilds the purple storm,
I look entranced on thy painted cloud:
And what wild eye with nature's beauties charm'd,
That hang enraptur'd o'er each 'witching spell,
Can see thee, Winter, then, and not be warm'd
To breathe thy praise, and say, 'I love thee well!'

John Clare (1793–1864)

HOW TO READ A POEM

Many people feel poetry is an exclusive or difficult art, meant for discussion amongst pretentious people in black polo necks, but it's actually one of the oldest forms of human expression and in many places back in history was publicly recited. Here are some tips for getting the most out of poems you encounter.

Keep an open mind; poetry takes many different forms, from telling stories, to expressing a mood or an emotion, to making political statements.

Poems can be like puzzles but you don't need to 'solve' them to enjoy them.

Pay attention to the vocabulary. As a generally short form, each word is very carefully selected by the poet to give the effect they want.

Read poems through twice. Often reading a poem out loud will also help with appreciation of the rhythm and meaning.

31 JANUARY

How to Tell Your Sumerians from Your Akkadians

Marvellous Mesopotamia has been the site of numerous crucial steps forward in history – it's believed to have been the place where the wheel was first invented, along with multiplication tables, writing, irrigation, the sail, the twenty-four-hour day and beer. But who were these clever people?

'Mesopotamia' means 'between the rivers' and refers to the fertile land between the Tigris and the Euphrates, now Iraq and parts of Syria, Iran, Kuwait and Turkey, which has been inhabited since 10,000 BCE. The first literate inhabitants of Mesopotamia were the Sumerians, who rose in the sixth millennium BCE and dominated the region with their city-states – they invented our system of time and schools before disappearing from history until they were rediscovered by eighteenth-century archaeologists.

The Akkadian Empire rose in the twenty-fourth century BCE and lasted until the twenty-second century BCE and was more unified than Sumer, starting with the rule of Sargon the Great. The Akkadians invented the postal system, the use of clay tablets and envelopes. So next time you pop a birthday card in the post, remember to thank the Sumerians for the gift of writing and the later Akkadians for their envelopes (happily no longer made of clay).

February

1 FEBRUARY

Sonnet 29

When, in disgrace with fortune and men's eyes,
I all alone beweep my outcast state,
And trouble deaf heaven with my bootless cries,
And look upon myself and curse my fate,
Wishing me like to one more rich in hope,
Featured like him, like him with friends possessed,
Desiring this man's art and that man's scope,
With what I most enjoy contented least;
Yet in these thoughts myself almost despising,
Haply I think on thee, and then my state,
(Like to the lark at break of day arising
From sullen earth) sings hymns at heaven's gate;
For thy sweet love remembered such wealth brings
That then I scorn to change my state with kings.

William Shakespeare (1564–1616)

As in many of Shakespeare's poems, the final rhyming couplet provides a shift in perspective, or volta (Italian for 'turn'). This romantic sonnet, and many others in Shakespeare's collection of 154, is addressed to an unknown 'fair youth' thought by many scholars to be either Henry Wriothesley, Earl of Southampton, or William Herbert, Earl of Pembroke: the collection is dedicated to 'Mr W. H.' Twenty-eight of the other sonnets are addressed to a 'dark lady' whose identity is equally mysterious.

2 FEBRUARY

All that Glitters

What is so special about gold? You can't eat it, it is too soft to be used to make tools, and it's not as rare as platinum, which is also pretty. Yet across millennia, cultures and continents, gold's warmth, brightness and colour has enthralled human beings. Think of the spectacular glowing masks of Agamemnon, Tutankhamun and Sanxingdui, the legendary Aztec cities of gold, the Hoen Farm Viking hoard, the Golden Rhino of Mapungubwe, the King of Na gold seal from Japan . . .

Gold is valuable because we have all agreed it's valuable. And there are good reasons why: it is very easily workable into different shapes and stampable for coinage, it doesn't corrode, it's rare enough to be scarce but common enough to be used worldwide. It is thought that there's enough gold in the earth's core to cover the whole surface of our planet with a 45-centimetre layer. So far, 30% of the world's discovered gold has come from the Witwatersrand Basin of South Africa.

For centuries, ancient chemists tried to create gold out of base metals using alchemy, looking for the elusive 'philosopher's stone', a substance that could transform things into gold, and by some accounts also grant eternal life. Modern alchemy is possible, although not by chemical means. You need a particle accelerator to create gold and it costs infinitely more to use one than the value of the microscopic amounts of gold produced.

3 FEBRUARY

Say Thank You

'The happy phrasing of a compliment is one of the rarest of human gifts, and the happy delivery of it another.'

Mark Twain (1835–1910)

Research has shown that we overestimate how awkward people will feel if we compliment them and underestimate what a positive difference it will make to their day. Because many people naturally seem to take criticism to heart more easily than praise, praise has to work harder to have an effect: both business psychologists and relationship experts encourage people to give out five positive pieces of feedback for every one negative in order to keep bonds and motivation high.

Saying a heartfelt thanks or telling someone what you appreciate about them not only creates a warm glow for the recipient: studies show that demonstrating gratitude improves your own mental and physical health too.

4 FEBRUARY
Beam Me Up

Wouldn't it be great to be able to travel anywhere in the world almost instantly? Sci-fi tales have often used a teleportation device to allow this to happen, generally to avoid having to describe boringly lengthy journeys through space. Sadly, scientists are sceptical that humans could ever really experience this without being destroyed and then rebuilt as a new entity in our desired location, which feels like too much of a risk in almost every scenario we can think of.

However, steps have been made on a more microscopic level. In 2016, Chinese scientists transferred the properties of a photon – a light particle – from earth to a satellite 300 miles away. They used a process called 'quantum entanglement', whereby two identical particles are created and share the same quantum state, which means that a change to one of them by another particle also affects the other in the same way, however far apart they are. The scientists used this to teleport the state of one electron to the other.

This doesn't mean we're any closer to beaming ourselves across the universe but it's an exciting step towards a super-speedy and secure quantum internet, which would allow unprecedented levels of complex research and communication to take place at great speed, bringing potentially great innovations in many different fields.

5 FEBRUARY

How Many Stars and Stripes?

The original US flag, established in 1777, had thirteen stars (in varying layouts) and thirteen stripes, representing the Thirteen Colonies (New Hampshire, Massachusetts, Connecticut, Rhode Island, New York, New Jersey, Pennsylvania, Delaware, Maryland, Virginia, North Carolina, South Carolina and Georgia) who declared independence from Britain. As more states joined over time the number of stars went up to fifty to match, but today's flag still has thirteen stripes. The original flag is sometimes referred to as the Betsy Ross Flag after the seamstress said to have sewn the first official flag – although historians consider this an unfounded legend.

6 FEBRUARY

Throwing Shapes

That stalwart staple of the hurried evening meal, pasta, is thought to have first come to Italy via Sicily thanks to the ninth-century Arab settlement there, but it only became a common food in the 1700s. Nowadays we have access to hundreds of types of pasta. Different consistencies of sauce work best with certain shapes – for example, creamy sauces are best with smooth shapes, ridged ones hold thinner sauces better and smaller pasta shapes work well in soups.

Rigatoni means 'ridged'

Orecchiette means 'little ears'

Farfalle means 'butterflies'

Ditalini means 'small thimbles'

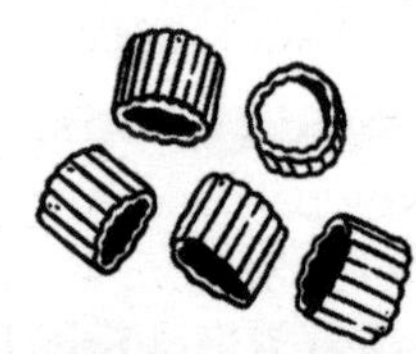

Campanelle means 'little bell flowers'

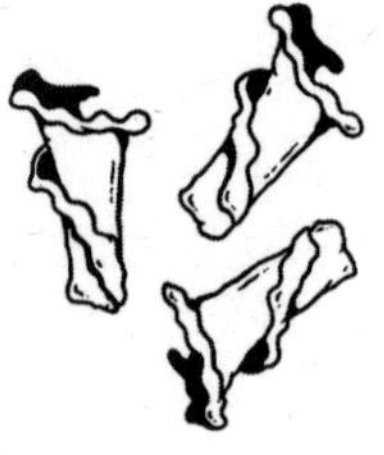

Mafaldine means 'little Mafalda', named in honour of the birth of Princess Mafalda of Savoy in 1902

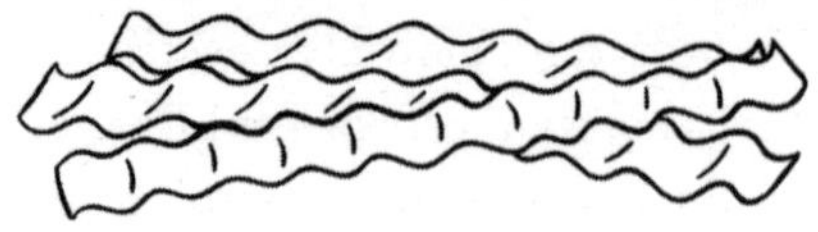

7 FEBRUARY

What the Dickens!

Charles Dickens was born on 7 February 1812. Despite his impoverished childhood he became a voracious reader and grew up to become one of the most popular English novelists of all time. Works such as *Great Expectations*, *David Copperfield*, *A Christmas Carol* and *Oliver Twist* are still taught in schools and repeatedly made into TV shows and films. Trademarks of his work include: satirical humour, concern for the conditions of working people, sentimentality, energetic language and wicked caricature. He is particularly known for his vivid and suggestive character names. Here are a few of our favourites:

- **Uriah Heep** – The creepy and obsequious Uriah is a fraudulent law clerk whom the hero David Copperfield exposes.
- **Thomas Gradgrind** – How much fun do you think a school run by someone called Gradgrind would be? Not very, is the answer in *Hard Times*.
- **Wackford Squeers** – An even less fun teacher than Mr Gradgrind, Squeers gets into a fight with Nicholas Nickleby after Nicholas discovers he's been mistreating his pupils.
- **Reverend Melchisedech Howler** – A minister 'of the Ranting persuasion' who unsuccessfully predicts the end of the world in *Dombey and Son*.
- **Pleasant Riderhood** – In *Our Mutual Friend*, Pleasant is the pleasant daughter of Rogue Riderhood (who is not so pleasant) and the eventual wife of Mr Venus the taxidermist. Of course.
- **Lord Lancaster Stiltstalking** – A diplomat in *Little Dorrit*, memorably described as 'This noble Refrigerator [who] had iced several European courts in his time, and had done it with such complete success that the very name of Englishman yet struck cold to the stomachs of foreigners.'

8 FEBRUARY

Brass Neck

As a legacy of colonisation, a truly shocking 90% of Africa's historical cultural treasures are held in collections and museums outside of Africa. One of the most famous examples is the collection of the Benin Bronzes, which comprise over three thousand sculptures and ornaments created in the ancient Nigerian kingdom between the fourteenth and nineteenth centuries. They were made of brass, bronze, wood and ivory by the master artisans of the Edo people and displayed in the royal palace of the King, the Oba. These extraordinary works have great cultural, artistic and commercial value: a piece that came up for auction recently sold for £10 million. They are currently split between 161 different museums around the world, with the British Museum holding over 900.

The Bronzes were seized from the Oba's palace in 1897 by British soldiers after a dispute between the British colonial Niger Coast Protectorate and the Oba of the time. The troops set fire to the buildings and annexed the entire kingdom into their colony. Eerie photographs exist of them sitting amongst piles of ivory and the sculptures they had chiselled off the walls of the palace. The British government took some of these as compensation for the cost of the military expedition and donated them to the British Museum, and others were looted by the soldiers and sold on privately.

A new museum, the Edo Museum of West African Art, is being built in Benin City near the restored Oba's palace, ready to receive the Bronzes, in the hope that they will eventually be returned to their homeland.

9 FEBRUARY

Teach an Old Dog New Tricks

The 1523 farming manual *The Book of Husbandry* contains an instruction for shepherds about how to train their sheepdogs: 'He must teach his dog to bark when he would have him, to run when he would have him, and to leave running when he would have him; or else he is not a cunning shepherd. The dog must learn it, when he is a whelp, or else it will not be: for it is hard to make an old dog to stoop [find a scent].' This is thought to be the first printed example of what became the phrase 'You can't teach an old dog new tricks'. However, modern experiments have shown that, though it may take longer, you can actually teach your more senior doggo pals new habits if you put your mind to it.

10 FEBRUARY
Under the Lid

What we call a piano or pianoforte was most likely invented by Bartolomeo Cristofori in the first decade of the 1700s in Florence. He developed it from the harpsichord, adding the capability to play the keys at different volumes – 'piano' is Italian for 'soft' and 'forte' means 'loud' – by changing the method of playing from plucking the strings to striking them with hammers. Before late-eighteenth-century innovations, this expensive instrument was usually called a 'fortepiano'.

Bach famously played an early example made by an instrument-maker called Silbermann. According to one of his contemporaries, he apparently praised its tone but 'complained that it was too weak in the high register and too hard to play. This was taken greatly amiss by Mr Silbermann, who . . . was therefore angry at Mr Bach for a long time.' Luckily for us others felt differently and the old joanna has gone on to become one of the most beloved instruments in the world.

11 FEBRUARY

Fecund February

February often gives us a 'fool's spring', where the weather improves briefly as the days get lighter only to be followed by another stretch of cold. However, there is brightness to be found, not least in the flowers and vegetables that come into their own.

Irises, violets and primroses are traditionally linked to February but aconites, snowdrops and crocuses are some of the earliest spring flowers in the northern hemisphere, along with cyclamens, daffodils and hellebores, and of course the blossom that starts to dress the trees. Finding these delicate blooms as you walk in a park or look out on a bleak back garden is a special spring gift of hope.

The best seasonal vegetables for February are parsnips, leeks, savoy cabbage, kale, Brussels sprouts and cauliflower. If you cook recipes using seasonal vegetables, grown locally, rather than imported from abroad, you will be helping to protect the environment: a quarter of all heavy goods traffic in the UK comes from food transport, and the further your shopping has travelled, the greater its negative impact.

The best things to plant in February are cosmos, cranesbills, lily and agapanthus bulbs, Jerusalem artichokes and fruit trees. It's also a good time for pruning and preparing your soil for spring planting.

12 FEBRUARY

Burn It Up

ardour: great enthusiasm or passion.

'After ten years together, their ardour for one another remained undimmed.'

The word 'ardour' came to the English language, via French, from the Latin verb 'ardere', meaning 'to burn'. Fire is often associated with ideas of intense emotion – as in phrases like 'fired up', 'get on like a house on fire', 'blazing row' and 'burn with passion' – as it conjures up ideas of chaotic energy that match extreme feelings.

13 FEBRUARY

Why a Heart Is Not a Heart

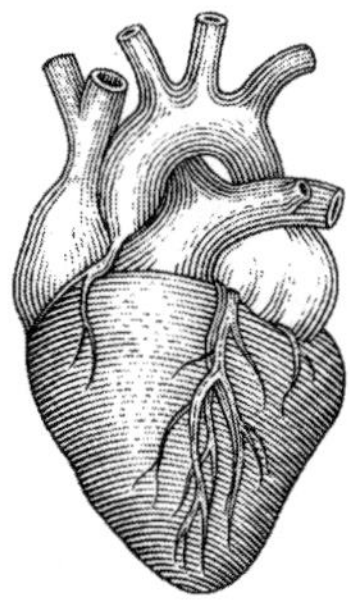

The heart has been connected with love for a long time. Back in ancient Greece, passion was thought to originate in the chest, perhaps because our hearts beat faster in situations of heightened emotion. But this doesn't explain why the heart shape as we know it came to be associated with romance. The people of ancient societies knew what real hearts looked like – the first recorded autopsy took place in around 300 BCE – and they don't look terribly heart-shaped.

The romantic heart motif started to appear in this context in the Middle Ages. One theory is that this shape came from artistic interpretations of written descriptions by scientists like the second-century Greek doctor Galen. Others propose that the shape developed from the outline of ivy leaves, which were considered by some to represent fidelity.

One of the most widely discussed theories suggests that it developed from the seed shape of a now-extinct North African plant called silphium, which was very profitably sold in the city of Cyrene, in modern Libya. The Greeks and Romans used silphium for all kinds of health concerns including as a contraceptive. It was so popular that some people believe its seed shape became symbolic of sexual love.

14 FEBRUARY

Love

'Love has nothing to do with what you are expecting to get – only with what you are expecting to give – which is everything.'

Katharine Hepburn (1907–2003), whisky-loving, trouser-wearing, multi-Oscar-winning Hollywood actor

15 FEBRUARY

Bubbling Away

Every person has an individual community of microorganisms living inside them, mainly in the gut. You have trillions of microorganisms inhabiting you, from around one thousand different species. All together they weigh about as much as your brain. Your microbiome is very individual: all humans share about 99.7% of the same DNA but we only share about 20–30% of our microorganisms.

Fermented foods, like live yogurt, kefir, sauerkraut and kimchi, are altered by microorganisms like yeast and certain bacteria to give them a particular flavour or help preserve them naturally for longer. Eating these foods adds these microorganisms to the diverse ecosystem of your gut and helps keep your microbiome healthy. Because the gut is linked to other aspects of our well-being like our immune system, anything that benefits it can improve overall health.Eating lots of different kinds of plants is the best way to keep your gut microbiome healthy. Top nutritional scientist Tim Spector notes that the Hadza people of Tanzania eat about six hundred different species of plant and animal products over a year and their microbiome is 30% more diverse than the average UK microbiome. The Hadza have very low incidence of obesity, allergies, cancer and heart disease. Dr Spector recommends that we try to eat thirty different plant foods each week.

16 FEBRUARY

Water, Water Everywhere

A staggering 71% of the earth's surface is water and the last remaining geographical mysteries of our planet lie under the oceans. Mapping bodies of water is called hydrography and studying submarine topography is called bathymetry. From our earliest seafaring days we've needed maps that show safe shipping routes and we now need them for laying undersea cables, mining for minerals that are running out on land, and conservation research. So far scientists have only mapped a fifth of the ocean floor.

Once you get to the twilight world of 200 metres below the surface, you are officially in the 'deep sea'. The deepest region of the ocean – 6 to 11 kilometres below the surface – is called the 'hadal zone', after Hades, the Greek god of the underworld. The immense pressure and huge variations in temperature here make it very difficult to explore, even for robotic vehicles, but amazingly certain living organisms have adapted to survive in this tough environment, like the cusk-eel. Many hadal creatures survive by eating 'marine snow' or 'ocean dandruff', whatever drops down through the ocean to their dim habitat, or by absorbing the chemicals that come from incredibly hot underwater volcanic vents. Organisations such as NASA are interested in exploring the hadal zone as they think it may help them with exploration of other planets.

The deepest measured point on the ocean floor is the Challenger Deep in the Mariana Trench, in the Pacific Ocean east of the Philippines, which is 10,924 metres deep. For context, Mount Everest is 8,849 metres high.

17 FEBRUARY

The Catcher in the Rye

J. D. Salinger's *The Catcher in the Rye* is the classic hymn to the most awkward of ages: our teens. Holden Caulfield is a kid in crisis, playing truant on a three-day walkabout in New York City.

But where does a novel set in the ultimate urban jungle get its pastoral title from? It's lifted from a line of the poem 'Comin thro' the Rye' by Scotland's Robert Burns **(see 25 January)**.

Gin a body meet a body
  Comin thro' the rye,
Gin a body kiss a body —
  Need a body cry.

Holden overhears a little kid mis-reciting the poem as he wanders down the street with his parents, and the boy's unfettered exuberance lifts Holden momentarily from his cynicism towards the world around him. When his sister Phoebe asks him what he wants to be when he grows up, Holden replies that he wants to be the catcher in the rye. He imagines the rye as a field overlooking a cliff, and his job will be to stop all the kids falling off the edge and into the abyss of adulthood. But, as Phoebe helps him to realise, Rabbie Burns's poem is actually about a casual sexual encounter, it's just that Holden's myopic world view has led him to interpret it in a different light; he's failed to see that there is no pure innocence, whether it's in childhood, teenage years or adulthood. Despite his flaws, Holden Caulfield remains an iconic teenager, still calling out the corny phonies three quarters of a century on.

18 FEBRUARY

Pineapple Passion

Pineapples originate in South America and were brought to Europe by Christopher Columbus in the fifteenth century. The fruits were named 'piña' after the word for 'pinecone' because of their resemblance. Their dramatic form and rarity meant they were lusted after as a luxury item in Europe – King Charles II even had his portrait painted with one and in Georgian times they were displayed as centrepieces at posh parties.

19 FEBRUARY

The Language of Flags

Flag semaphore is a signalling system of waving flags, torches or the signaller's arms to send messages over a visible distance. It was the main means of naval communication in the nineteenth century and it is still occasionally used on ships, by lifeguards and in the mountains. People assume the famous cover for the Beatles' *Help* album shows the Fab Four spelling out the word 'HELP' in semaphore, but the photographer, Robert Freeman, said he abandoned that idea to get the best possible shapes, so it actually spells a meaningless 'NUJV'. The CND (Campaign for Nuclear Disarmament) peace symbol uses the semaphore positions for 'N' for 'Nuclear' and 'D' for 'Disarmament' in its design.

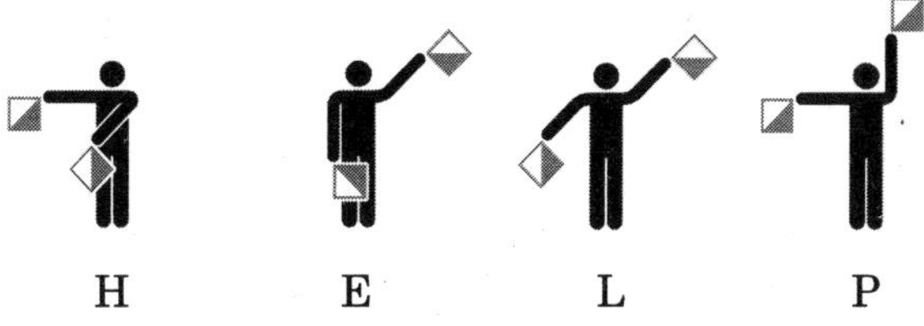

20 FEBRUARY

Your Brain on Jazz

'Life is a lot like jazz . . . It's better when you improvise.'
George Gershwin, composer (1898–1937)

Inspired by the work songs of the slave plantations of the US, mixing with other influences along the way, the blues developed in the southern states in the late nineteenth century. Around the same time in St Louis, Missouri, ragtime, which is composed primarily for the piano, started growing in popularity. In the early 1900s these forms in turn influenced the birth of a mind-blowingly creative and influential new form: jazz. New Orleans is most closely associated with the rise of this new genre, which is characterised by mixing improvisation and composition, often with elements of syncopation (the use of off-beat rhythms).

In the 1920s there were anxieties that the hot new fashion for jazz was overstimulating and could make fans sick, fidgety and nervous, but nowadays it's widely accepted that listening to music of all kinds is good for our brains, enhancing well-being and keeping our neural connections strong, and playing music also helps with focus and creativity.

Scientists at Johns Hopkins University studied the brain waves of jazz musicians while they were improvising using a special keyboard that could go inside an MRI scanner. They noted that the inhibiting and planning regions of the musicians' brains slowed down and the free and expressive areas lit up when they played. So jazz really is good for creativity!

21 FEBRUARY

The World's Weirdest-Named Fish

1. Asian sheepshead wrasse
2. Blobfish
3. Sarcastic fringehead
4. Cookiecutter shark
5. Slimehead
6. Spotted stargazer
7. Psychedelic frogfish
8. Wahoo
9. Coffinfish
10. Bombay duck

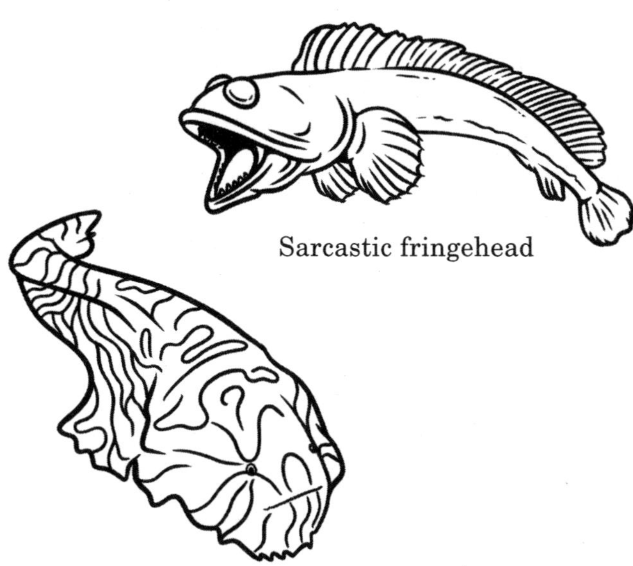

Sarcastic fringehead

Psychedelic frogfish

22 FEBRUARY

Crime Scene Analysis

When the grizzled police detective in a cop drama says they need to wait for crime scene analysis to 'come back from the lab', whose insight might they be waiting for? Here are a few of the practices involved in modern forensic science.

1. A **forensic odontologist** focuses on teeth. Teeth are extremely useful for confirming the identity of bodies that are too damaged for other methods. Standard dental X-rays from visits to the dentist are used as all of us have unique dentition. Perpetrators can also be identified from tooth marks – one robbery suspect was caught because he'd eaten a piece of cheese in the house he was robbing and left his unique tooth print at the crime scene.

2. **Fingerprint analysis** is one of the oldest and best-known elements of forensic science. We each have a unique pattern of whorls and lines on our fingertips and the oils on our skin can imprint them on surfaces. The first fingerprint databases were set up in the 1980s, and the UK database contains the fingerprints of over 8 million people. Every time someone is convicted of a crime, or even just arrested for certain offences, their fingerprints are added and kept for a set period of time.

3. **DNA** is our individual genetic code and it's contained in all the cells of our body. The UK police have a database of forensic DNA containing the profiles of over 5 million people, collected – usually by swabbing inside mouths to pick up skin cells – in similar situations to fingerprints.

DNA analysis was first used in criminal cases in the 1980s and the technology has improved rapidly since then. But while it has been used to exonerate and convict many, it is not foolproof: DNA can be planted on crime scenes and contaminated during investigations. There are also privacy concerns about keeping individuals' DNA on databases, because, unlike fingerprints, it also contains information about their family and health.

4. A **forensic pathologist** is a doctor who examines a body to ascertain cause and time of death. Aspects of a corpse's appearance such as the extent of livor mortis can help establish time of death: this is caused when the victim's circulation stops and their blood pools at the lowest point of their body, causing swelling and darkening.

5. A **forensic palynologist** is a specialist in pollen and spores and can help work out if a victim or suspect was in a particular area based on which species are found on their clothing. In one famous case from the 1950s, a palynologist helped locate a missing body after finding 20-million-year-old fossil hickory pollen grains on the boots of a suspect, which could only be found in a tiny stretch of the banks of the River Danube in Austria.

6. A **forensic entomologist** can help determine time and place of death from the presence of specific insects and bugs in or on the body. Fly larvae can even be used to determine if drugs or poison were used on a body that is too damaged to be analysed for this itself.

23 FEBRUARY

A Gaming Glossary

The old stereotypes about video games being just for teenage boys are well out of date. The average age of gamers worldwide is now thirty-four, and across the many device formats the male/female split is roughly 50/50. Over 3 billion people worldwide play, and that number is ever-rising – it's estimated that by 2026 gaming will hold around a 10.9% share of the global entertainment market.

Whether you spend hours each day on *Fortnite* or just a few minutes of your commute on *Candy Crush* on your phone, video game lingo is an increasing part of mainstream culture. Here are some key terms and acronyms to help you navigate the gaming world.

AAA – A 'triple-A' game is one made by a big-budget games studio.

Buff – A boost given to a player's health, abilities, weapons or equipment that improves them.

Class – A type of character in a game with a certain skill set. For example a barbarian is a big, tanky, physically aggressive class, whereas a rogue is more stealthy and agile.

Crit – A 'critical hit' is an attack that deals an unusually hefty amount of damage.

Cutscene – An animated scene that you don't play in, which usually involves storytelling.

E-sports – 'Electronic sports' are the tournaments played by professional players of certain games, often for large monetary prizes.

Farming/Grinding – Repeating a task or action in a game to amass resources or XP (experience points).

NPC – 'Non-playable characters' are exactly that.

24 FEBRUARY

Jean Genie

The tiny copper rivets you find on your jeans were invented by the Levi Strauss company for their first-ever pair of jeans in 1873. They were used to hold pockets on firmly, making the trousers suitable as tough workwear. During the Second World War the pockets stopped having rivets as metal was in short supply because of the need to make weapons. The little front pocket you still find on many pairs of jeans was also part of an original Levis 1890 design, and was intended to hold pocket watches.

25 FEBRUARY

Look Up

We spend a lot of time looking down at our phones but it's good for our eyes and our souls to look up and out every so often. You might also develop your own sense of what the weather has in store if you familiarise yourself with the ten different types of clouds found in our skies – they are categorised according to their basic shape and how high up in the troposphere they hang out. (The troposphere is the area stretching to roughly 13 kilometres above the earth's surface where most weather happens.) Clouds are made of water droplets and ice crystals caused by water vapour condensing in the cool air high in the sky.

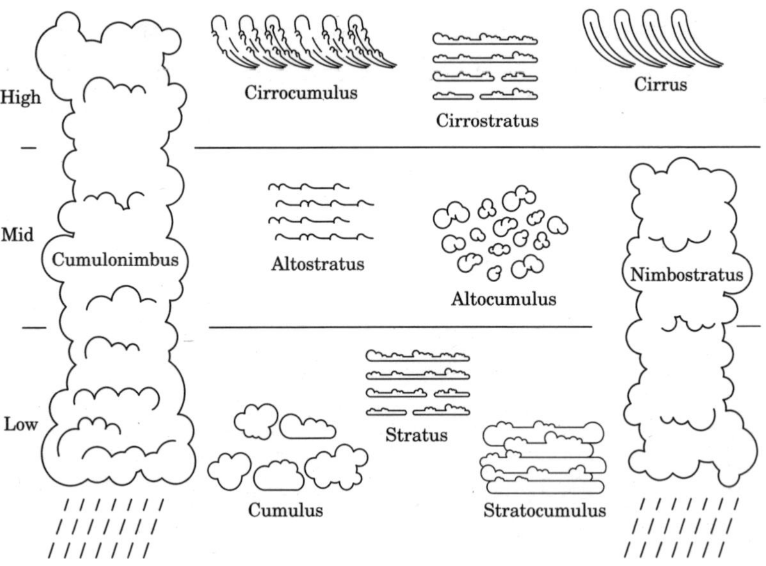

26 FEBRUARY

The Thirteenth Olympian

The twelve Olympians get their name from Mount Olympus, the highest mountain in Greece, where they lived. They are the big guns of ancient Greek religion: Zeus, the king of the gods; Hera, his queen and goddess of marriage and childbirth; Poseidon, god of the sea; Demeter, goddess of harvest; Apollo, god of the sun, art and music; Athena, goddess of wisdom; Aphrodite, goddess of love; Artemis, goddess of the moon and hunting; Hephaestus, god of fire and smithing; Ares, god of war; Hermes, god of travel and communication; and Dionysus, god of wine and fertility. (Hades, the other top god, of death, lived under the earth rather than on Olympus so doesn't get included.)

Some lists exclude the glamorous Dionysus and instead bring in the more humble goddess of the hearth and home, Zeus's sister Hestia. Less lusty and fighty than her siblings, Hestia was a protector of the family, the home, and by extension the state. Sacrifices were often offered to her first as a sign of her significance. In some cities there was a communal hearth dedicated to Hestia, the prytaneion, which had set rituals around its regular lighting, extinguishing and relighting.

This reverence for the hearth developed into the Roman custom of keeping the flame burning in the Temple of Vesta (Hestia's Roman equivalent) in the Roman Forum at all times. If the fire went out unexpectedly it was considered a terrible omen for the city. Six virgin priestesses, called the Vestals, looked after this temple and they had to keep a vow of chastity for thirty years in the goddess's honour. If they broke their vow they were buried alive, because it was taboo to spill their blood.

27 FEBRUARY

Box Breathing

Scientists have shown that there is a connection between our breathing and the arousal centre of the brain, which is why slow, deep breathing can deactivate stress responses that naturally kick in when we feel anxious. Box breathing is an effective way to recentre yourself if you want to focus your concentration or calm yourself if you are feeling panicky or overwhelmed. It's taught to many people who work in high-stress occupations and is a quick and simple exercise to calm your mind and your body's physical responses to stress.

1. Exhale as much air as possible from your lungs.
2. Imagine a box.
3. Inhale slowly and deeply through your nose while counting to four, imagining you are tracing along one side of the box.
4. Hold your breath for four, as you imagine tracing along the next side of the box.
5. Exhale through your mouth for another count of four while you trace the next side.
6. Hold your breath, with your lungs empty, for a final count of four as you finish the last side of the box.

Repeat four times and feel better.

A GOOD PAIR

If you spread your lungs out flat they would nearly cover the area of a tennis court.

28 FEBRUARY

Heaven Scent

To make perfume, essential oils are extracted from blossoms, fruit peels and leaves; their very concentrated versions are called absolutes. Four tons of roses, equating to about 1.6 million rose blossoms, yields only 1 kilogram of rose oil. These oils tend to evaporate very quickly, losing their scent, so they are mixed with fixatives to slow this down. Fixatives also often contribute base notes to the overall perfume. Less glamorous animal products such as ambergris from whales, musk from the genitals of musk deer, civet from glands on the backside of the civet cat and castoreum from glands on the backsides of beavers have been popular fixatives in the past, but many perfume companies now use synthetic alternatives.

The first thing you smell when you sniff a perfume is the fresh top note, which lasts for about half an hour; this blends with the more substantial middle note and the longest-lasting base note to give the overall olfactory experience. Perfumes are classified by type of dominant fragrance: floral, fresh, ambery or woody.

Perfumes come in different intensities, ranging from parfum through eau de parfum, eau de toilette to eau de cologne, and the lightest, eau fraîche. Parfums tend to have greater sillage – the technical term for how long a perfume follows you in the air. We put perfume on our pulse points because these are the parts of the body where the blood runs closest to the skin, warming the perfume up and increasing its sillage.

29 FEBRUARY

Take a Leap

Every four years, February has twenty-nine days instead of twenty-eight – and if you have an annual salary you give your boss an extra day's work for free. This 'leap' is designed to get us back on track with the astronomical year, which doesn't exactly fit neat mathematical units of days. The earth actually takes 365.242 days to orbit the sun rather than the clean 365 in a common year. If we didn't add in the extra day every four years, eventually our calendar would cut adrift from the seasons. However, even the four-year-leap system isn't quite accurate, so every hundred years, on the century year, we skip a leap year – unless the year is divisible by 400. In 2100 we will not have a leap year but we did have one in 2000.

March

1 MARCH

Dydd Gŵyl Dewi Hapus!

St David, or Dewi Sant in Welsh, is the only one of the United Kingdom's patron saints to be born in his actual homeland, and he died on this day in 589 CE. Legend has it that his birth was quite the drama: he was born on a clifftop during a storm on the coast of Pembrokeshire in the year 500, just as a lightning bolt split a huge rock there in two. A holy well believed to have curative powers is located nearby and is a site of pilgrimage even now.

David went on to found a monastery at Glyn Rhosyn, now known as St Davids, in Pembrokeshire in Wales. Life in the monastery was extremely ascetic **(see 15 January)**; he was famed as an abstemious vegan who consumed only water and leeks and was fond of reading from scripture whilst submerged to his neck in a freezing lake. His reported miracles include restoring a blind man's sight and bringing a dead boy back to life by splashing tears in his face. He travelled extensively as a missionary, founding another monastery at Glastonbury and even making it to Jerusalem, bringing back a stone that resides today at Glyn Rhosyn.

David's deathbed words were said to be beautiful and uplifting: 'Be joyful, keep the faith, and do the little things that you have heard and seen me do.' That phrase 'Gwnewch y pethau bychain mewn bywyd' – 'do the little things in life' – is a maxim that still resonates in Wales today.

So loop a daffodil in your lapel and brandish your leek all day long. Happy St David's Day!

2 MARCH

Once Upon a Time

Countless studies have proven that reading boosts children's cognitive development; it's also great for reducing stress by unlocking creativity and emotions. The act of reading with your child, niece, nephew or grandchild releases a gorgeous flow of love and bonding. Here is a heavily biased top five children's books of all time.

1. *Not Now, Bernard* by David McKee (for babies and up). A classic morality tale for parents, warning of the monstrous ramifications of ignoring your children. McKee recalled that, upon publication in 1980, some libraries banned it for the violence at the heart of the story. It has sold over 5 million copies to date and has never been out of print.

2. *Goodnight Moon* by Margaret Wise Brown (for babies and up). A soporific incantation for lulling even the liveliest of little ones at bedtime. Brown's storytelling genius lies in her ability to reflect the world just as young children still experience it even eighty years after publication, but one extremely influential librarian at the New York Public Library took against it and refused to stock it, causing other libraries across America to follow suit. It very nearly fell out of print. Happily, word of mouth trounced the gatekeepers' taste, and the book has now sold 48 million copies around the world.

3. *The Very Hungry Caterpillar* by Eric Carle (for babies and up). This wonderful interaction of art, texture and story, which first appeared in 1969, was said to be inspired

by some absent-minded hole-punching. At its heart it's a story of glorious gluttony and transformation that continues to resonate with children across the world.

4. *Pig-Heart Boy* by Malorie Blackman (for nine- to twelve-year-olds). Who would have thought a novel exploring the concept of xenotransplantation could deliver such an emotionally rich read? Cameron is a dying thirteen-year-old boy who can only survive if he receives the heart of Trudy the pig. But what if the world around him isn't ready to accept such a concept? This is a powerful tale of otherness and acceptance from a woman whose first novel received a whopping eighty-nine rejections from short-sighted publishers.

5. *The Tiger Who Came to Tea* by Judith Kerr (for babies and up). Another colourful tale from the 1960s, but when read against the backdrop of Judith Kerr's traumatic past – her family were Jewish Germans hounded out of Berlin by Hitler's Nazi regime, and her father later took his own life – this beloved story of a tiger who arrives in a little girl's house, eats all her food and then disappears into the night, takes on rather darker undertones.

6. *The Cat in the Hat* by Dr. Seuss (for three- to seven-year-olds). Here is the ultimate disrupter cat, causing joyous, exuberant chaos in a little sister and brother's home while their mother is away on a rainy day. Theodor Geisel, the man behind Dr. Seuss, created it in 1957 in response to onerous traditional primers like the extremely un-fun *Fun with Dick and Jane*. His challenge was to create a fantastic story using just 236 words that all young children would understand. It was an instant classic.

3 MARCH

Ramadan Mubarak

'Allah is with those who restrain themselves.'
Qur'an 16:128

Ramadan is the Holy Month observed by most of the world's 1.8 billion Muslims. Because the Islamic calendar is arranged around the lunar cycle, the exact date on which it falls shifts by around ten days each year. It is a time of fasting and spiritual reflection, lasting for twenty-nine or thirty days, where able-bodied Muslims abstain from food, drink and some other activities, from dawn until sunset, having one meal (Suhoor) just before dawn and another (Iftar) directly after sunset. One of the five pillars of Islam, Ramadan is a month of self-discipline, increased prayer and acts of selflessness and charity.

Ramadan commemorates the revelation of the holy text, the Qur'an, to the Prophet Muhammad and is considered a time for purification and strengthening of one's faith, fostering a sense of unity, empathy and gratitude among Muslims. The end of Ramadan is celebrated with the three-day joyous festival of Eid al-Fitr, marking the breaking of the fast, where Muslims come together to feast, exchange gifts and pray.

MIDNIGHT SUN

With Muslim communities increasingly growing in places like Finland, Sweden and Norway, which sit within the Arctic Circle, there's an interesting ethical dilemma. How do you observe Ramadan when the sun doesn't set? Most Muslims facing this issue decide to follow Mecca's timetable, or Turkey's, which is the closest Muslim country.

4 MARCH

Lights, Camera, Action!

Ever wondered exactly what some of those weird-sounding job titles that appear in film credits actually mean? Here's how to tell your best boy from your child wrangler.

Gaffer: The Gaffer oversees the entire electrical department for a movie production. The name probably comes from an old British theatre term for the man who adjusted the lighting in the theatre using a 'gaff' – a type of hooked pole.

Grip: At its simplest level, the grip is the person who moves lighting equipment around.

Best boy: Gaffers and grips each have a second-in-command – this person is called the best boy electric and best boy grip respectively. It's considered a gender-neutral term; there are no best girls.

Focus puller: The focus puller works for the cinematographer (who delivers the director's vision through visual storytelling via various technical processes) and is responsible for maintaining and controlling the focus of a shot as it is filmed.

Foley artist: A Foley artist creates sound effects in post-production. The position is named after Jack Foley, who was part of the sound crew on *Show Boat* (1929), a film that proved Universal Pictures was more than capable of making the transition from silent pictures to talkies. Jack Foley was a master of invention, stomping on crushed-up rolls of film for footsteps in dry leaves, or using coconut shells cut in half for the clopping of horses' hooves.

Child wrangler: This is a truly saintly person whose job it is to keep child actors, babies and toddlers entertained and well behaved on set.

5 MARCH

The Inward Places of the Soul

'Rhythm and harmony find their way into the inward places of the soul.'

Plato (c. 427–348 BCE)

Music-fan superstar Greek philosopher and student of Socrates, Plato started out as a soldier before devoting himself to studying the world.

6 MARCH

Tut-Mania

Egyptomania has had worldwide influence for centuries – the ancient Greeks and Romans were fascinated by ancient Egyptian society, Napoleon's foray into Egypt in 1798 sparked a European wave of curiosity, and Howard Carter's discovery of Tutankhamun's tomb in 1922 reignited a global passion that continues today.

There is a lot we don't know about 'The Boy King', but we do know he was the son of Akhenaten, also known as Amenhotep IV, an ancient Egyptian pharaoh who reigned during the fourteenth century BCE. His mother was possibly Akhenaten's co-ruler, Queen Nefertiti, and he became king at the age of nine, dying just nine years later.

The discovery of King Tut's tomb – the most intact tomb ever found – very nearly didn't happen. After years of searching, financial backer Lord Carnarvon was becoming frustrated by Carter's lack of progress and told him he had one last chance. Legend has it that a boy carrying water tripped on a stone that would turn out to be the beginning of a flight of steps to a doorway covered in hieroglyphics. Two weeks later Carnarvon and Carter opened the door that had been sealed for over three thousand years. More than five thousand priceless artefacts were found, including King Tut's solid gold coffin, a gaming board, gold sandals and his magnificent death mask.

In one of the first examples of an exclusive scoop, Carter sold the rights to document the excavation to *The Times*. The world was transfixed and the Roaring Twenties embraced all things Egypt, in fashion, art, architecture and song. US President Herbert Hoover even named his dog King Tut.

7 MARCH

Plant Power

Today new medicines are designed and created in laboratories but chemists often look to the natural world for inspiration. Plants spend a lot of time fighting off attacks from fungi, aphids and other threats, after all. Here's a list of the most powerful medicines bequeathed to us by Mother Nature.

- Ancient Egyptian medics and Hippocrates himself mention treating fever and pain using willow bark, and in the mid-nineteenth century German doctors figured out how to extract the compound salicin from the tree. Over time, chemists worked to produce the synthetic version acetylsalicylic (a fun Scrabble word), better known as aspirin.
- Morphine is derived from the opium poppy, and was first discovered by German pharmaceutical chemist Friedrich Sertürner in 1804. Sertürner carried out experiments on stray dogs and rats, though his discovery remained unrecognised until he took some himself whilst in the grip of a terrible toothache and experienced instant relief. He named it morphium, after the Greek god of sleep. He was also a poster boy for the dangers of this new drug, eventually becoming hopelessly addicted.
- Obtained from the bark of the Pacific yew tree, paclitaxel is an effective chemotherapy drug used in the treatment of various cancers. And while scientists first tested vinblastine and vincristine, derived from the pretty Madagascar periwinkle, for diabetes, it transpired that they are more effective in treating lymphoma and leukaemia.
- Quinine, derived from the bark of the cinchona tree, has long been used to treat malaria. Indigenous tribes in South America used cinchona bark to treat fevers, and in the seventeenth century Europeans adopted it.

8 MARCH

Window of Opportunity

Who doesn't love a window box? Planted windows are said to date back to the Hanging Gardens of Babylon, one of the Seven Wonders of the Ancient World **(see 21 July)**, built by order of King Nebuchadnezzar II. The ancient Roman philosopher Pliny reminisces about them in his first-century book *Naturalis Historia*, which is credited with being the very first scientific encyclopaedia. And whilst flowers are pretty and mood-enhancing, nothing quite beats the satisfaction of pimping up your prandial experiences with your own home-grown herbs, and spring is the time to get sowing.

Choose sturdy, durable herbs: we recommend oregano, rosemary and sage. Get a good-quality planter with drainage holes in the bottom and fill it with soil containing perlite for drainage. You can grow from seed but no one will slap your wrists if you choose young plants as an easy shortcut. Place in a sunny spot and prepare to be admired by all.

HERBALICIOUS

Oregano was said to have been created by the goddess Aphrodite as a symbol of joy and happiness, and some Greek couples getting hitched today still wear a wreath of it in their hair. Rosemary was used by ancient Greek scholars to boost memory, and it is now being investigated for potential efficacy against Alzheimer's. Sage was regarded by the Romans as a holy herb that could heal, and in medieval times it was used as a meat preserver. It was thought to bestow immortality on whoever ate it every day for the month of May.

9 MARCH

The Father of Economics

In 1776, Scottish economist Adam Smith published *An Inquiry into the Nature and Causes of the Wealth of Nations*, which, for the first time, argued that the distribution of wealth was not decreed by God, but was a system controlled by various influences – politics, technology, nature, society – working together.

At 950 pages, his book is a pretty turgid affair, but it explains how free trade without government interference leads to healthy competition. Smith explains the concepts of division of labour, and the 'invisible hand': when people are free to pursue their own trading agendas, they unintentionally help others whilst benefiting themselves. So, on one extremely gentrified road two shops compete for customers: the Authentic Grocer and the Village Larder. As the Authentic Grocer decides £25 is a reasonable sum to charge for a bunch of biodynamic tulips, the Village Larder offers a bunch of daffs for £2.50. The Larder pulls in customers looking for affordability, whilst the Authentic Grocer improves its quality, attracting a more niche market. The invisible hand balances prices and quality, satisfying different customer wants and needs.

Smith believed that if governments let people trade freely without too many rules and restrictions, it would lead to prosperity and wealth for the whole country. Et voilà, the theory of capitalism and the free market was enshrined in the pages of history.

Not only did Adam Smith write one of the most influential and unreadable books ever written, but he was also the first Scotsman to make it onto an English banknote. A notable Scot indeed.

10 MARCH

Poets' Corner

The earliest form of literature made by humans was poetry, and from George MacDonald's 'The Shortest and Sweetest of Songs' ('Come/ Home.') to the 1.8 million words of the *Mahabharata*, people have been writing, declaiming and reading poetry the world over for centuries.

Poets combine words and rhythms in dazzling arrays of combinations but there are some formal patterns that are popular enough to have their own definitions. If you flick ahead to 'Time Does Not Bring Relief' on 1 October you can see that it takes the form of a Petrarchan sonnet, following the rhyme scheme ABBA ABBA CDE ECD. It is also written in one of the most popular metres for English poetry – the famous iambic pentameter. ('Metre' is simply the official term used to describe poetic rhythm – the magic ingredient which sets verse apart from prose.) A pentameter is a line of poetry made up of five feet. Each foot in poetry is a particular pattern of stressed and unstressed syllables that is repeated a set number of times. In an iambic pentameter each foot has a pattern of one unstressed syllable (often marked as –) followed by one stressed syllable called an iamb (marked as /).

Shakespeare's 'Shall **I** | com**pare** | thee **to** | a **summ** | er's **day**?' is a perfect iambic pentameter. Iambic pentameter is so popular because it closely resembles the rhythms of ordinary speech and is also easy to memorise because of its repeated patterns of stress. It is often described as replicating the rhythm of a heartbeat.

11 MARCH

Wet, Wet, Wet

Make no mistake about it, the British Isles are wet. And some places get more than their fair share – the Lake District has an average of 200 days of rain per year. It's no wonder, then, that there are several words for rain in the Cumbrian dialect. '**Mizzling**' (raining with very small drops), '**spitting**' (light, just visible rain), '**syling**' (from the Scandinavian word for 'sieve', so, as if through a sieve), '**smirring**' (like drizzle), '**hossing**' (a heavy downpour), '**stotting**' (from the old Scottish and northern English word for 'bouncing') and '**hoyin it down**' (torrential rain) are all employed in the local lingo to describe different meteorological conditions from a fine mist to a drenching downpour.

Other gems from across the nation (some estimates suggest we have over a hundred) include:

Bange (East Anglia): A damp hovering that can last for days.

Plothering (Midlands): A heavy, windless rain.

Mae hi'n brwr hen wragedd affyn (Wales): Raining old women and sticks.

Dreich (Scotland): Dreary and bleak.

Letty (Somerset): From the old word for 'disallow', if the weather is letty it's just wet enough to make outdoor work hard-going.

12 MARCH

OMg: The Periodic Table

The giant cheat sheet on every science classroom wall shows the arrangement of the earth's chemical elements, organised by atomic number, electron configuration and recurring chemical properties. Consisting of rows called periods and columns called groups, each element is represented by its symbol, its atomic number and its atomic mass. The table was invented by Russian chemist and political economist Dmitri Mendeleev, who also, according to myth, standardised the alcohol content of vodka at 40%. Mendeleev has a volcano, an underwater ridge, the 101st element in the periodic table and a Moscow metro station named after him. Its genius lies in how it organises an array of mind-boggling elemental information in an exquisitely elegant form that can be read and understood immediately. It also allows scientists to predict relationships between the elements based on where they lie in the table.

1 H HYDROGEN 1.008																	2 He HELIUM 4.002
3 Li LITHIUM 7.0	4 Be BERYLLIUM 9.012											5 B BORON 10.81	6 C CARBON 12.011	7 N NITROGEN 14.007	8 O OXYGEN 15.999	9 F FLUORINE 18.998	10 Ne NEON 20.180
11 Na SODIUM 22.989	12 Mg MAGNESIUM 24.305											13 Al ALUMINUM 26.981	14 Si SILICON 28.085	15 P PHOSPHORUS 30.973	16 S SULFUR 32.07	17 Cl CHLORINE 35.45	18 Ar ARGON 39.9
19 K POTASSIUM 39.098	20 Ca CALCIUM 40.08	21 Sc SCANDIUM 44.955	22 Ti TITANIUM 47.87	23 V VANADIUM 50.941	24 Cr CHROMIUM 51.996	25 Mn MANGANESE 54.938	26 Fe IRON 55.84	27 Co COBALT 58.933	28 Ni NICKEL 58.693	29 Cu COPPER 63.55	30 Zn ZINC 65.4	31 Ga GALLIUM 69.72	32 Ge GERMANIUM 72.63	33 As ARSENIC 74.921	34 Se SELENIUM 78.97	35 Br BROMINE 79.90	36 Kr KRYPTON 83.80
37 Rb RUBIDIUM 85.468	38 Sr STRONTIUM 87.6	39 Y YTTRIUM 88.905	40 Zr ZIRCONIUM 91.22	41 Nb NIOBIUM 92.906	42 Mo MOLYBDENUM 96.0	43 Tc TECHNETIUM 97.907	44 Ru RUTHENIUM 101.1	45 Rh RHODIUM 102.905	46 Pd PALLADIUM 106.4	47 Ag SILVER 107.868	48 Cd CADMIUM 112.41	49 In INDIUM 114.82	50 Sn TIN 118.71	51 Sb ANTIMONY 121.76	52 Te TELLURIUM 127.6	53 I IODINE 126.904	54 Xe XENON 131.29
55 Cs CESIUM 132.905	56 Ba BARIUM 137.33	56-71 LANTHANOIDS	72 Hf HAFNIUM 178.5	73 Ta TANTALUM 180.947	74 W TUNGSTEN 183.8	75 Re RHENIUM 186.21	76 Os OSMIUM 190.2	77 Ir IRIDIUM 192.22	78 Pt PLATINUM 195.08	79 Au GOLD 196.966	80 Hg MERCURY 200.59	81 Ti THALLIUM 204.383	82 Pb LEAD 207	83 Bi BISMUTH 208.980	84 Po POLONIUM 208.982	85 At ASTATINE 209.987	86 Rn RADON 222.017
87 Fr FRANCIUM 223.019	88 Ra RADIUM 226.025	89-103 ACTINOIDS	104 Rf RUTHERFORDIUM 267.122	105 Db DUBNIUM 268.126	106 Sg SEABORGIUM 271.134	107 Bh BOHRIUM 274.144	108 Hs HASSIUM 277.152	109 Mt MEITNERIUM 278.156	110 Ds DARMSTADTIUM 281.165	111 Rg ROENTGENIUM 282.169	112 Cn COPERNICIUM 285.177	113 Nh NIHONIUM 286.183	114 Fl FLEROVIUM 289.191	115 Mc MOSCOVIUM 290.196	116 Lv LIVERMORIUM 293.205	117 Ts TENNESSINE 294.211	118 Og OGANESSON 294.214
		57 La LANTHANUM 138.905	58 Ce CERIUM 140.12	59 Pr PRASEODYMIUM 140.907	60 Nd NEODYMIUM 144.24	61 Pm PROMETHIUM 144.912	62 Sm SAMARIUM 150.4	63 Eu EUROPIUM 151.96	64 Gd GADOLINIUM 157.2	65 Tb TERBIUM 158.925	66 Dy DYSPROSIUM 162.50	67 Ho HOLMIUM 164.930	68 Er ERBIUM 167.26	69 Tm THULIUM 168.934	70 Yb YTTERBIUM 173.04	71 Lu LUTETIUM 174.967	
		89 Ac ACTINIUM 227.027	90 Th THORIUM 232.038	91 Pa PROTACTINIUM 231.035	92 U URANIUM 238.028	93 Np NEPTUNIUM 237.048	94 Pu PLUTONIUM 244.064	95 Am AMERICIUM 243.061	96 Cm CURIUM 247.070	97 Bk BERKELIUM 247.070	98 Cf CALIFORNIUM 251.079	99 Es EINSTEINIUM 252.083	100 Fm FERMIUM 257.095	101 Md MENDELEVIUM 258.098	102 No NOBELIUM 259.101	103 Lr LAWRENCIUM 262.110V	

13 MARCH

Caffe Culture

It's only in recent years that the UK has embraced a credible coffee culture, where your average cup does actually taste rather good. For those of us baffled by the options, here is a handy guide to help you tell your macchiato from your marocchino, so you never need be intimidated by your trendy barista again.

Espresso

A concentrated coffee made with finely ground coffee beans

Lungo

An espresso with double the amount of water

Ristretto

An espresso with half the amount of water

Macchiato

An espresso with a small amount of foamed milk on top

Cortado

A double espresso with equal parts steamed milk

Marocchino

An espresso poured into a small cup lined with cocoa, topped with foamed milk, with cocoa powder on top

Corretto

An espresso with a small amount of grappa, sambuca or brandy poured on top

Romano

An espresso with a slice of lemon and an optional teaspoon of sugar

Affogato

An espresso poured over a scoop of vanilla ice cream

Irish coffee

A long coffee with Irish whiskey and sugar, topped with cream

Frappuccino

An espresso blended with ice, milk and a syrup of choice, poured into a glass with whipped cream on top

Freddo

Your choice of coffee shaken with ice and poured into a glass with ice cubes

Mocha

An espresso poured over cocoa, topped with steamed milk, and sometimes whipped cream, with cocoa powder on top

Bicerin

A layered drink with hot chocolate at the bottom, then espresso, then topped with foamed milk, served in a wine glass

14 MARCH

Fight Domestic Entropy

The second law of thermodynamics states that, when converting energy into work, some will always be lost and become disordered. Over time the amount of useful energy in a system will decrease and the amount of random, unusable energy will increase: nothing can be totally energy-efficient.

This is a nice metaphor for how our homes gradually get more and more knackered and untidy, despite our efforts to keep things clean and fixed. We can't help you with the piles that seem to build up no matter how many storage solutions you invent, but here are some home hacks to help quickly improve aspects of your living environment.

- Nasty ring of scum round your bath tub? Rubbing used coffee grounds over it will help get it off.
- Stinky dishwasher? Run it with a cup of white vinegar inside to freshen it up.
- Clogged showerhead? Soak it in white vinegar to loosen the deposits – tie a plastic bag full of vinegar round the head with an elastic band.
- Cooking trays and grills sticky with burned-on food? Soak them in your sink with a dishwasher tablet dissolved in hot water to loosen up the gunk.
- White water rings on wooden furniture? Rub them with mayonnaise and leave it to sit for a few hours before buffing off to remove them. Other scuffs on wooden furniture can look better if rubbed over with a shelled walnut.
- Whiffy fridge? Put a small cup of baking soda in there to absorb the odours.

15 MARCH

Renaissance

From the French word 'renaître', 'to be born again', the Renaissance refers to the incredible blooming of arts and letters that had its genesis in fourteenth-century Italy and soon spread across Western Europe through the fifteenth and sixteenth centuries. It was the age of da Vinci, Michelangelo, El Greco and van Eyck, and it was also a time of incredible scientific progress and human invention – some items we can't imagine living without were dreamed up by Renaissance figures. Amongst them are the printing press, the pencil, the parachute, the flushing toilet, helicopters, machine guns, aeroplanes, overdrafts, paperback books and, most crucially, ice cream.

Bernardo Buontalenti was a true Renaissance Man, a multitasking genius of the sixteenth century who was as skilled at art and architecture as he was at military engineering, set design and firework arranging. He is also credited with inventing ice cream. Buontalenti entered the service of the court of the Medici in Florence as a youth and remained there through his life, tasked as a designer and architect with creating the spectacular mood that was the envy of all of Europe. At a reception for the Spanish ambassador, he created a cold cream of lemon, sugar, egg, honey, milk and a drop of wine, flavoured with bergamot and orange. But this wasn't merely some sweet cooking – Buontalenti also used his architectural expertise to design cold storage cellars covered with isolating cork and wood panels to keep his new dessert chilled.

16 MARCH

A Lexicon of Leaf Shapes

A tree's leaf is where the magic of photosynthesis takes place, whereby plants change energy from the sun's light into glucose to feed themselves, happily creating oxygen as a by-product. Without trees and their leaves, there would be no life on our planet. Let's repeat that, shall we? Without trees and their leaves, there would be no life on our planet. Leaves come in a dazzling array of shapes and sizes, as each species of plant has adapted to its environment to produce leaves that capture the optimum amount of light. They are categorised by botanists based on various characteristics, including shape, arrangement on the stem, venation pattern (the arrangement of veins in the leaf) and margin (the edge of the leaf). From the tiniest mini-leaf of the aquatic duckweed, at a piffling 0.5 centimetres, to the raffia palm leaf which can loom over 25 metres, it's time to admire the vivid vestments of our arboreal cousins.

SIMPLE

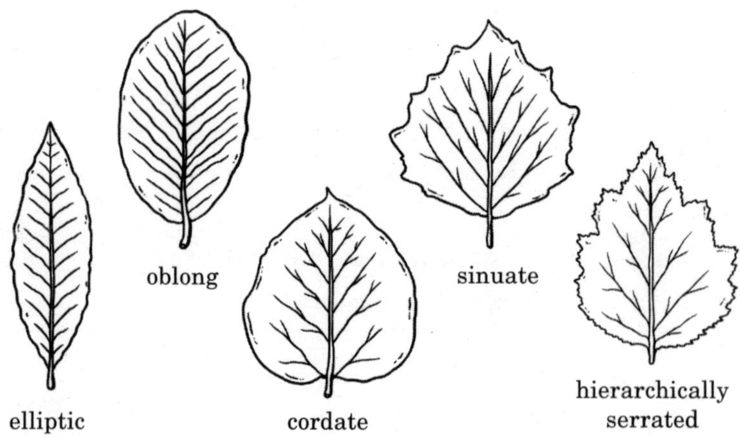

LOBED

palmately lobed

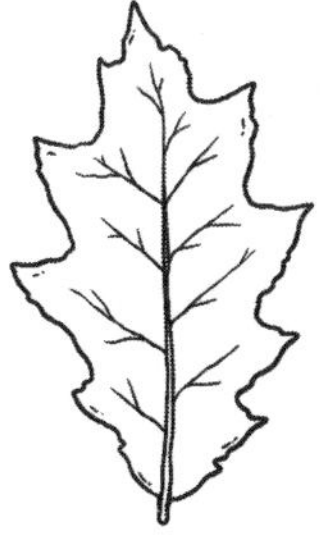
pinately lobed

hierarchically lobed

COMPOUND

sessile leaflets

petiolulate leaflets

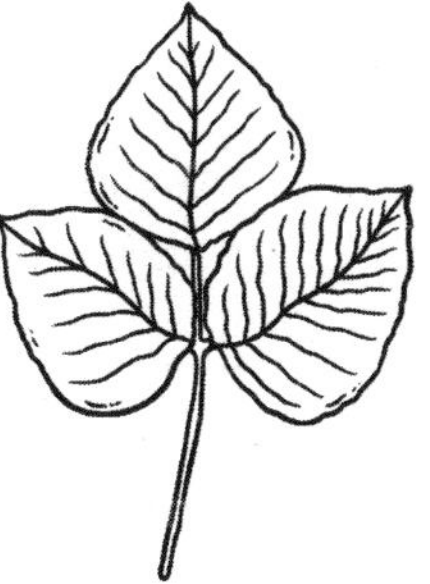
ternate

pinnate

17 MARCH

May Your Blessings Outnumber the Shamrocks That Grow

You wouldn't know it from St Patrick's Day celebrations today but it turns out Ireland's patron saint wasn't Irish, wasn't called Patrick, didn't wear green and didn't get rid of any snakes.

St Patrick is thought to have originally been called Maewyn, and was born in Roman Britain at the start of the fifth century. He was kidnapped as a teenager and brought to Ireland as a slave, where he was forced to work as a shepherd for five bleak years. Still, he writes that this is where he cleaved to God most strongly, finding huge solace in his faith. He experienced a vision in which a man handed him a letter: 'I found it contained these words: "The voice of the Irish", and while reading it I thought I heard, at the same moment, the voice of a multitude of a multitude of persons . . . and they cried out, as if with one voice, "We entreat thee, holy youth, to come and henceforth walk amongst us."'

After a bout of impostor syndrome during which Patrick feared that his lack of education would mean he wasn't up to the job of bringing Christianity to the pagan Irish, he set about his task with gusto, converting thousands and spreading his message across the land. His success in driving out paganism is thought to be behind the legend about him banishing all the snakes from Ireland – as archaeologists think Ireland hadn't had any snakes for thousands of years. Early depictions of him usually have him wearing blue rather than green but the stories do associate him closely with shamrocks. He used the three-lobed leaves of the plant to help explain the Holy Trinity to his flock.

18 MARCH

Curl Up and Dry

The hairdryer was invented in 1888 by French coiffeur Alexandre Godefroy. It was a seated device, which consisted of a large bonnet attached, rather alarmingly, to the chimney pipe of a gas stove. In the 1920s, the first electric hairdryers were introduced, but they were still heavy and exhausting to use; some even came with a support for tired arms. It wasn't until the 1950s that more compact and efficient hairdryers became available, thanks to advancements in technology and the introduction of plastic components.

Today there are added features such as adjustable heat settings and ion technology (where the hairdryer blows negative ions onto the hair, where they naturally cling to the positive charge coming from each follicle, reducing frizz). They have also become far less dangerous, with deaths due to hairdryer incidents now at an all-time low. And nowadays, even if you dropped your hairdryer in the bath, it wouldn't necessarily be fatal: you will only be electrocuted if your body completes an electrical circuit between the dryer and the metal drainpipe. Because bathwater is more conductive than the human body, the current would likely flow from the hairdryer to the ground through the water. Let's not test this hypothesis, though.

19 MARCH

The Mother of Modern Physics

The physicist and chemist Marie Curie was born in Poland in 1867. She changed the world and the face of medicine with her groundbreaking research on radioactivity, and was the first woman to win a Nobel Prize (which she actually won twice).

Not only was Marie a queen in the world of science; she had a pretty fabulous way with words of inspiration too. Here is a selection of her finest.

'Be less curious about people and more curious about ideas.'

'I am among those who think that science has great beauty. A scientist in his laboratory is not only a technician: he is also a child placed before natural phenomena which impress him like a fairy tale.'

'One never notices what has been done; one can only see what remains to be done.'

'Nothing in life is to be feared; it is only to be understood.'

20 MARCH

Black Gold

The sturgeon is a remarkable fish with a history as long as a river. Its prehistoric lineage can be traced back millions of years, and we know that sturgeon were around long before the dinosaurs. They settled into their current size and shape around 150 million years ago and haven't found the need to evolve much since. They can grow up to 2.5 metres long, weigh up to 136 kilograms and live up to 150 years. They are living fossils.

We humans have been obsessed with this majestic fish for centuries, and most especially with the unfertilised eggs (roe) of certain sturgeon species, particularly beluga, ossetra and sevruga sturgeon. The first mention of caviar is by Aristotle in the fourth century BCE, and in 1324 the English king Edward II declared sturgeon to be a 'Royal Fish' which could only be nibbled by people in the royal court. Even today, all wild sturgeon found within the foreshore of the United Kingdom are decreed the property of the monarch. But it was the Russian courts that established caviar as an elite gourmet dish and a symbol of luxury and sophistication in the mid-1800s.

Needless to say, overfishing over the next 150 years pushed sturgeon stocks to fall dramatically, leading to conservation efforts to protect these ancient fish. Today, all the legal caviar that we eat is farmed. It's still eye-wateringly expensive: you could expect to pay £110 for a few bites' worth of 50 grams. The world's most expensive food is Almas beluga caviar: 1 kilogram of this fishy wonder is regularly sold for £20,000. It comes from the eggs of the rare albino sturgeon, which swims in the relatively unpolluted southern Caspian Sea.

21 MARCH

The First Rain

petrichor: the pleasant, earthy smell associated with rain falling on very dry ground.

'I love the smell of petrichor in the morning.'

This word combines 'petri', the Greek for 'stone', and 'ichor', the ethereal fluid that was believed to flow through the veins of Greek gods and goddesses.

22 MARCH

The Prince of Stars

Ulugh Beg, born in 1394, was a ruler and astronomer of the Timurid Empire, in what's now Central Asia. As well as being a prince, he was a philosopher and mathematician and he was obsessed with astronomy. He built an extraordinary observatory in Samarkand, where he constructed a huge sextant, used for measuring the positions of celestial objects. It consisted of a large arc with a sighting mechanism, and it had a radius of over 40 metres. He compiled his spookily accurate star positions into an exhaustive set of astronomical tables called the *Catalogue of the Stars*, which was the first comprehensive catalogue of the stars since Ptolemy's of over a thousand years earlier. Ulugh Beg's catalogue remained the primary reference for scholars and astronomers for centuries to come. And he achieved all of this two hundred years before the invention of the telescope.

Ulugh Beg's visionary observatory was razed to the ground after his death (at the hands of an assassin appointed by his own son), and its remains were only discovered by an Uzbeki-Russian archaeologist in 1908. Today, Ulugh Beg is a national hero in Uzbekistan, with a main-belt asteroid and a crater on the moon named after him.

23 MARCH

Unexpected Impacts

On this day in 2020 the UK entered its first lockdown because of the Covid-19 pandemic. Here are some strange and unexpected after-effects of historical pandemics.

- The Black Death ended serfdom. When at least a third of Europe's population was wiped out in the fourteenth century, it created a labour shortage that inflated wages and gave power to the peasants.
- Isaac Newton's WFH led to a science revolution. During the Great Plague of London in 1665–66, Cambridge University sent its students, including Newton, home. Left to his own devices, he had his 'annus mirabilis': sorting out the foundation of calculus, musing on light spectra and spending huge amounts of bored time in his garden underneath that apple tree dreaming up gravitational theory.
- Haiti's fight for independence was in part won by yellow fever. During the Haitian Revolution (1791–1804), mosquito-borne yellow fever decimated Napoleon's troops, leading to Haiti's successful rebellion and the establishment of the first independent Black republic in 1804.
- The Plague of Florence led to great literature: the immensely influential *Decameron* by Giovanni Boccaccio, published in *c.*1353, charts a group of wealthy young Florentines who escape the city to laugh, drink and tell each other stories – one hundred in all.
- The 'Spanish flu' boosted women's rights. The Great Influenza epidemic that started in 1918 killed more men than women, and this, combined with the terrible casualty rates of the First World War, led to vast labour deficits. As women entered the workforce, they demanded more rights.

24 MARCH

The Fashion Police

Velvet's origins can be traced back to ancient China, and it reached Europe in the fourteenth century via trade routes including the Silk Road. Originally woven from silk, velvet was an exclusive fabric reserved for royalty and the nobility due to its high cost and labour-intensive production process. Henry VIII even commissioned a velvet toilet seat, which must have been very comfortable, if tricky to clean. With the advent of the Industrial Revolution, and the invention of the power loom, velvet became much more accessible, and whilst it's still associated with glamour and glitz, any one of us today can grab a little scrap of luxury.

FASHION FELONS: THE SUMPTUARY LAWS

By 1574, Queen Elizabeth I and her court had become so annoyed by the riff-raff (well, mainly newly minted merchants) parading around in gorgeous threads that she extended her sumptuary laws to include clothing. She forbade the wearing of certain clothes to those below a certain social standing and rank. 'Only the King, Queen, King's Mother, children [and] brethren' could wear 'any silk of the color purple, cloth of gold tissued, [or] fur sables.' Outside of the royal family, it was law that no woman could wear 'damask, taffeta, or other silk in any cloak or safeguard: except knights' wives'. It's hard to find much evidence of anyone actually being punished for violating the sumptuary laws but in 1565 one Richard Walweyn, a peasant, was imprisoned for wearing 'a very monsterous and outraygous greate payre of hose'.

25 MARCH

Warring Celts

The Giant's Causeway is an extraordinary UNESCO World Heritage Site that stretches four miles along Northern Ireland's northern coast. Made up of around forty thousand basalt columns, each regularly shaped with five to seven sides, it was created by an ancient volcanic eruption some 50 million years ago. It's no surprise, given its majestical and utterly otherworldly appearance, that it inspired one of Ireland's greatest myths.

The story goes that the causeway was created by the Irish giant Finn MacCool, who, enraged at the Scottish giant Benandonner's claim on Ireland, tore up bits of the Antrim coast to build a bridge to Scotland for a bit of confrontation. However, when Finn arrived, he saw he'd underestimated his opponent, and Benandonner was heftier than he had imagined. He realised his only way out was trickery, so he beat a quick retreat back across the waves and arranged for his wife to dress him up as an enormous baby. When Benandonner arrived, only to be confronted with the giant baby who was said to be Finn's child, he was filled with horror at the thought of what size the father must be, and quickly fled back to the island of Staffa, smashing up the causeway as he went so that Finn could not cross. And so the Emerald Isle was saved.

26 MARCH

Why Do the Clocks Go Back?

British clocks change on the last Sunday in March, moving forward by one hour, meaning we lose some snooze but gain an extra dose of mood-boosting light as we make our way into British Summer Time (BST). As a concept, the changing of the clocks to chime with the seasons has been ticking around since Roman times, but it was a builder from South-East London named William Willett (the great-great-grandfather of Coldplay's Chris Martin, don't you know) who really pushed for daylight saving.

A lover of golf and other outdoor pursuits, William's self-published pamphlet, 'The Waste of Daylight', appeared in 1907 and quickly gained high-profile fans in David Lloyd George, Arthur Conan Doyle and Winston Churchill, who agreed with its argument for the health benefits and fuel-saving ramifications of more daylight hours. But it wasn't until the horrors of the First World War became clear – with coal running desperately short – that Willett's proposal gathered true momentum. And in fact the Germans, suffering their own fuel crisis, went first, passing their Daylight Saving Bill in April 1916. Great Britain passed its own a month later.

27 MARCH

Sacred Stones

There is a long history of stones being associated with places of power and authority. The Benben stone in the temple of the sun god Ra at Heliopolis in ancient Egypt marked the first part of the temple touched by the sun each day. The stone at the centre of the Dome of the Rock in Jerusalem is considered by Muslims to be the place from which the Prophet Muhammad visited heaven, while many Jewish people believe the rock is the Foundation Stone from where the world was created. Across the world there are countless stones of significance, like the thousands-year-old ones at Stonehenge and the omphalos stone at Delphi in Greece. This was once thought to be the centre of the world ('omphalos' means 'navel').

The Stone of Scone (pronounced Scoon) is a very special 152-kilogram block of sandstone. Legend has it that Jacob rested his head on it when he had his visions of a ladder of angels, before it made its way to Scotland. It was used during the coronations of the kings of Scotland until 1296, when it was seized by King Edward I of England and put in the coronation chair at Westminster Abbey.

After various excitements, including a suffragette bomb attack in 1914 and theft by Scottish nationalists in 1950, in 1996 the British government finally returned the stone to Scotland but it journeys back to Westminster for coronations. It's not the only regnal stone around, however. There is a Coronation Stone in Kingston-upon-Thames, which was apparently where various Anglo-Saxon kings were crowned in the tenth century, and the Stones of Mora in Sweden were used in similar ceremonies there in the Middle Ages.

28 MARCH

The King's Whistle

King Henry VIII had a vast appetite: for food, hunting, political machinations, gambling, the theatre, women, divorces and beheadings, and also for music. He could play the lute, the lyre, the harpsichord and the organ, but this larger-than-life figure was particularly passionate about the humble recorder. He is said by the time of his death to have owned a whopping seventy-six of them. *King Henry's Songbook* is a manuscript dating from 1518 that contains thirty-three of the King's own compositions: he was widely regarded as a consummate composer – though it's equally likely that no one felt minded to critique his work, given his penchant for an execution. One ditty that is *not* in the book is 'Greensleeves'; apocrypha has it that Henry wrote it to woo Anne Boleyn, for whom he would break with the Catholic Church to divorce his wife of twenty-four years, Catherine of Aragon. In fact, 'Greensleeves' first appeared in 1580, thirty-three years after Henry's death.

29 MARCH

Cosmic Connectedness

The Fibonacci Sequence is a numerical sequence that was most famously written about by Leonardo Fibonacci, the Italian medieval mathematician, who uncovered it when studying the exponential breeding habits of rabbits. It's a series of numbers where each number is the sum of the two preceding numbers. 0, 1, 1, 2, 3, 5, 8, 13, 21, 34, and so on infinitely.

This sequence brings about a rather wonderful feeling of cosmic connectedness when it is expressed as the golden ratio. This refers to the relationship between a number in the sequence and the number that precedes it; dividing the former by the latter settles into a constant 1.61803, a ratio symbolised by the Greek letter phi Φ. For example, 610 ÷ 377 = 1.61803, just as 987 ÷ 610 = 1.61803.

The golden ratio seems to be some kind of infinitely unifying ordering number, because it can be seen in the way that nature arranges itself in patterns: how plants order petals on a flower, in seedheads, pinecones, whorls on pineapples and cauliflowers, the logarithmic spirals that we find in shells, goats' horns, spiderwebs, the twisting we see in the shapes of hurricanes and even in the shapes of our galaxies. Examples of the golden ratio can be found in human faces too: beauty is commonly perceived in those faces that are 1.61803 times as long as they are wide, with the mouth and nose positioned within golden ratio parameters. Even the DNA molecule follows the Fibonacci Sequence, measuring 34 angstroms long by 21 angstroms wide for each full cycle of its double-helix spiral, at a ratio of 1.6190476, very close to phi.

30 MARCH

Emoti-Can

We think of emoticons as a thoroughly modern invention, the first example being credited to computer scientist Scott Fahlman, who proposed using :-) to denote a joke and :-(to indicate something meant to be taken seriously. Fahlman introduced these symbols in a message on an online bulletin board at Carnegie Mellon University in 1982. But in fact there are examples of text-based visual expressions being used a hundred years earlier – in 1881, to be precise, when *Puck* magazine (a satirical publication famous for its biting social commentary) published the emoticons for –

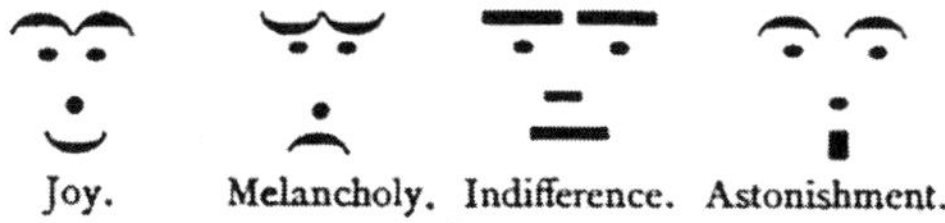

31 MARCH

The Truth

'The truth will set you free, but first it will piss you off.'

Gloria Steinem (1934–present)

Gloria Steinem is an American writer and feminist activist who became famous for going undercover as a Playboy Bunny as part of her investigative journalism work in the 1960s. She later co-founded the influential *Ms.* magazine and helped establish Take Our Daughters to Work Day in the 1990s.

April

1 APRIL

More Fool You

No one knows where the tradition of playing pranks on 1 April comes from but the date has been widely celebrated in different ways in different countries for centuries. The French try to pin paper fish to each other's backs, the 'poisson d'avril'; in Scotland it is sometimes still known as 'Huntigowk Day' or 'Hunt the Gowk Day', with 'gowk' meaning 'cuckoo' or 'fool'; in Britain and Ireland victims were historically sent on 'fool's errands' to deliver important letters, which, when opened, read 'send the fool further', or instructed them to buy 'pigeon's milk' or 'a left-handed monkey wrench'. In England, Ireland and Wales it's still generally only accepted to play tricks before midday, otherwise you become the fool.

Some people think the tradition of April Fool's Day developed from the Roman festival of Hilaria, celebrating the mother goddess Cybele and the coming of spring at the vernal equinox. People began the festival solemnly and ended it joyfully, dressing up and feasting.

2 APRIL

The *Enuma Elish*

The *Enuma Elish* is one of the oldest stories in the world and is thought to have influenced the writing of the Bible's book of Genesis. Written in Akkadian, it is estimated to have been composed around the fourteenth century BCE, but perhaps developed from an even earlier Sumerian myth. It was discovered on clay tablets in 1849 during an archaeological dig of the ancient Library of Ashurbanipal in what is now Iraq by the Assyriologists Sir Austen Henry Layard and Hormuzd Rassam, who were searching for evidence to support stories from the Bible. The *Enuma Elish* was a spectacular and controversial find: before these excavations, people believed the Bible to be the oldest book in the world and no one knew anything at all about the Sumerians.

The story tells of the creation of the world and the triumph of the Babylonian god Marduk:

> In the beginning was water and chaos which separated into the gods Apsu and Tiamat, whose children became the other gods. When Apsu got cross with the noisy younger gods he decided to kill them, but Tiamat warned her oldest son, Enki, who killed Apsu instead. This enraged Tiamat, who then declared war against her children and sent eleven monsters to fight them. Enki's son Marduk finally killed Tiamat by trapping her with the winds and shooting her with an arrow. He established order and created heaven and earth out of her body. He then created humans from the blood of Tiamat's ally Quingu.

3 APRIL

Give It Away Now

Could your clutter be someone else's treasure? April is a traditional time for spring cleaning and setting your house in order. Famed tidying expert Marie Kondo advises freeing your home from unwanted clutter by methodically going through your belongings by category and only keeping those which 'spark joy' – and then making sure they are always kept in their designated space. Anything you decide to get rid of could find an affectionate new home via the network of treasure troves that are charity shops.

DIAMONDS IN THE ROUGH

Eye caught by that odd flowery brown cup you see languishing on a dusty shop shelf? Or that quirky animal print on the floor behind the counter? Or that pretty turquoise bowl? Some lucky shoppers have found themselves surprised by the value of what they've picked up at their local charity shops. In 2013 a man from Sydney got himself a bargain when he bought what turned out to be a rhinoceros horn libation cup for $4, which went on to sell for $75,640. In 2015 a woman from Swindon unknowingly bought a print by the artist Ben Nicholson for 99p, and then sold it at auction for £4,200. And another woman from Hindhead picked up a modest little bowl that turned out to be a Chinese censer worth £21,000.

4 APRIL

What Do Angels Look Like?

The word 'angel' comes from the Greek 'angelos', meaning 'messenger'. In many religions including Judaism, Christianity and Islam, angels are the ethereal intermediary spirits who help people understand the truth about the world and come closer to God, and in some traditions they act as guardians. In their malevolent form they are usually called demons and encourage bad behaviour or cause disasters.

When you think of angels you likely think of white-dressed, glowing, flying people, possibly playing harps or trumpets. In Christian tradition there are nine 'choirs', or types, of angel: cherubim, seraphim, angels, archangels, principalities, powers, virtues, dominions, and thrones or ophanim. They aren't all described but those that are don't look at all like our sweet Christmas-card image of an angel, which has actually developed more from classical depictions of the winged god of love, Cupid. In the Books of Isaiah and Ezekiel, cherubim have two pairs of wings, hooves, and four faces: ox, lion, human and eagle. Seraphim have six wings, and thrones are described as wheels full of eyes.

5 APRIL

Nineteen Eighty-Four's Gift to Language

'It was a bright cold day in April, and the clocks were striking thirteen' is the opening sentence of George Orwell's seminal dystopian novel, *Nineteen Eighty-Four* (the first-edition title is written out in words not digits). It immediately sets the scene that the world of the story is slightly twisted. Original readers in 1949 were thirty-five years away from the future Orwell imagined, and we are now more than forty years beyond it. But the society Orwell's hero, Winston Smith, lives in is more like ours than that of the real 1984: mass surveillance, policing of what people say, falsification of historical facts, domestic tech giving and receiving information, the encouragement of group outrage, and AI writing music and literature. No wonder Orwell's name is mentioned in news stories every week.

Orwell also invented terms that we still use, from 'Newspeak' to 'Room 101' to the 'Thought Police', 'unperson' and 'doublethink': Doublethink means the power of holding two contradictory beliefs simultaneously, and accepting both of them. This term was developed after the novel's publication into the terms 'groupthink', to describe bad decisions made by a group because of the dynamics within that group, and 'doublespeak', meaning language designed to hide the truth. The test of a true classic of literature is that it continues to have something to say to readers long after its publication.

6 APRIL

Minty Fresh

Why is it that when you drink a glass of water after brushing your teeth or chewing gum it tastes colder? This is down to a naturally occurring chemical in mint that makes your brain think things are colder than they are, creating a thermal illusion: menthol. Eucalyptus and tea tree contain a similar chemical called eucalyptol.

We all have proteins in the sensory systems on our skin and in our mouths that transfer information about temperature to the brain. The protein for sensing cold, TRPM8, reacts to menthol in such a way that it sends cold signals to the brain even though your mouth or skin isn't actually made colder. This effect lingers so that water you drink straight afterwards will also seem colder. Capsaicin in hot peppers works in a similar way, with the opposite effect. Both probably developed as defence mechanisms for the plants, to discourage animals from eating them.

However, it isn't menthol that makes orange juice taste disgusting after you brush your teeth. This is because of the sodium lauryl sulfate foaming agent found in many toothpastes. (Sensitive-teeth toothpastes often don't have it.) This chemical suppresses taste buds' sweetness receptors and also breaks up the natural compounds in OJ that reduce its bitterness. This means you get a full-on bitter hit if you clean your teeth just before drinking it. The good news is it only takes about half an hour for the effects of sodium lauryl sulfate to dissipate, and then you are free to glug joyfully at will.

7 APRIL

Zip It

The zip was patented in the USA in 1893 by the inventor Whitcomb L. Judson, who called it a 'clasp locker', and it was mainly used on shoes. This design was refined by European manufacturers but it wasn't until the 1920s that the zip took off. Most clothes zips today are made by Japanese company Yoshida Kōgyō Kabushikigaisha, which is why you'll see the letters YKK on them.

8 APRIL

A Problem Well Stated

'A problem well stated is a problem half-solved.'

Charles F. Kettering, inventor and engineer

Kettering's problem-solving flair is clear from the fact he is listed as the inventor on 186 patents (sadly one of these was for leaded petrol, which turned out to be a problem of its own).

9 APRIL

Where the Hell Is Elmet?

A poisoned father, a daughter with magical powers, a vanished kingdom: it sounds like the plot of a great fantasy series, but it is actually a real mystery from history. Archaeologists and historians discover more about medieval Britain every year, but one conundrum that continues to frustrate and evade them is what happened to the lost kingdom of Elmet.

Yr Hen Ogledd, or the Old North, was a stretch of land in what is now northern England and southern Scotland. It was populated by Celtic British people, in amongst Anglo-Saxons, Picts and Scots. The people of this area spoke a Brittonic dialect like that of the nearby Welsh. Hen Ogledd included the kingdoms of Strathclyde, Gododdin (centred around Edinburgh), Rheged (south of Hadrian's Wall, covering Cumbria) and the lost kingdom of Elmet, which they think was possibly somewhere near Leeds.

According to the seventh-century monk Bede, King Ceretic of Elmet, 'King of the Britons', drew the wrath of the powerful Anglo-Saxon King Edwin of Northumbria after his relative, Hereric, was poisoned while staying in Elmet. (Hereric was the father of a devout young daughter who would become St Hilda of Whitby, who, legend says, freed Whitby from all dangerous snakes by driving them over a cliff, explaining the wealth of ammonites on the shores nearby.) In revenge for Hereric's death, Edwin invaded Elmet and absorbed it into Northumbria in 617 CE. Although some historians believe it did regain its independence for a time after this, the kingdom's exact fate thereafter, and even the borders of where it originally existed, are lost to time.

10 APRIL

Follow Your Nose

Before modern medicine, aromatic massages and baths were commonly used as health treatments around the world. Nowadays, 'aromatherapy' is the name for the use of essential plant oils to help improve physical and mental health. Clinical trials have not decisively shown clear benefits, and some oils can be dangerous if not used correctly, but many users say inhaling certain scents helps them deal with conditions like anxiety, nausea, insomnia and headaches. The idea is that scent molecules from the oils send signals down the olfactory nerves to the brain, where they have a particular effect on the amygdala. (The amygdala is a small almond-shaped part of your brain that is particularly associated with processing emotions and stress responses.) The term 'aromatherapy' was invented in 1937 by a French chemist called René-Maurice Gattefossé, who popularised the therapeutic use of essential oils after burning his hand badly in his lab and discovering that treating it with lavender oil helped it heal. He then devoted himself to finding out more about the beneficial properties of plant oils, especially lavender, which is still one of the most widely used and popular oils in aromatherapy today, and is especially good for instilling calm and promoting sleep.

11 APRIL

The Day's Eye

Daisies are in bloom now in the northern hemisphere, heralding the start of warmer weather. They belong to the plant family Asteraceae (from the Greek word 'aster', meaning 'star'), which includes plants as varied as thistles, chrysanthemums, zinnias, marigolds, dahlias, dandelions, sunflowers, lettuce and artichokes. Asteraceae are thought to have first developed in Argentina over 50 million years ago.

Daisies look like a central button surrounded by long petals, but the button is actually made up of tiny individual flowers and each petal is also a flower. Ox-eye and Shasta daisies grow quite tall but the archetypal English daisy (Bellis perennis) is tiny. Its English name is thought to mean 'day's eye', from the Old English 'dæges eage', because it opens with sunlight in the morning and closes at night. Daisies are small but hardy flowers, which is why you commonly see them in parkland and popping up on lawns.

In medieval times the daisy was also called 'bruisewort' and its leaves were mixed with butter to heal wounds. It was also believed that feeding them to puppies would stop them growing into large dogs. Counterintuitively, Daisy is sometimes used as nickname for people called Margaret. This is in reference to the French word for the flower, 'marguerite'. The game of 'He loves me, he loves me not', where you pick off the individual petals of a daisy to establish whether the object of your affection returns your feelings, was originally called 'effeuiller la marguerite', or 'pluck the daisy'.

12 APRIL

Head Over Heels

limerence: a euphoric and obsessive state of mind resulting from romantic attraction, including the desire to have one's feeling reciprocated.

'What started as a crush developed into full-blown limerence she referred to as "love at first sight".'

The word 'limerence' was invented by the American psychologist Dorothy Tennov in her 1979 book *Love and Limerence: The Experience of Being in Love*. She came up with the term to describe a common feeling she had observed over many years of studying romantic love but which she felt had not been adequately defined before.

13 APRIL

Metric vs Imperial

Before 1824, the UK's official measurement system was based on the 'Winchester measure' of bushels, pecks, gallons and quarts, but with the passing of the Weights and Measures Act the imperial system (inches, miles, ounces, acres) came into regulation. In 1965, in a bid for international cooperation, the UK started to use the French metric measurement – based around units like the metre, which was originally designed in 1791 to embody one ten-millionth of the distance between the equator and the North Pole. This shift had been a long time coming and was not without controversy – back in 1863, Parliament had nearly voted for the UK to convert to metric, to much wailing and fear-mongering in the media, *The Times* warning of 'perplexity, confusion and shame' should the vote go through.

Metric developed into the SI (Système International), which is now most commonly used worldwide. However, many countries still use a mixture of their old-fashioned systems (miles for road signs in the US and UK, pints in UK pubs) and the SI system (seconds, metres, kilograms, amperes, kelvins, moles and candelas). This can cause confusion – as with the Mars Climate Orbiter mission of 1998, where different suppliers of components used both the metric and SI systems, causing the $125 million probe to fail.

14 APRIL

The World's Deadliest Sins

The world's major religions often lay out behaviours their followers should avoid. Particularly well known is the classic office-party combo, the seven deadly sins of lust, gluttony, greed, sloth, wrath, envy and pride. In Christian thought, committing any of these nasties inevitably leads to further immoral behaviour, so they are the most dangerous.

Judaism has 613 mitzvahs, or commandments, that it is considered transgressive to break, and Islam also has a list of major sins, but Hinduism and Buddhism do not hold the same concept of sin. They do both uphold the idea of 'dharma', which refers to living the right way, and 'ahimsa', which means 'non-violence'. For non-religious people, 'The Golden Rule' is an ethical standard most strive to live by, often summarised as: 'Do as you would be done by.'

THE LAST JEDIS

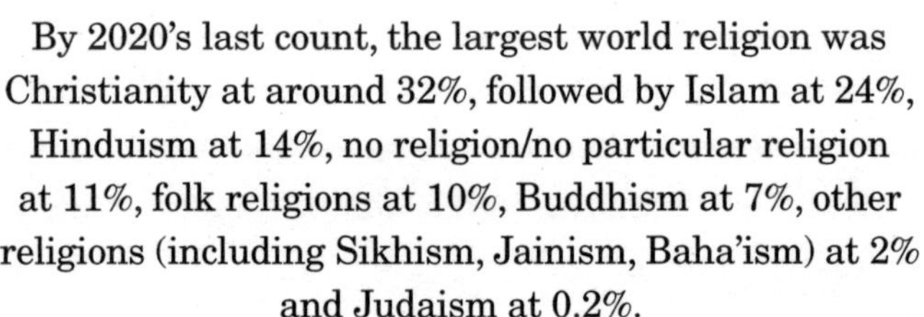

By 2020's last count, the largest world religion was Christianity at around 32%, followed by Islam at 24%, Hinduism at 14%, no religion/no particular religion at 11%, folk religions at 10%, Buddhism at 7%, other religions (including Sikhism, Jainism, Baha'ism) at 2% and Judaism at 0.2%.

Famously in the 2001 UK census 390,127 people logged their religion as Jedi Knight, making it the most popular faith in the 'other religions' category. The Force seems to have weakened in subsequent censuses, and Jedi had dropped to below 1,600 by 2021.

15 APRIL

'I Wandered Lonely as a Cloud'

What many consider England's finest Romantic poem was inspired by a post-prandial walk William Wordsworth took with his sister Dorothy. (So his description of himself as being lonely needs to be taken with a pinch of poetic salt.) She describes it beautifully in her *Grasmere Journal* of 15 April 1802.

> 'When we were in the woods beyond Gowbarrow Park we saw a few daffodils close to the water-side. We fancied that the sea had floated the seeds ashore, and that the little colony had so sprung up. But as we went along there were more and yet more; and at last, under the boughs of the trees, we saw that there was a long belt of them along the shore, about the breadth of a country turnpike road. I never saw daffodils so beautiful. They grew among the mossy stones about and above them; some rested their heads upon these stones, as on a pillow, for weariness; and the rest tossed and reeled and danced, and seemed as if they verily laughed with the wind, that blew upon them over the lake; they looked so gay, ever glancing, ever changing.'

16 APRIL

Shirley Temple Black

Named after the famous Hollywood child star of the 1930s, who found it sickly sweet, the Shirley Temple is the most famous mocktail of all time. Its alcoholic variant, the Shirley Temple Black, is named after the adult Shirley and takes her married name. Shirley is famous for being the youngest-ever winner of an Oscar. She made her film debut at the age of three, starring in a series of films with the now inappropriate-sounding name of *Baby Burlesks*. Less well known is that, when her popularity with audiences waned as she grew up, she went on to become the first female US ambassador to Ghana and Czechoslovakia, among other senior diplomatic roles.

SHIRLEY TEMPLE BLACK (ALCOHOLIC)

50ml dark rum
150ml ginger ale
a splash of grenadine
a maraschino cherry
ice

SHIRLEY TEMPLE (NON-ALCOHOLIC)

200ml ginger ale
a splash of grenadine
a maraschino cherry
ice

17 APRIL

The Here and Now and the There and Then

We are all time travellers, moving through time at one second per second. According to Einstein's special theory of relativity, time is relative rather than absolute. Both gravity and speed can affect time. At very high speeds, the faster you travel the slower you experience time, and the stronger gravity is the slower you experience time. GPS satellites out in space, where gravity is weaker, experience time slightly faster than one second per second and have to be corrected to give us accurate GPS information on earth.

But could we ever travel back in time? A black hole's gravity is so intense that, in theory, it could make space-time fold back on itself, creating a wormhole which would allow you to travel through it to a previous point in time (but not into the future). But only if you could find a way of stopping its gravitational effect from tearing you apart. Scientists call this a 'closed timelike curve', or CTC. In the concept of CTCs, someone time-travelling into the past this way would always have been part of this past so they could not change it.

So time travel is theoretically possible but currently far beyond our capabilities. And many celebrated scientists, including the late genius Stephen Hawking, don't believe it will ever happen – citing as evidence the fact that we've never had anyone visit us from the future. However, humans, apparently uniquely among animals, can mentally time-travel to experience memories of the past and imagine our futures.

18 APRIL

Crossing the Line

Charles Darwin's five-year voyage aboard HMS *Beagle* in the 1830s is well known for inspiring his theories of evolution. It is less well known that at one point on the ship's journey the celebrated scientist was shaved, drenched, lathered with pitch and paint and then ducked in a large tub of water. Strangely enough, this was a common fate for travellers and sailors crossing the equator for the first time – who were known as 'tadpoles' or 'griffins'.

The naval tradition of crossing-the-line ceremonies stretches back at least to the eighteenth century. They are both tests of new sailors' endurance and fun opportunities for the crew to let off steam. Dressing up, pranks and feats of endurance are usually involved: tadpoles are invited to join the court of King Neptune, often by his attendant 'bears' or 'constables'. They are usually 'baptised' in some way by being immersed in water – sometimes even dunked in the sea.

In the past the ceremonies have been violent, involving tadpoles being beaten as well as dunked, but nowadays the rituals are more controlled – although they still involve a lot of outlandish fancy dress.

THE EQUATOR'S MUFFIN TOP

There is a bulge in the earth's diameter at the equator; this means that if you measured the height of mountains by distance from the earth's core, rather than from sea level, the peak of Mount Chimborazo in Ecuador would be the highest point on earth, rather than Everest.

19 APRIL

What Are Taxes For?

What do Bermuda, Monaco, the Bahamas and the UAE have in common? They do not collect any income tax from their citizens. However, for the rest of the world, the true certainties in life are death and taxes. Governments generally collect a share of their citizens' earnings and invest in shared resources we can sometimes take for granted, like education, roads, policing, healthcare, waste collection, libraries, defence and social care.

For example, in 2023 the UK goverment spent 19.8% of the income tax and national insurance revenue it received on health, 19.6% on welfare, 12% on national debt interest, 10.3% on state pensions, 9.9% on education, 7.6% on business and industry, 5.2% on defence, 4.1% on public order and safety, 4.1% on transport, 2% on government administration, 1.7% on housing and utilities; 1.3% on culture, 1.3% on environment, 0.6% on payments to the EU and 0.5% on overseas aid.

Depending on the government's priorities, taxes can also be adjusted to address social concerns. But government priorities can sometimes be eccentric. The Roman emperor Vespasian (9–79 CE) famously taxed the sale of pee, which was collected from public urinals to be used as a chemical by tanners and as a bleach for laundries. And in the eighteenth century, the Russian tsar Peter the Great (1672–1725) had an unusual plan to modernise Russian culture by taxing beards. He wanted his country to become more European and adopt the clean-shaven fashion popular there, so his citizens had to pay and carry an exemption token if they wanted to keep their beards.

20 APRIL

Take a Bath with the Trees

For centuries, taking in the sea air has been considered beneficial, but there are other ways to bring nature therapy into your life. Since the 1980s in Japan, the Forestry Agency has developed a practice called *shinrin-yoku*, or forest bathing.

To forest-bathe you don't need your swimming trunks. You just need to spend regular time – ideally two hours a week – walking slowly, without looking at your phone, through a woodland or quiet local park, concentrating on your sensory response to the environment. Trees, sky and birdsong have been shown in studies to improve mental well-being, and research about spending time in nature has shown it may reduce anxiety, improve blood pressure and decrease the incidence of diabetes.

THE WOOD WIDE WEB

It may seem fanciful but while you're enjoying their splendour on your forest dip, the trees are talking to one another. They are linked through their roots by a network of fungus called a mycelium. They use the mycelium to send nutrients to their seedlings and other trees in need. Mycorrhizal networks also connect other plants: scientists have found that broad bean plants connected by mycelium put out the same chemical response if one of them is attacked by aphids, implying the victim plant is alerting its neighbours.

21 APRIL

Not-Quite-Danish Pastries

Danish pastries should really be called Austro-Danish pastries. The story goes that they were invented in the mid-nineteenth century when the Danish Bakers' Association went on strike and bakers came to the country to take over their work and feed the nation. They taught Danish bakers new ways of layering pastry and the Danish added fruit and butter to the Austrian recipes, creating what we think of as a Danish pastry. The Danes call their pastries 'Wienerbrød', or 'Viennese bread'. Several other famous foods also have misleading geographical monikers.

- Baked Alaska is not from Alaska but is thought to have been invented in New York in 1876, to celebrate the USA buying Alaska from Russia in 1867. It was originally called Alaska Florida to refer to the cold ice cream and hot meringue covering it.
- French fries, which are called 'pommes frites' ('fried potatoes') in France, were named by US soldiers in the First World War. They discovered the dish in Belgium but called them French because that was the language their Belgian brothers in arms spoke.
- Hawaiian pizza, with pineapple, was apparently originally invented in 1962 by Greek-Canadian chef Sam Panopoulos, who simply named it after the brand of pineapple he used.

22 APRIL

Screw-Down Cocks

If you showed a medieval peasant a kitchen tap and told them that we have instant access to hot and cold clean running water, they would be amazed. It's easy to take this wonderful technology for granted. Before 1613 the only way to get drinking water in the UK was from wells and rivers and by collecting rainwater. This was hard to do in busy cities like London. Then an entrepreneur called Hugh Myddelton built the New River canal to bring water into London from Hertfordshire, and connected it to various rich people's houses. Others began to follow suit and advances were made when iron pipes replaced the original wooden ones in the early 1800s, allowing for greater water pressure (created by steam pumping stations) and broader supply. The New River canal continues to supply water to London today.

The Romans had a form of tap for their advanced water supplies but the precursor to the tap we know today was the 'high-pressure loose-valve screw-down cock' invented in 1845 in Rotherham by the Guest and Chrimes company.

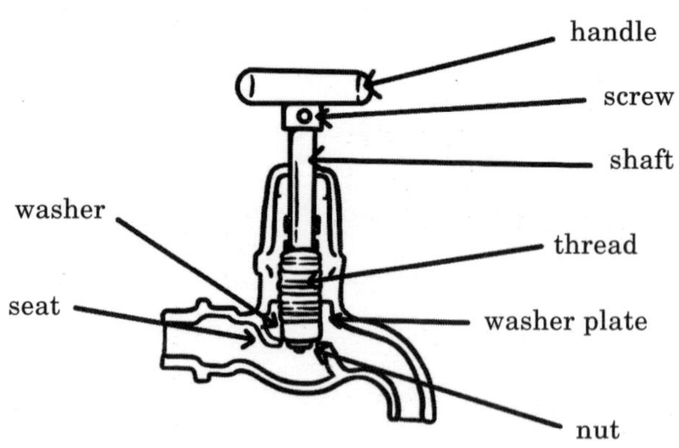

23 APRIL

How English Is St George?

For many centuries, this day has been celebrated as the feast day of St George, the patron saint of England . . . and Georgia, Aragon, Catalonia, Lithuania, Palestine, Portugal, Germany, Greece, Moscow, Istanbul and Genoa, soldiers, farmers, riders, sufferers of leprosy and plague, and Scouts. There is no reliable history of St George but tradition says he was born to Christian parents in what is now Turkey in the third century CE and became a soldier for the Roman Empire. He left the army in protest against the persecution of Christians by the Emperor Diocletian and was arrested and tortured, before being beheaded on 23 April. He never visited England.

George was canonised in 494 CE but it wasn't until the ninth century that his story started to feature a man-eating dragon that he was said to have defeated in Libya. It's likely George's story came to England with knights returning from the Crusades in the Middle East, and he is usually depicted as a Crusader knight himself, on horseback wearing a tunic with a red cross on a white background (which now makes up part of the design of the Union Jack). When King Edward III set up the Order of the Garter for his best knights in 1348, he picked St George as its guiding light.

As a warrior, George has been said to appear to inspire English armies on the battlefield, including at Antioch and during the Great Retreat from Mons during the First World War; in 1940, King George VI set up the George Cross as an award for outstanding acts of courage in war.

24 APRIL

The First Sonnets

The first sonnet sequence in English was published in 1560 by the Calvinist religious poet and translator Anne Locke (c. 1530–c. 1590) and called *A Meditation of a Penitent Sinner.* As you can tell from the title, Anne's poems were a bit less hearts-and-flowers than we'd usually associate with sonnets, including lines like 'The lothesome filthe of my disteined life'. Locke wrote her collection in the English sonnet form popularised by her contemporary the Earl of Surrey, which uses the rhyme scheme ABAB CDCD EFEF GG, later used by Shakespeare too.

Surrey and fellow aristo Sir Thomas Wyatt brought the sonnet form to England from Italy, where it had been popularised by the poet Petrarch. Petrarch spent twenty years writing over three hundred poems of unrequited love about a woman he noticed in church called Laura. (The Petrarchan sonnet follows a different scheme: an octet of ABBA ABBA and then a sestet with a pattern like CDC DCD or CDE CDE.)

Wyatt had a rather more wild time and was imprisoned for having an affair with Anne Boleyn. (He was being held in the Tower of London when she was beheaded there.) Some of Wyatt's poems have been interpreted to be about Anne, including one featuring the lines:

And graven with diamonds in letters plain
There is written, her fair neck round about:
Noli me tangere, for Caesar's I am,
And wild for to hold, though I seem tame.

'Noli mi tangere' is Latin for 'Do not touch me' and 'Caesar' is taken to mean Henry VIII.

25 APRIL

Cunning Stunts

In myriad action movies we enjoy the gasp-inducing work of highly skilled and ingenious stunt coordinators, yet there is still no Oscar for stunt performance. Here are a few moves to look out for next time you're at the cinema or relaxing with a box set.

- **The Full Body Burn** is when a character is fully on fire. This often happens to unfortunate henchmen. Fireproof clothes, gloves and hoods are worn and any exposed areas are soaked in a high-water-content gel. Then a special flammable gel is applied and lit and the performer moves forward in a choreographed way to avoid inhaling the smoke before they are swiftly extinguished.
- **A Texas Switch** is when a stuntperson and actor swap places while obscured by scenery during the action. If you see someone run past a pillar or drop down out of screen and then pop up again before or after an amazing stunt, you've seen a Texas Switch.
- **An air ram** is a high-pressure device for launching a stunt performer into the air, as if they've been blown up by a bomb or some other force. These are carefully calibrated so the performer lands on deep crash mats to cushion their fall.
- **Stunt cars** are fitted with extra safety devices and frames to strengthen them for rolls, to allow cameras to be fixed to them and to prepare for any accidents. Sometimes an air ram is attached to a car to help launch it into the air.

26 APRIL

Flare Flair

Flared trousers were first popularised by American sailors in the nineteenth century because the wide-leg bell-bottomed style made it both easy to roll the trousers up when working in water and to take them off when they got wet.

27 APRIL

Immigrant Species

What makes an animal or plant native to the UK? The short answer is that if it wasn't introduced by humans, it's native. But it's more complicated than that, as wildlife populations have changed with geographic conditions over millions of years, so often the boundary is counted as the end of the last ice age, about eleven thousand years ago. Here is a surprising list of species categorised as non-native.

- Rabbits were thought to have come to the British Isles with Norman invaders in the eleventh century CE, but in 2019 archeologists discovered a rabbit bone on a Roman dig site in Sussex, although there is no evidence that they were common at this time.
- Leeks were introduced when Britain was part of the Roman Empire (43–410 CE). The Romans also brought walnuts, carrots and cherries, and made chickens popular.
- Carp were introduced at an unknown point before 1496 when they were first listed in a fishing guide as 'a deyntous fysshe' and 'an euyll fysshe to take'.
- Grey squirrels were first imported from North America to Britain in the 1870s, but the great conservationist Herbrand Russell, Duke of Bedford, is considered particularly responsible for their conquest of the native red squirrel population. He brought ten greys to his home in Woburn and let them loose, and gave away a few as presents, releasing them into London's Regent's Park.
- House mice in the north of the British Isles have DNA connections to Norwegian, Icelandic and Greenlandic populations, implying that the Vikings brought their mice with them.

28 APRIL

Ill Humour

From ancient Greece and Rome up to the nineteenth century, many people in Europe believed that the balance of 'humours' in your body affected your health and personality. Too much blood, phlegm, yellow bile/choler and black bile/melancholy could throw you out of harmonious balance and make you sanguine, phlegmatic, choleric or melancholic. The word 'humour' meant 'body fluid' and only came to our modern sense of something funny via the word's meaning extending to include 'state of mind' and eventually an amused state of mind.

Lovesickness was originally thought to stem from having too much black bile and could supposedly be cured through the use of laxatives. Nosebleeds meant you had too much blood, which naturally meant you should submit to bloodletting or leeches to rebalance you. A runny nose meant too much phlegm so you needed to be steamed, and too much yellow bile was fixed by taking a cold bath. Diet also influenced your humours, so too much phlegm could be fixed by eating watery veg.

29 APRIL

Algorithms and Bone-Setting

Most of us are familiar with algebra from school, where letters stand in for values in mathematical equations. The 'Father of Algebra' was Muhammad ibn Musa al-Khwarizmi (c. 780–c. 850 CE), an astronomer and mathematician from Baghdad. We get the word 'algebra' from the title of his famous book about it, *Al-Kitāb al-mukhtasar fī hisāb al-jabr wa'l-muqābala* or *The Compendious Book on Calculation by Completion and Balancing.* The Arabic 'al-jabr' in the title means 'the reunion of broken parts' or 'bone-setting', referring to the work required to manipulate equations.

Al-Khwarizmi's influence on today's world extends even further than algebra. He also helped popularise the use of Hindu-Arabic numerals throughout the Islamic world, which then spread to Europe. These are the numbers we use today instead of unwieldy Roman numerals. 888 + 112 is much clearer than DCCCLXXXVIII + CXII.

Another of his texts also had a big impact: his *Kitāb al-hisāb al-hindī* came to Europe with the Latin title *Algoritmi de numero Indorum,* meaning *Al-Khawrizmi's Principles of Hindu Reckoning.* This transliteration of his name is where we get the word 'algorithm' from.

30 APRIL

The Periodic Table of Your Mobile Phone

Mobile phones contain around thirty of the ninety-eight natural elements in the periodic table **(see 12 March)**. For example, tungsten is used in the vibration mechanism, lithium is great for storing energy in your battery, aluminium and silicon are used in the glass screen, yttrium, along with terbium and dysprosium, helps makes the colours on your screen bright, indium makes it work as a touchscreen, and bromine is used to make the case flame-retardant.

Several of these naturally occurring elements are due to run out in the next few decades due to our failure to recycle and our regular rush to replace our phones. Many phone ingredients like tin, gold, tungsten and tantalum are also 'conflict elements'. These are often mined in war zones and involve child labour. The extraction of these elements often has a negative environmental effect too, so next time your magpie eye is distracted by a shiny new model, ask yourself: do you really need that upgrade?

May

1 MAY

Crowdfunding Calamity

In the late seventeenth century, the Company of Scotland, an overseas trading monopoly, attempted to colonise the Darién Gap between Colombia and Panama. The brainchild of banker William Paterson, the plan was to establish a port on the narrow strip of land that connects North and South America, to control the trade between the Atlantic and Pacific Oceans. Paterson sold the dream to his countrymen: they would build New Caledonia there, a paradise of wealth and happiness. The English were originally involved in the investment too, but pulled out after King William III succumbed to pressure from the East India Company and the Spanish. Undeterred, between the government and countless individuals pouring their life savings into the venture, the Scots raised £400,000 (about £56 million today).

The expedition was an unmitigated disaster. Around 1,200 souls left Leith Harbour on 12 July 1698 in five boats. Many perished on the journey, including Paterson's wife, and they arrived to find a mosquito-infested patch of swampy land with few supplies, fighty Spanish neighbours and an Indigenous population who weren't best pleased with their new guests. After seven months, the company decided to abandon its dream. However, communications were tricky and the next two convoys had no idea things had gone to pieces. Out of sixteen boats that left Leith, only one returned; two thousand people died and Scotland bankrupted itself. This paved the way for Scotland to accept the Act of Union, and its clause that promised 'The Equivalent', a financial payment of nearly £398,000, as compensation both for taking on a share of England's national debt and for the losses suffered on the doomed expedition.

2 MAY

When the Flower Blooms

'When the flower blooms, the bees come uninvited.'

Ramakrishna (1836–86), Hindu spiritual leader who taught that all religions are different paths to the same destination

3 MAY

Floriography: The Language of Flowers

The language of flowers – a coquettishly cryptic means of communication – bloomed in Victorian Britain and America in the nineteenth century. Its roots lie in the traditional language of flowers known as 'Selam', which originated in Turkish harems as far back as the thirteenth century. It allowed for secret sexy communication between the (often illiterate) women of the harem and their lovers.

Lady Mary Wortley Montagu, wife of the British ambassador to Turkey in the early eighteenth century, wrote in a letter that 'There is no colour, no flower, no weed, no fruit, herb, pebble or feather that has not a verse belonging to it; and you may quarrel, reproach, or send letters of passion, friendship, or even news, without ever inking your fingers.' It's thought that the posthumous publication of her letters in 1762 kickstarted the Western craze that allowed lovers to declare their feelings within a society that frowned upon such communication. In 1884, Routledge published its *Language of Flowers* – a lexicon of love that ensured everyone was singing from the same flowersheet.

Some – curiously particular – definitions:

- deep-red rose = bashful admiration
- gum rockrose = I shall die tomorrow
- adonis = sorrowful reminiscences
- cactus = I shall not survive you
- carnation, withered = sadness
- fuchsia = anxiety
- iris = my compliments
- myrtle = I love you
- night-scented jasmine = watchfulness

4 MAY

Perfect Flow

太极拳

Could tai chi be the perfect form of exercise? It's suitable for any age group, for any level of fitness, no equipment is needed and it is as good for the mind as it is for the body. Tai chi has its roots in Chinese Taoism, the ancient belief system that celebrates the delicate balance between yin and yang, where yin energy is receptive and dark, and yang is active and expansive. In Taoism, a central belief is that humans and animals should strive to live in harmony with Tao, or the universe. According to legend, tai chi was created by a Taoist monk who watched a battle between a crane and a snake, and was struck by their graceful movements and flowing energy. The idea is that two forces should work in harmony to achieve balance, and that by performing fluid movements one can reach a state of meditation in motion.

There are several different styles of tai chi with slightly different sequences. The widely practised Yang style, named for its founder, Yang Luchan, has 108 moves, but you can start with the basics, like the Single Whip Move, involving a fluid motion with one hand extended while the other hand forms a whip-like shape, which is great for boosting your chi energy.

5 MAY

Finding Roots

Crafting a family tree is an immensely rewarding activity, boosting compassion for, and connection with, those who came before us. And besides, you might uncover some juicy family secrets or remarkable relatives. A recent study of Y chromosomes showed that around 16 million men today share genetic material with the thirteenth-century Mongolian warrior king Genghis Khan.

Building a family tree involves a few steps, but one of the most enjoyable aspects of ancestry research is talking to your older relatives, who can give you the colour and context that public records can't. Begin with yourself at the bottom of a large piece of paper, and work upwards, adding names, birth dates and relationships.

You can pack it with genealogical gold dust like marriage dates, occupations and locations to bring your family history to life. And a big bonus is that you are guaranteed to uncover a venerable royal connection: pretty much everyone with British ancestry is descended from Edward III, according to geneticist Adam Rutherford, while most Europeans are related to Charlemagne, King of the Franks and Christian Emperor of the West.

6 MAY

Rhubarb Rhubarb Rhubarb

The origin story of what we think of as a quintessentially British foodstuff is surprisingly packed with misadventure and intrigue. Rhubarb originates in Asia and has been used in Chinese medicine for over five thousand years. But in the seventeenth century, Russia's rulers took advantage of their role in the trade routes to Europe and created a monopoly by banning the sale of rhubarb seeds outside of Russia – at one point, they were more valuable than gold. A Scottish physician, one James Mounsey, is responsible for breaking this stranglehold. Mounsey had been a leading court physician to Peter III, who was allegedly murdered by his wife, Catherine the Great, in a coup d'état. After Peter's death in 1762, Mounsey realised his position at court was fragile, and persuaded the Empress Catherine to allow him to return to Scotland due to his failing health. He smuggled several pounds of rhubarb seeds home with him and, as cultivators worked to master the art of growing rhubarb, the UK's love affair with it began.

In fact, growers managed to get one up on their Russian rivals by discovering a way to extend the vegetable's growing season. The story goes that a worker at the Chelsea Physic Garden accidentally placed an upturned bucket on top of a crown of rhubarb, and when it was removed gorgeous pale stems had grown. By 'forcing' the rhubarb out of its natural winter hibernation, growers invented forced rhubarb, and prolonged its season into January, February and March. Today, the 'Rhubarb Triangle' of West Yorkshire, a nine-square-mile area between Leeds, Bradford and Wakefield, has been awarded protected status by the EU.

7 MAY

Nul Points!

The Eurovision Song Contest, or, in the spirit of the thing, Le Grand Prix Eurovision de la Chanson Européenne, was invented by a Swiss television executive named Marcel Bezençon and first broadcast in 1956, featuring solo singers from just seven countries. It quickly became famous for its flamboyant performances, eccentric costumes and deeply cynical voting blocs. Love it or loathe it, you can always rely on the song contest to deliver quite bonkers performances. Our favourites include:

- Luxembourg, 1980, 'Papa Pingouin' (56 points) – A penguin-themed revel-in-the-silliness-of-it song, in which two sisters croon while a large man in a penguin suit waddles amongst them.
- Ukraine, 2007, 'Dancing Lasha Tumbai' (235 points) – Dressed entirely in silver foil, this drag act created a whole new genre of techno-accordion, and bagged second place.
- Montenegro, 2013, 'Igranka' (41 points) – Rap is always an outlier in the song contest, but this performance by established duo Who See really pushed the boundaries as they dressed in astronaut suits and excelled at slow-mo dancing during the main singer's chorus.

(UN)LUCKY COLOURS

There are many peculiar things about the contest. One of the most curious is that acts whose performances feature the colour green tend not to do well. The curse was broken when Katrina (of 'and the Waves') wore a green shirt in Dublin and stormed to top of the podium in 1997.

8 MAY

Lift-Off

Humanity's obsession with flight is stitched into our very being. The Greeks immortalised it in the myth of Icarus, and in the ninth century the Muslim inventor Abbas ibn Firnas briefly achieved flight after he created a bird-like flying machine. He fell almost immediately and really hurt his back, but he did manage it more than a thousand years before the Wright brothers. But if the idea of hurtling through the air at 36,000 feet in a cramped metal tube gives you the heebie-jeebies, understanding the physics behind flight might soothe your nerves.

In simple terms, aeroplanes fly because of the principles of aerodynamics. As pilot and chronicler of the skies Mark Vanhoenacker so beautifully puts it, these act as 'a kind of natural sculptor' to create the graceful shapes of aircraft design and work with the four main forces at play: lift, thrust, weight and drag.

- **Lift** is the upward force that allows an aeroplane to overcome gravity and stay up.
- **Thrust** is the forward force that propels the plane through the air.
- **Weight**, or gravity, is the unhelpful force pulling the plane down towards the ground. The other forces, particularly lift, must be greater than the weight to keep it airborne.
- **Drag** is the resistance or force that opposes the forwards motion of the plane. Clever designers and engineers work to minimise drag by designing beautifully aerodynamic shapes.

It's all a question of balance, and pilots are highly skilled at using things like the ailerons, elevators and rudders to hold the four forces in perfect harmony, so we can take off, stay up and land safely.

9 MAY

Cruciverbal Conundrums

Crosswords seem to thrive in times of upheaval, when people look for distraction and relaxation: the first was published in December 1913 by Liverpudlian Arthur Wynne, an editor at *New York World*'s 'Fun' section, just as tensions in Europe began gearing up towards the First World War. Crosswords hit another high in the 1930s as war loomed again.

There was even a suspected spy-puzzle leak during the Second World War. The story goes that, in the weeks before D-Day, certain unusual code words like 'Neptune' and 'Mulberry' appeared in the *Telegraph* crossword. The setter, a headmaster named Leonard Dawe, was horrified to be accused by the authorities of a security breach. When no evidence was found, Leonard went back to his innocent acrostical ways. Forty years later, a former pupil of Dawe's claimed that he and the other boys had overheard the words from an army base adjacent to the school, and then fed them to Mr Dawe as interesting clue answers.

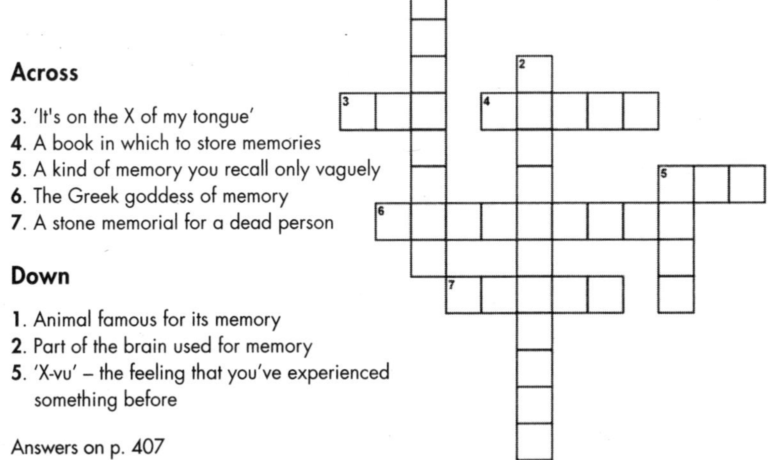

Across

3. 'It's on the X of my tongue'
4. A book in which to store memories
5. A kind of memory you recall only vaguely
6. The Greek goddess of memory
7. A stone memorial for a dead person

Down

1. Animal famous for its memory
2. Part of the brain used for memory
5. 'X-vu' – the feeling that you've experienced something before

Answers on p. 407

10 MAY

The Theory of Colours

Ever slept in a red room and woken up feeling curiously furious? That's because red elicits an excited and aggressive response in human beings, according to some theories. Scholars have been fascinated by the link between colour and psychology for centuries. Giant of literature Johann Wolfgang von Goethe's *The Theory of Colours* (1810) is a key text on the subject, and in it he proposes the idea that colours are not inherent in light but are instead a result of the interplay between light and darkness, and that they are linked to emotional responses (a pretty radical refutation of Isaac Newton's mathematical ideas about the colour spectrum). Based on his own experiences with his perception of colour, Goethe stated that yellow is associated with serenity and 'gladdening', and you might notice that primary schools and hospitals are often painted yellow. And as for the room you spend the most time in, Goethe says: 'The eye experiences a distinctly grateful impression from this colour . . . Hence for rooms to live in constantly, the green colour is most generally selected.'

11 MAY

Mary's Tears

The flower most associated with the month of May is the lily of the valley (*Convallaria majalis*), an achingly delicate and perfumed flower known for its bell-shaped blooms, symbolic of sweetness, purity and joy. Legend has it that the lily of the valley was created by the slightly creepy god Apollo, who laid it down as a carpet in the woods to protect the delicate feet of his nine nymphs. In Christian lore, it's said that Mary shed tears at the foot of Jesus's cross and they transformed into beautiful lilies of the valley; they are also sometimes held to represent Eve's tears after she was expelled from the Garden of Eden. In medieval England, as part of traditional May Day celebrations, a dance took place in which likely lads would place a bloom of lily of the valley on the front door of girls who'd caught their eye. If the object of their affections turned up at the party later with the flowers in her hair, it meant the game was on, romantically speaking.

12 MAY

Astronomical Alignment

syzygy [*sizz-eh-gee*]

'I can't believe how perfect that syzygy was last night.'

'Syzygy' is a fabulous word derived from the Greek 'syzygos', meaning 'yoked together'. Astrologists and stargazers use it to describe the partial or complete alignment or configuration of three celestial bodies. The most common type of syzygy (but deeply exciting for us mortals) is the alignment of the earth, moon and sun during lunar and solar eclipses.

13 MAY

Wild Rides

Evolution is a thing of wonder. As well as designing more perfectly adapted beings, evolution has also thrown up some truly wild animal genitals and reproductive habits.

1. **The Argentine blue-bill** (*Oxyura vittata*) is a type of duck which possesses a corkscrew-shaped penis that can extend up to 40 centimetres in length, helping it to navigate the equally complicated reproductive tract of the female blue-bill.
2. **The spiny anteater** (*Tachyglossidae*) has a red four-headed penis. During mating, two heads become active, alternating between use, giving an echidna's junk better efficiency in navigating the female's two-branched vagina.
3. **The male bedbug** (*Cimex lectularius*) uses the grim technique of traumatic insemination, whereby it pierces the female's abdomen and ejaculates into her body cavity. This can often prove fatal for the female.
4. **Some species of flatworms** engage in extraordinary penis fencing. These hermaphroditic organisms use their sharp, stubby, swordlike penises to spar and attempt to pierce their partner's skin. The first one to be successfully inseminated assumes the female role, while the other becomes the male.
5. **The female hyena** (specifically, the spotted hyena – *Crocuta crocuta*) has a pseudo-penis that is very similar in size and appearance to the male's actual penis. It is in fact an elongated clitoris, which serves as a birth canal and is used for urination, mating, and can even become erect when she gets excited.

14 MAY

Harlem

What happens to a dream deferred?

Does it dry up
like a raisin in the sun?
Or fester like a sore—
And then run?
Does it stink like rotten meat?
Or crust and sugar over—
like a syrupy sweet?

Maybe it just sags
like a heavy load.

Or does it explode?

Langston Hughes (1901–67)

Langston Hughes was a writer of fiction, non-fiction, plays and children's books, and was one of the key figures of the Harlem Renaissance, an explosion of Afro-American art and culture that took place in New York City in the 1920s and 1930s. In this devastating protest poem, Hughes interrogates the idea of the American Dream – the idea that anyone can make a success of their life – and asks if that is really true for the Black community, given the obstacles they face. He wonders what happens when dreams and hopes are put on hold, using visceral imagery to bring his ideas to life. The final line is ambivalent: is the question simply a musing, or is it a prediction?

15 MAY

Yes You Cannes

Cinema's story began with the Lumière brothers' glimmering wonders and, from indie flicks to dazzling blockbusters, its storytelling allure never fades to black. Expand your cinematic journey with some lesser-known genres.

1. **Mumblecore**: A low-budget genre characterised by naturalistic acting and improvised dialogue, and rooted in the everyday. Richard Linklater's *Slacker* (1990) is considered a mumblecore masterpiece.
2. **Slow Cinema**: Known for its deliberate pacing, long takes and pared-back storytelling, this genre challenges you to interpret subtle changes. *From What Is Before* (2015) directed by Lav Diaz, a five-and-a-half-hour-long epic which bears witness to a tragedy that befell a Philippine village in the 1970s, is a consummate example.
3. **Mockumentary**: This genre presents fictional stories in a documentary-style format, blurring the lines between reality and fiction, in order to satirise its subject. Rob Reiner's *This Is Spinal Tap* (1984) hilariously sends up the world of rock stars.
4. **Lynchian**: Influenced and inspired by the works of filmmaker David Lynch, these movies are long on strange, dreamlike narratives and opaque symbolism. Richard Ayoade's *The Double* (2013) is a disturbing Kafkaesque nightmare.
5. **Kaiju**: The clue is in the name, which means 'monstrous creature'. This Japanese genre celebrates gigantic monsters engaging in epic battles. Nacho Vigalondo's *Colossal* (2016), in which an alcoholic Anne Hathaway manifests a giant monster to terrorise Seoul, is a gem.

16 MAY

Bee First Aid

Bees matter. Along with other pollinators, it's been calculated that they are responsible for one in every three bites of food we eat.

On top of their propagating prowess, bees have many astonishing characteristics. These tiny animals, with brains the size of sesame seeds, have been shown in various experiments to be capable of adding and subtracting, understanding the concept of zero, playing football (by moving balls to get a sugar treat), dancing, and being capable of flying at the height of Mount Kilimanjaro (around 5,895 metres).

We can all help to protect our apian amigos and create bee-friendly environments.

- Whether you have a window box or a wild meadow, make sure you plant native flowers that bloom through the year: bees can be active from February to November. Think snowdrops, crocuses and forget-me-nots in spring; sunflowers, geraniums, rosemary and lavender in summer; and ivy, winter honeysuckle and winter clematis in the colder months.
- Emancipate yourself from the tyranny of a well-mown lawn. Allowing a little wildness provides a playground for flowers and weeds, which will encourage all sorts of insects.
- Plant a tree – bees get most of their nectar from trees. Apple and crab-apple trees are particular favourites.
- Make a bee bath. Put out a small bowl with some rocks or stones that sit above the waterline to break the water's surface.
- Inspire the next generation: involving children in the buzz is soul-enriching and helps to future-proof our green spaces.

17 MAY

The Body's Defence Systems

Our *Avengers*-style immune system of cells, tissues and organs protects us from harmful invaders, such as bacteria, viruses and other pathogens, and it even remembers specific pathogens it has encountered before, so that if the same nasty attacks again it can assemble and launch a quick response.

There are actually two immune systems: the innate and the adaptive. The innate system is the Black Widow of the piece: the body's first line of defence. It includes the skin and mucous membranes, as well as immune cells like phagocytes, natural killer cells and complement proteins, which all work together to quickly eliminate invaders.

The adaptive immune system is Hulk: it takes longer to kick in but it generates strong and long-lasting immunity. It involves specialised white blood cells called lymphocytes, including B cells and T cells. B cells are your Tony Starks, beavering away to produce antibodies that bind to specific pathogens, marking them for destruction. T cells are like a flexible Dr Strange, playing various roles, such as directly killing infected cells or coordinating immune responses. T and B cells are the most quickly evolving cells in the human genome – this is how we can keep up with flu strains that evolve and mutate very quickly.

18 MAY

Bordering on Insanity

Have you ever stopped to notice the map of Africa? Around 30% of the borders on the continent consist of straight lines, and they have a dark and tangled past. The 'Scramble for Africa' was a period in the second half of the nineteenth century when European powers raced each other to secure treaties from Indigenous rulers (or their supposed representatives) to allow the plundering of natural resources. The Berlin Conference of 1884–85 represented the peak of the scramble. Lasting 104 days, it was attended by representatives from every European country except Switzerland, as well as the United States. There were no Africans at the table. It laid down the principles for free trade and set out the framework for future European claims. As European powers divided and colonised the African continent, they carved out nations with little thought for the actual terrain, let alone ethical, tribal and cultural boundaries. For example, mistakes about the shape of the Akwayafe river, which was designated as the boundary between Cameroon and Nigeria, have caused long-lasting problems. As the river demarcates the oil-rich Bakassi peninsula, its shape really does matter, and the two West African countries spent years attempting to claim it as their own, even taking their case to the International Court of Justice.

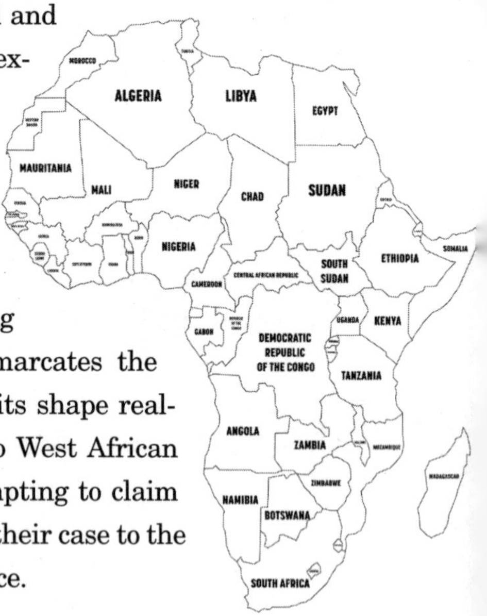

19 MAY

Quantum What Now?

Quantum mechanics is the branch of physics that deals with things that are extremely tiny: the size of an atom and smaller. Much of what happens at this microscopic level makes no sense, even to the cleverest of scientists. In fact, quantum mechanics' most famous (and fun) scientist, Richard Feynman, once said, 'I think I can safely say that no one understands quantum mechanics.' Things happen at atomic levels that sound like they belong in science fiction, yet experiments have repeatedly proven that they do occur. One of the principles of quantum mechanics is that, if you observe subatomic particles, their behaviour will completely change – so it's impossible to observe them in their unobserved state. You can find out where a particle is or how fast it's moving but not both of those things: this is called Heisenberg's uncertainty principle. Particles exist in a range of potential states until they are observed: their situation before they are observed, when they can be in two places at once, is called 'superposition'.

The most famous illustration of the weirdness of quantum behaviour is the Schrödinger's Cat paradox. In this thought experiment, if you lock a cat in a box with a poison which will eventually kill it, you cannot tell until you open the box whether the cat is dead or alive, so the cat is in a superposition state of being simultaneously both dead and alive until it's observed.

The concept of quantum computers was first imagined in 1982 by Feynman, who speculated that by harnessing the bonkers principles of quantum mechanics, quantum computers could work far more efficiently than classical computers. In 1985, David Deutsch, another influential physicist, expanded on Feynman's concepts and proposed the idea of a universal quantum computer. Since then, researchers and scientists have been building machines that harness the unique properties of quantum bits, such as superposition and entanglement, to explore many possibilities simultaneously and process information in parallel. This means that complex problems in fields like cryptography, optimisation and scientific simulation can be performed vastly more efficiently: in 2023, Google claimed its latest model could carry out in seconds a calculation it would take a standard supercomputer forty-seven years to do. So mind-bendingly complicated is all this science that in over forty years only a few dozen, quite rudimentary machines have successfully been built.

THE COUNTERINTUITIVE GENIUS

Richard Feynman was a groundbreaking physicist, avid bongo player and artist who started his career as part of the Manhattan Project, whose mission was to build the atomic bomb before Nazi Germany could.

He won the Nobel Prize for his work in furthering understanding of quantum mechanics, but he also had a refreshingly candid approach and was able to brilliantly communicate complex ideas in a fun and accessible way. Feynman also helped investigate the 1986 Space Shuttle *Challenger* disaster, cracking the mystery of why it had failed using a simple demonstration with store-bought O-rings (a type of gasket or seal) and iced water. His famous diagrams used simple aesthetics to illustrate incredibly complex theories. Feynman drove a customised Dodge Tradesman Maxivan, which he customised with his diagrams. It had a personalised number plate which read 'QUANTUM'. Obviously.

20 MAY

Mapping the World

Flemish cartographer Abraham Ortelius produced the first modern atlas in 1570. He called it *Theatrum Orbis Terrarum* (*Theatre of the World*). It's a fascinating document; Australia is not included, but there is a 'Great South Land', which demonstrates travellers suspected the continent would be there; much of western America is also speculative.

Ortelius was one of the first cartographers to raise the idea of continental drift **(see 6 January)**, as he noticed that there was a mirroring of the eastern coasts of the Americas with the western coasts of Europe and Africa. His atlas is a remarkably precise scientific document, but it also allowed for delicious flights of fancy: Ortelius included a section called Tabulae Novae, or New Tables, which featured maps of imaginary places and islands. There you can see maps depicting mythical lands such as Atlantis and Utopia, and he also added fantastical creatures such as serpents, unicorns, mermaids and dragons. This blend of science and whimsy caught the public imagination, and his atlas was a huge bestseller.

In Greek mythology, Atlas was the leader of the Titans who led a rebellion against the Olympian gods. After the Titans' defeat, Atlas was punished by Zeus and condemned to an eternity of holding up our celestial sphere on his shoulders. Gerardus Mercator, the sixteenth-century cartographer who changed the face of the map world, used a beautiful illustration of Atlas with the heavens on the frontispiece of his maps, and they soon became known as atlases.

21 MAY

Time for Tea

Teabags as we know them were invented accidentally in 1908 by a tea merchant named Thomas Sullivan, who sent tea samples to his customers in small silk bags, assuming they would open the bags before brewing.

Today, tea is the second-most consumed beverage in the world, after water. Tea leaves come from the *Camellia sinensis* plant, and different types of tea (such as green, black, white and oolong) are produced through variations in processing methods. The most important of these is the oxidising of the leaves after they've been crushed. They are left exposed to the air for different lengths of time to alter the flavour – black tea is oxidised for the longest. Tisanes are not teas, but rather herbal infusions made by steeping various herbs, flowers and leaves in hot water.

Your daily cuppa is thought to deliver a range of health benefits. Tea is rich in plant compounds that protect our body's cells from illnesses like cancer, diabetes and heart disease, and studies have found tea can reduce stress and improve focus too. And we all know there are very few problems that can't be made better by having a nice cup of tea and a sit-down.

22 MAY

How Do 3D Printers Work?

The American inventor Chuck Hull was the first to patent 'stereolithography', or 3D printing, in 1986: the first thing he made with his printer was a modest eyewash cup. 3D printers work by melting a filament of a material like plastic to make it soft and malleable and then extruding it into layers that build up a shape transmitted to the printer from a computer design. Nowadays, 3D printing is used in the manufacture of incredibly sophisticated parts for cars, medical equipment and fashion, and it is possible to print elaborate foodstuffs and build houses using massive printers that extrude concrete. 3D printers have even been used to create viable mouse ovaries. In 2017, fertility researchers successfully created gelatin ovaries that were implanted in seven infertile mice, leading to three of them giving birth.

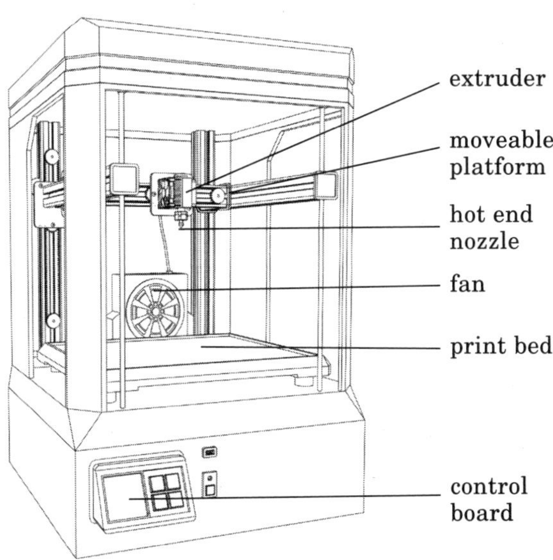

23 MAY

Spider-Man: How Anansi Brought Stories to Life

Anansi, also known as Ananse or Kwaku Ananse, originates in West African folklore, and is a trickster teacher celebrated for his cunning and mischievousness. He loves to help humankind almost as much as he loves fooling us, and he is often depicted as a spider.

In one of the most famous Anansi adventures he notices that humans' lives seem boring and bleak, and decides to liven things up a little by bringing the magic of stories to them. Knowing that the sky god, Nyame, has plenty of stories up in his palace, Anansi spins his web into the sky to ask him to send some down to earth. Nyame isn't keen to share, but because he doesn't want to seem selfish he sets Anansi a series of impossible tasks: capturing Mmoboro the deadly hornet swarm, Onini the lethal python, Osebo the sly leopard, and Mmoatia the impish fairy. After consulting with his equally clever wife, Aso, Anansi devises a way to trick each of his opponents into captivity – and brings them back to Nyame, who reluctantly sticks to his part of the bargain and gifts humanity with the joy of storytelling.

24 MAY

The Best Medicine

Invented by legendary mixologist Sam Kivelenge aka Dr Dawa in the 1980s, Kenya's favourite boozy tipple is the dawa, a twist on Brazil's famous caipirinha. It's always served with a dawa stick, a wooden muddler, which is coated with honey to sweeten the drink. The word 'dawa' is Swahili for 'medicine', and this one is bound to make you feel better.

DAWA

60ml vodka
1 tsp brown sugar
1 whole lime, quartered
2 tbsp honey
crushed ice

Place the lime quarters and brown sugar into a short lowball glass. Crush the limes slightly, then add the ice and vodka. Twist a dawa stick (or the wrong end of a wooden spoon) in the honey. Roll it around until it's coated and add the stick to the drink. Muddle the limes with the dawa stick, and stir. The more you stir, the more honey gets infused into your drink – you are in charge.

25 MAY

Once Removed

Trying to figure out your first, second and third cousins is tricky, so here is a beautifully simple and elegant visual guide for the next family get-together.

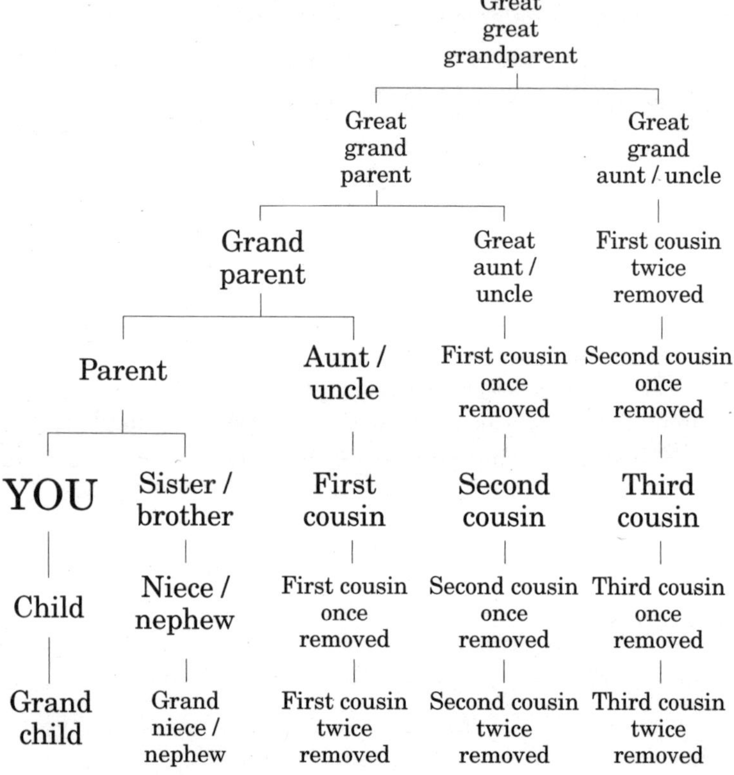

First, second and third cousins (and so on and on and on) are an equal number of generations removed from the common ancestor. First cousins are both the second generation removed from shared grandparents, second cousins are the third generation removed from shared great-grandparents, etc. So rule of thumb: cousin plus one is the number of generations back.

26 MAY

Shhhhhh

- Britain's Secret Intelligence Service – MI6 – is known for its eccentric code names. C is the chief, and he or she is allowed to sign their name in green ink. Ian Fleming's enduring icon James Bond is MI6's most famous fictional agent, code-named 007.
- Mossad, the national intelligence agency of Israel, has a fearsome reputation for its willingness to carry out high-risk missions, including targeted assassinations. One of its most famous assignments was 1960's Operation Finale, in which agents captured one of the 'Architects of the Holocaust', Adolf Eichmann, who was living as a factory worker in Argentina. They smuggled him out of the country and back to Israel, where he stood trial. He was executed in 1962.
- India's Research and Analysis Wing (RAW) goes to imaginative lengths in its methods, apparently employing animal spies, including pigeons and even a squad of spy cats.
- East Germany's Ministry for State Security, the Stasi, was the country's secret police agency during the Cold War. It infiltrated all aspects of society – turning neighbours, friends, lovers and family on each other in a vast network of informants. At one point, one in every sixty-three citizens was an informer, and the number of files held by the secret police was greater than the number of documents held for the entirety of German national history.
- America's CIA is believed to have spent around $20 million in the 1960s on Project Acoustic Kitty, tooling up a cat with a radio antenna in its tail, a microphone hidden in its ears and a transmitter installed at the base of its skull. The operation is said to have ended in disaster when the moggy was run over by a taxi and killed.

27 MAY

Twinning at Life

In astrology, Gemini is the third star sign, represented by a pair of twins, most commonly identified as Castor and Pollux (or Polydeuces), the sons of Leda, a Spartan queen. There are variations on the story, but legend has it that they had different fathers: Castor's father was King Tyndareus, Leda's husband; Pollux's father was Zeus himself, who had assumed the form of a swan to 'seduce' Leda. Castor was mortal while Pollux was immortal, but together they were inseparable, jaunting off on missions on the *Argo* with Jason, and rescuing their sister, Helen of Troy, from Minotaur-slaying Greek warrior Theseus. But when Castor was killed, Zeus offered Pollux a choice: spend the rest of his time on Olympus, or share his immortality with his brother and alternate between Olympus and Hades. He chose the latter and the brothers became the constellation Gemini.

Famous Geminis include Donald Trump, Paul McCartney, Marilyn Monroe, John F. Kennedy, Bob Dylan, Queen Victoria, Anne Frank, Jeffrey Dahmer, Che Guevara, Peter the Great, Stan Laurel, Aurelia Cotta (mother of Julius Caesar), Arthur Conan Doyle, Josephine Baker, Boris Johnson, Carl Linnaeus, Geronimo, Harriet Beecher Stowe, Tenzing Norgay, Miles Davis, Ice Cube and Fats Waller.

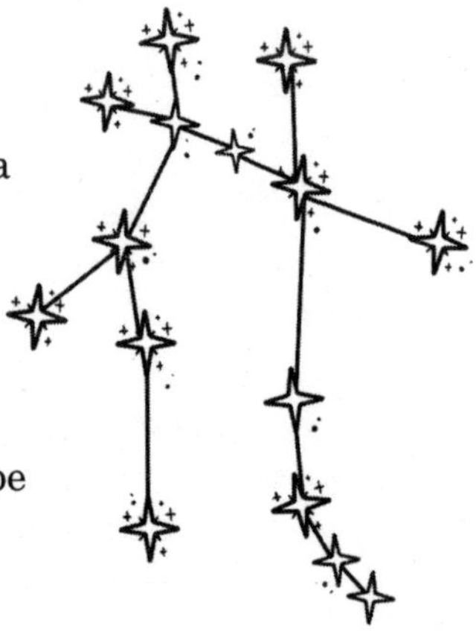

28 MAY

The Crescent and the City

The Fertile Crescent is a boomerang-shaped region in the Middle East that curves through modern-day Iraq, Syria, Lebanon, Jordan, Israel and Palestine. Known for its rich soil, it's where archaeologists believe agriculture began for *Homo sapiens* as they transitioned from hunter-gatherer communities to complex societies. And, as food security led to population growth, the first cities sprung up here too. Cities are where nearly every human concept was advanced: technology, science, writing, mathematics, domestication of animals, cultivation of food systems, the notion of time, law, the wheel, astronomy, religion . . . The list goes on.

- Çatalhöyük in southern Anatolia in Turkey was probably founded over nine thousand years ago. There were no streets, and dwellings were clustered together in a honeycomb formation, each house having a ladder reaching up to a hole in the roof. To move around, people would range over the rooftops. Dwellings were all the same size, which has led some historians to surmise that it was an egalitarian society.
- 'Ain Ghazal was a settlement that began around 10,000 BCE to the east of Jericho in modern-day Jordan. The people of 'Ain Ghazal loved a statue – over 195 have been found there.
- The Sumerian city-states of Eridu, Uruk and Ur can be traced back as far as 6000 BCE, each famous for its extraordinary temples, or ziggurats.
- Mehrgarh is one of the earliest-known settlements in South Asia, in modern-day Pakistan, dating back to around 7000 BCE. Excavations at the site have revealed evidence of crop cultivation, domesticated animals and advanced pottery techniques.

29 MAY

Dear Diary

Not many of us would like the idea of our private diaries being shared with the world. One of the most famous diarists of all time, Samuel Pepys, considered burning his, but fortunately for us his million words of reflection were spared the flames.

Pepys made his first diary entry on 1 January 1660 and kept it up every day for another nine and a half years as a vibrant, joyful record of life in Restoration London. He ranged effortlessly from world events – the Great Plague, the Great Fire of London – to arguments with his long-suffering wife and accounts of his affairs. The final entry was written on 31 May 1669 as his eyesight began to fail and he decided to put down his pen. The glory of the diary lies in the details, which bring a distant period of history to vivid life. Like, for example, his entry of Tuesday 4 September 1666, which explains how he saved his Parmesan cheese as the Great Fire of London raged:

> Sir W. Pen and I to Tower-streete, and there met the fire burning three or four doors beyond Mr Howell's, whose goods, poor man, his trayes, and dishes, shovells, &c., were flung all along Tower-street in the kennels, and people working therewith from one end to the other; the fire coming on in that narrow streete, on both sides, with infinite fury. Sir W. Batten not knowing how to remove his wine, did dig a pit in the garden, and laid it in there . . . And in the evening Sir W. Pen and I did dig another, and put our wine in it; and I my Parmazan cheese, as well as my wine and some other things.

30 MAY

Perilous Provenance

In 2014 the literary world was set alight when a papyrologist claimed to have found sections of Sappho's previously unknown poetry in cartonnage in the possession of an anonymous London-based collector.

Though Sappho was a huge hit in her own times, named by Plato as 'The Tenth Muse' and honoured in the famous Library of Alexandria **(see 30 June)**, very little of this iconic poetess's work has survived, so this discovery was A Big Deal. Though it was eventually proven the papyrologist had acquired the material through less-than-honest means, happily there was never any doubt cast on the fragments' authenticity: critics agree these are most definitely Sappho's words shining out from the dark swirls of time.

Just send me along, and command me
To offer many prayers to Queen Hera
That Charaxus should arrive here, with
His ship intact,

And find us safe. For the rest,
Let us turn it all over to higher powers;
For periods of calm quickly follow after
Great squalls.

31 MAY

Hippo Hieroglyphics

Despite their rather adorable appearance, hippopotami are one of the most dangerous creatures in Africa, killing more humans than any other large animal. They are also – whilst appearing to be rotund and lumbering – incredibly fast on their feet: hippos can easily outrun a nimble human. Huge and aggressive they may be, but the females are protective and nurturing towards their calves. Hippos have been extinct in Egypt since the late nineteenth century, but the ancient Egyptians revered and feared hippopotami in equal measure. They were a constant threat to farmers (capable of consuming 40 kilograms of vegetation over the course of a single night), and a favourite sport as far back as 3000 BCE was harpoon hippo hunting – the Egyptians used the male animal's skin, fat, hide and teeth but the hunt also had a deeper symbolic meaning, representing the triumph of kingly order over chaos.

Female hippos were held in high esteem: they represented fertility, protection and the life-giving power of the River Nile. The goddess Taweret, often depicted as a pregnant hippo standing on her hind legs, was considered a protector of women during pregnancy and childbirth, and every home with an expectant mother or young child would have an amulet or carving of Taweret for protection.

June

1 JUNE

Dolly Mixture

Dolls aren't always just toys – they also express something about the culture that creates them. In the ancient world, dolls were often made for religious rituals – the earliest examples discovered are wooden paddle dolls with beaded hair found in ancient Egyptian tombs. The most famous doll today was made for play but she has grown in cultural significance. Toy company Mattel introduced Barbara Millicent Roberts to the world in 1959. The original Barbie was impossibly long-legged and slim-waisted and sported a full face of make-up. Contrary to popular opinion, Barbie was not always a blonde: her first iteration was also available in brunette.

Barbie immediately caused controversy for her unattainable figure but she was also feminist-forward in her very nature. In the 1950s most dolls were babies, encouraging little girls to develop their maternal instincts, but Barbie was an adult with her own exciting, independent life. (She has never had children herself.) She has gone on to have over two hundred different careers, from ice cream parlour server to astronaut, from ballerina to sign language teacher, from surgeon to beekeeper. She enjoys a lavish consumerist lifestyle in her Dreamhouse with her boyfriend Ken, various vehicles, pets and, of course, with her incredibly enviable wardrobe.

Barbie has adapted to the times: the first Barbie of colour was produced in 1980 and she now comes in a variety of body types and doesn't have to always wear punishingly high heels. According to Mattel, three Barbies are still sold every second. The bestselling Ken doll of all time was 1993's Earring Magic Ken, who immediately became a gay icon.

2 JUNE

The Nonsense of Nursery Rhymes

Most of the traditional nursery rhymes we know in the English- speaking world today come from the eighteenth century. In 1744 the first nursery rhyme collection, *Tommy Thumb's Song Book*, was published, followed by the influential *Mother Goose's Melody* in 1781.

In the early twentieth century, as interest in popular folklore became fashionable, people began to conjecture hidden meanings in our most popular nursery rhymes, none of which have been proven – apart from 'London's Burning', which does appear to be based on the Great Fire of London in 1666.

'Ring a Ring o' Roses' was said to be inspired by the Black Death (1346–53) or the Great Plague (1665–66). This interpretation sees the 'ring of roses' as a plague rash, the 'posies' as the flowers people wore to try to fend it off, and 'we all fall down' as the many deaths. But the rhyme was first recorded in the nineteenth century and had different, unplaguey words in regional variations, making this explanation unlikely.

It has also been claimed that 'Goosey Goosey Gander', with its 'old man who wouldn't say his prayers' getting thrown down stairs, is about the persecution of Catholics in the sixteenth century. Some have interpreted that line as being about hunting for Catholic priests who lived in hiding in some nobles' houses during the rules of the Protestant Tudor monarchs, Henry VIII, Edward VI and Elizabeth I. Another theory suggests that it refers to STIs, as geese were associated with sexual promiscuity.

3 JUNE

Make a Bee-Line for an A-Line

Wide skirts became very popular in the 1950s after Christian Dior's 1947 collection included exaggerated silhouettes. This was a reaction to the war years when material had been in short supply, so skirts had been narrow and suits had moved from double- to single-breasted.

Dior called his collection 'Corolle' after the petal part of a flower, because of the curved shape of the skirts, but it became popularly known as the 'New Look'. Many embraced its radical French chic but some found the vain waste of fabric so affronting that there was even an incident of a young woman wearing the style being attacked in Paris. Others, including Coco Chanel, considered the look regressively feminine and uncomfortable.

4 JUNE

How to Work with Your Circadian Rhythm

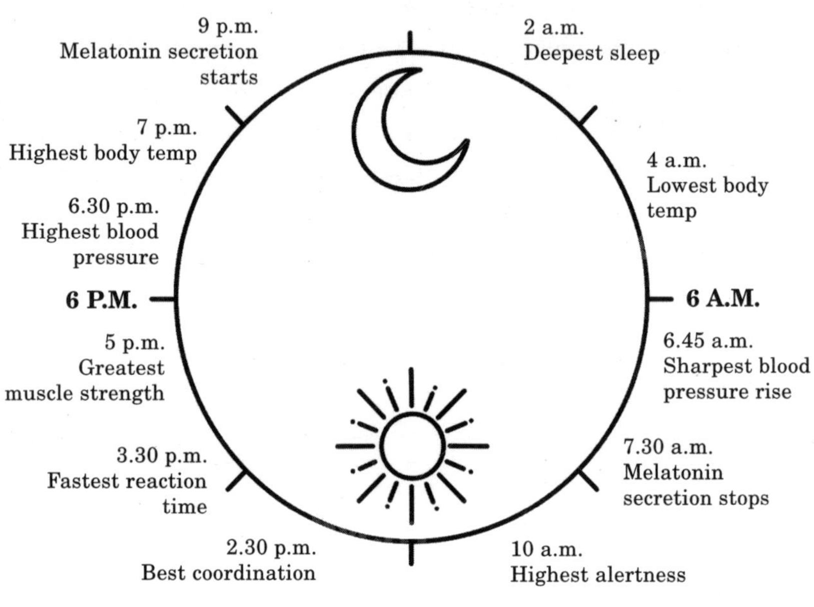

The circadian rhythm – named from the Latin 'circa diem', meaning 'around the day' – exists in plants, animals and humans to provide a sleep–wake cycle that regulates our psychological and physical systems. It's the twenty-four-hour clock that allows for restorative sleep and periods of activity – meaning our bodies are optimised for different times of the day. It's one of the most important processes in our lives and is thought to affect a vast array of physical and mental functions, from DNA repair to weight gain and depression.

Our master clock is situated in the hypothalamus in our brain, which sends signals through our body to align our periods of activity and inactivity with day and night. The master clock is extremely sensitive to light, so that when darkness falls our body is instructed to make melatonin, the hormone that promotes sleep. It's why many of us feel so inexplicably tired during the winter months.

Individuals do have different circadian rhythms. The wild hormonal fluctuations of teenagers affect the production of melatonin and mean they lean towards being night owls. As we age, our hypothalamus becomes less effective, meaning we secrete less melatonin, and that's why early-bird elderlies tend to go to sleep earlier in the day and wake up much earlier in the morning. Exposure to natural light is one of the main drivers of our circadian rhythm, so get out there, whatever the weather.

It's not just us humans who are Slaves to the (Circadian) Rhythm. Scientists have recently discovered some bacteria can tell the time too, opening up exciting opportunities around the precision timing of delivery of antibiotics for example.

5 JUNE

Flower Power

Ikebana is the Japanese art of flower-arranging. It is a serious discipline that has been studied in Japan for hundreds of years and is generally more minimalist in style than Western flower-arranging. Key elements are the mindful process of making the arrangement, a focus on reflecting the seasons, and the elegant and pleasing lines of the flowers' stems. Ikebana is underpinned by a philosophy of balance and harmony, and a celebration of the beauty of nature. June is a wonderful month for blooms so a perfect opportunity for trying your own arrangement. Flowers that are in season in the UK in June include sweet peas, lilies, alliums, marigolds, carnations, chrysanthemums, delphiniums, geraniums, peonies, alstroemerias, freesias, gerberas, hydrangeas, phlox and roses.

6 JUNE

The Family Tree of Music

When people draw family trees of music genres, it gets untidy fast. They tend to start with the first branches of early forms like classical, folk and blues, which split into further branches, which twist and merge and split again until, if you were a peppy squirrel, you could hop along the boughs of blues into rock, then metal, but connect from there again with hip-hop and grunge twigs to end up at the leaf of nu metal.

Musical artists constantly influence each other and develop in new directions. Before the twentieth century you had to choose between community folk music or classical 'art' music. Industrialisation and mass production and broadcast led to the unstoppable rise of pop music, which is, unsurprisingly, the world's most popular genre. But even this seemingly simple form has complex ancestors, as it developed from the music hall, jazz and country music of the early twentieth century, which in turn grew out of opera, blues and folk, before being revolutionised by the rise of rock in the 1950s and disco, hip-hop and dance in the 1970s.

Different leaves on the musical family tree are more popular in different geographical regions thanks to particular cultural heritages, but the rise in digital music availability has increased the variety people listen to globally. Music taste is also closely tied to personality, and it's been shown that it changes as we get older. A ten-year study of 25,000 people found that adolescents prefer 'intense' musical genres, early adults like danceable 'contemporary' and more 'mellow' styles, and older people move to 'sophisticated' genres like jazz and 'unpretentious' ones like country.

7 JUNE

Tune Out

Though some archaeologists have found evidence of meditation being practised as much as five thousand years ago, in the Western world it has only become mainstream relatively recently. Scientific studies have suggested that it leads to beneficial physical changes in the brain – including increased grey matter density, changes in neural pathways and improved connectivity between different regions. It's also believed to alleviate anxiety, promote relaxation and reduce stress. One study even found that, after an eight-week meditation course, participants had higher immune system function. The concept is simple: sit still, focus on your breath, and notice when your mind starts to wander.

- Find a quiet space where you can sit or lie down comfortably.
- Set a time limit – you can start with as little as five or ten minutes.
- Close your eyes or maintain a soft gaze, whatever feels more natural to you.
- Focus on your breath by observing the sensation of the air entering and leaving your body. Whenever your mind wanders – and it will – gently guide your attention back to the breath.

8 JUNE

Good Earth News

Sometimes efforts to save our planet can feel fruitless and frankly overwhelming, but it's worth remembering all the amazing steps forward we have achieved that give us hope for the future.

WE HAVE DRAMATICALLY REDUCED ACID RAIN

Between the 1960s and 1990s we had a major problem with acidic rain created by the burning of fossil fuels in North America and Europe. The rain weakened trees, poisoned lakes and corroded stone. Although acid rain is still a problem in parts of Asia, financial incentives led to industries in many parts of the world reducing their emissions, and nature is gradually recovering.

WE ARE RESTORING THE OZONE LAYER

The ozone layer is a region of our atmosphere that protects us from the harmful effects of the sun, which cause skin cancer and global warming. Over the 1970s and 1980s, scientists realised that human-made CFC gases used in aerosols and fridges were damaging the layer, creating a hole over Antarctica. In response, 197 countries banned CFC gases, and in 2023 it was reported that the layer is set to return to its whole condition by 2040.

WE'VE REDUCED PLASTIC BAG LITTER

Over one hundred countries have now banned single-use plastic bags and many others charge for them. Beach-cleaning initiatives have seen a drop in the number of plastic bags and straws clogging beaches.

WHALE POPULATIONS ARE RECOVERING

Blue whales were nearly hunted to extinction but populations have rebounded since the International Whaling Commission's ban came into effect in 1986, which most countries in the world adhere to. Things also look hopeful for humpback and southern right whales.

RENEWABLE ENERGY IS GROWING

Solar energy production grew by 24% in 2022, providing enough electricity to run a country the size of South Africa, and 2023 saw the first time global fossil-fuel production of electricity fell due to a rise in renewables, especially in China. According to the International Energy Agency, 'the amount of renewable energy capacity added to energy systems around the world grew by 50% in 2023'.

DEFORESTATION IN THE AMAZON IS SLOWING

Brazil is home to 60% of the world's largest rainforest and the government there reported that rates of deforestation fell by nearly 50% in 2023, hitting the lowest-recorded deforestation rate for the previous five years.

WE ARE CLOSER TO PROTECTING THE SEA

Before 2023 only 1% of the two-thirds of the world's oceans that are international waters (not belonging to any country) were protected. Now more and more nations are signing up to the UN High Seas Treaty, which aims to protect marine life there.

9 JUNE

A Rose by Any Other Name

Beloved for their beauty and heady scent, here are some other ways roses are special.

- Fossils show that roses have been around for more than 30 million years.
- Attar of Roses is the essential oil that is extracted from rose petals by steam distillation. The petals are harvested before sunrise. Rosewater used in cooking is a by-product of this process.
- Golabgiri is an Iranian festival of rosewater-making in early summer. Iran is a major producer of rosewater.
- The phrase 'sub rosa', meaning 'in secret', translates directly from Latin as 'under the rose'. This is said to have come from the Roman myth of Cupid giving a rose to the god of silence, Harpocrates (an adaptation of the Egyptian god Horus), to stop him talking about Cupid's mother, Venus's, affairs. Venus, and her Greek counterpart, Aphrodite, were often associated with roses. In the Middle Ages roses were carved into the ceilings of council chambers and outside confessionals to show that anything discussed in them was confidential.
- The quotation 'That which we call a rose by any other name would smell as sweet' is said by Juliet about Romeo in Shakespeare's play about their warring families, the Capulets and Montagues.
- The political slogan 'Bread and Roses' was coined by Helen Todd in 1911. Helen was a campaigner for votes for women in America, and she gave a speech asking for 'bread for all, and roses too', meaning basic pay, rights and security for women as well as the roses of life: culture, music and education.

10 JUNE

What's on the Cards?

Tarot has risen in popularity in recent years as people turn to its age-old guidance in times of uncertainty. Tarot cards were originally just an extension of regular card decks, known as Trionfi, for a particular game popular in 1400s Italy. Only in the eighteenth century were they adopted for fortune-telling or cartomancy.

There are many different ways to interpret the cards in the Tarot deck and it is considered a personal and intuitive exercise, but generally the session begins with the reader asking the deck a broad and open question and then shuffling the cards. Decks are divided into the twenty-two cards of the Major Arcana, which represent the big issues and themes in life, and the fifty-six cards of the Minor Arcana, which represent more specific challenges. Each suit of the Minor Arcana focuses on a different area: wands are associated with passion and creativity; cups with love and feelings; swords with thoughts and actions; and pentacles with career and finances. When you encounter the Major Arcana, do not be spooked by drawing the Hanged Man, who can mean release or pause, or Death, who famously means transformation and new beginnings, rather than a sinister obvious interpretation.

The most commonly used Tarot deck is the Rider-Waite-Smith one created in 1909 by Arthur Edward Waite and the artist Pamela Colman Smith, and published by the Rider Company. As well as being an illustrator, Pamela worked as a performer with Bram Stoker's theatre troupe; there she met the famous actress Ellen Terry, who is said to have inspired Colman Smith's design for the Queen of Wands.

QUEEN of SWORDS.

QUEEN of PENTACLES

QUEEN of WANDS.

QUEEN of CUPS.

11 JUNE

Making Eyes at You

Have you ever stared deeply into the eyes of a goat? If so, you will have noticed that they have horizontal rectangular pupils rather than the round ones that humans and most other vertebrates have. In fact, the animal kingdom exhibits a vast array of different pupil shapes, from our house cat's vertical slits that can expand into big cute circles, to the narrow vertical eyes of crocodiles, the blobby lines of the pupils of some geckos, the semicircular ones of stingrays and the wobbly 'W's of cuttlefish.

The purpose of the pupil is to control the amount of light entering our eyes and hitting the retina at the back of our eyeball, which sends sight signals to our brains. As you'll have noticed if you step out of a dark bar into a bright morning, for example, your vision will struggle for a second while your pupils contract to let the right amount of light in. The variety of animal pupil shapes remains quite mysterious, but scientists have theorised that they have most likely evolved into their individual shapes because of the animals' environments and lifestyles.

Foxes and cats are ambush predators who like to leap on their prey from close quarters, often in dim light, so it makes sense that they would have similar eyes. Their vertical pupils allow them to see well in these conditions. Snakes also have vertical eyes and hunt in a similar way. Wolves hunt in packs, so their round-pupilled eyes need to work differently. And at the other end of the food chain, poor old goats, sheep and deer are often being hunted, so they need to keep a wide range of vision while they're grazing, hence their horizontal pupils.

12 JUNE

A Glorious Gimlet

The word 'gimlet' generally refers to a small tool for boring holes, so no one really knows why it became the name of this cocktail. One theory relates it to the British navy's efforts to combat scurvy by putting lemon and lime juice into its sailors' rations. (This is thought to be why British sailors, and later British people generally, were referred to by Americans as 'limeys'.) The juice was mixed with the rum or gin the sailors drank, and the barrels containing these were likely opened using a gimlet.

GIMLET

2 limes
200g sugar
50ml gin (swap for soda or sparkling water for a non-alcoholic rendition)
ice

Grate the limes so that you get all their zest into a small saucepan. Cut one slice to use as a garnish later and then juice the limes into a measuring jug. Top up with water to 100ml. Add this to the pan and add the sugar. Heat gently until the sugar has dissolved and leave to cool. Chill a Martini or coupe glass in the fridge.

When the syrup is cool, add two ice cubes to a jug, gin if you're using, and top up with 50ml of the syrup. (Any remaining syrup will keep in the fridge for a month.) Stir until the mixture is very cold and then strain into your glass. Add soda or sparkling water if you've opted for a mocktail and top your glass with your slice of lime.

13 JUNE

Mountain High

Many people know that modern yoga developed from an Indian philosophical practice delineated hundreds of years ago and designed to achieve deep focus and clarity. But not everyone knows that, out of the steps involved in this practice, the asanas, or poses, were originally a minor component, less important than the spiritual and meditative element. In most modern postural yoga classes, stretching and exercise are the main event and many of the asanas used in these classes were invented in the twentieth century in a fusion with gymnastics, including the wonderfully simple Mountain Pose, so named because it evokes the stillness and strength of mountains.

This is a fantastic move to get yourself aligned at the start of the day or to sort out your posture if you've been slumped at a desk for hours. It takes seconds and you can do it whenever you're standing around for a moment: in a queue at the shops, perhaps, or waiting for the pedestrian crossing lights to change. Stand with your feet hip-width apart. Lift your toes and spread them out on the ground to make a firm base, with your weight evenly distributed. Don't lock your knees, and tip your pelvis so that you're not sticking your bum out. Pull your tummy in a little. Breathe in and lengthen your neck so that you feel taller. Make sure your chin is neither tucked in nor tilted out. Breathe out and drop your shoulders down. Stretch your fingertips towards the floor. Take a few more slow breaths here if you have time.

14 JUNE

Feeling Hot Hot Hot

The Scoville organoleptic test measures the potency of chilli peppers. ('Organoleptic' means 'relating to the qualities of a substance that affect the senses', such as texture, taste, colour and odour.) The test was invented by an American scientist called Wilbur Scoville in 1912.

Peppers contain a chemical called capsaicin, which produces a feeling of burning in mammals, and this is what makes chilli peppers spicy. We vary in our sensitivity to capsaicin, but the Scoville scale gives a rough idea of how hot any type of pepper will be: the classic bell pepper scores a 0, jalapeños are about 5,000 and Scotch bonnet chillies can measure up to 350,000 units, but avoid the Carolina Reaper at all costs, because at 1.6 million units it is hellfire.

Capsaicin is also sometimes used in topical pain relief. In the 2008 Olympics, four showjumpers were disqualified because their horses tested positive for capsaicin, which is a banned substance in the event because of this effect.

15 JUNE

Silky Bulletproof Vests

In the Wild West of the 1880s, a doctor working on survivors of gunfights made an interesting observation: three of his patients had been saved by the folded silk handkerchiefs in their pockets or tied around their necks. Silk is the strongest freely available natural fabric in the world. Spider silk is, in its individual strands, stronger than silk, but it's very hard to farm.

Silk is usually made from the cocoon fibres of the silkworm – the caterpillars of the *Bombyx* moth. Each little cocoon contains about a kilometre of thread. Silk cultivation (sericulture) began in China around the third millennium BCE and its secrets were closely guarded. From the second century BCE China traded silk with the Roman Empire via the Silk Road, a trade network that ran from Xi'an through Afghanistan to Turkey and the Mediterranean. Legend has it that in around 552 CE the Emperor Justinian I persuaded two monks to smuggle silkworms from China to Constantinople in their bamboo canes, and thus began silk production in Europe.

By this time in China, officials were already using padded silk uniforms to protect them against attack. In 1897 in Chicago, a Polish priest called Casimir Zeglen started producing and marketing 'soft armour' made of layers of silk. It wasn't long before royalty, politicians, law enforcement officers and criminals started wearing it. The Archduke Franz Ferdinand, whose assassination started the First World War, apparently owned one of the vests but wasn't wearing it on the day he was attacked (and he was shot in the throat anyway).

16 JUNE

Amazing Mae

'You only live once, but if you do it right, once is enough.'

Mae West (1893–1980),
actor, screenwriter and singer

When Mae West was arrested and convicted for corrupting the youth, on account of her 1926 play *Sex*, she hired a limo to take her to jail. She donated the money she made from subsequent magazine articles about her experience to set up a library for the prison.

17 JUNE

Four on the Floor

'Four on the floor' or 'four to the floor' is a rhythm pattern that has been much used in pop, disco and dance music from the 1970s onwards. It is a simple rhythm in 4/4 time with a uniformly accented beat and a bass drum hit on each beat. It is used in a wide range of classic songs, from Blondie's 'Heart of Glass' to Bob Marley's 'Exodus' and Queen's 'Another One Bites the Dust'. 4/4 is also often used in classical, jazz and rap music. But what is it?

The first historical example of written music is on a four-thousand-year-old clay tablet from Sumer so we've been recording how to play our music for a long time. Different cultures use different kinds of musical notation: Western written music usually has a time signature indicated at the start of the piece and is divided into 'bars' by vertical lines that break it up into manageable units. The time signature indicates how many beats there are in the bars and the duration of each beat. In 4/4 the top 4 shows that there are four beats per bar in the piece of music and the bottom 4 shows that each beat lasts for a quarter note – also known as a crotchet. Sometimes 4/4 is indicated by just a letter 'C', meaning 'common time'.

A huge percentage of Western pop music is in 4/4, but the traditional music of India, the Middle East, Bulgaria and many other regions of the world is a completely different story. In these cultures, asymmetric metres such as 7/8 are more widespread.

18 JUNE

A Glossary of Sushi

Maki: Sushi rice wrapped in seaweed (nori) with a filling in the middle.

Nigiri: Sushi rice pressed into a rectangle with a topping.

Sashimi: Fish or shellfish on its own, usually raw.

Uramaki: A Western-originated variation of maki where the seaweed is wrapped around a filling with sushi rice on the outside of the seaweed.

Temaki: Seaweed rolled into a cone with rice and filling inside.

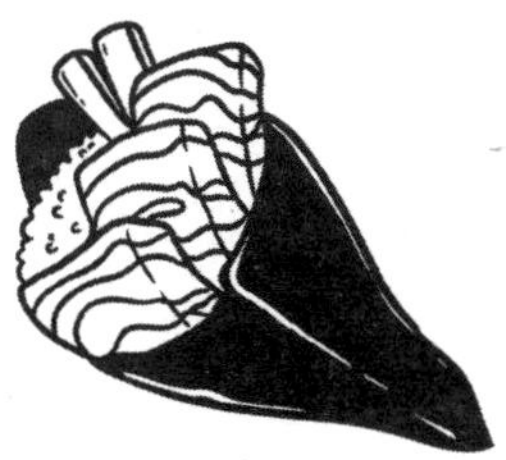

Temarizushi: Balls of rice with the topping on top.

Inarizushi: Sushi rice inside deep-fried tofu pockets. Inari is the Shinto god of rice and foxes, and the fried tofu is considered a favourite food of the fox; in some regions inarizushi is triangular rather than rectangular and considered to reflect the shape of foxes' ears.

Gunkan maki: Long ovals of rice with the topping on top, wrapped round the edge with seaweed.

Fillings and toppings include toro (fatty tuna), tako (octopus), ebi (shrimp/prawn), tamago (egg omelette), maguro (tuna), ika (squid), sake (salmon), unagi (eel), uni (sea urchin), ikura (salmon eggs), tai (red snapper), hotate (scallop) and saba (mackerel).

Sushi rice: Rice flavoured with vinegar.

Wasabi: Green horseradish (*Eutrema japonicum),* usually mixed with soy sauce as a dip for sushi. Japanese wasabi is naturally green but in the West a different kind of horseradish (*Armoracia rusticana)* is often used to make the paste and then dyed green.

Pickled ginger: Eaten between different types of sushi to cleanse the palate.

19 JUNE

The Secrets of the Fourth Page

If you look at the opening pages of this book you'll find they don't start with page 1. Page 1 is usually the first page of the main text and the pages before this are called the 'prelim' (for preliminary) pages and are numbered using Roman numerals. On pages i–iii you'll find a half title page, a list of the authors' previous books and a full title page, but the page with the most information, often in tiny type, is the 'copyright page' on p. iv.

When you see © it means that a creator is asserting their rights over a piece of work and no one else can copy it without their permission. Copyright laws only started protecting authors in 1710. In the UK, copyright generally lasts for seventy years after your death. After that anyone can print and sell your book – which is why there are so many versions of *Pride and Prejudice* available.

Under the copyright line is a row of numbers. These refer to the number of printings the book has had. To save time adjusting the copyright page significantly on every printing, the first edition has numbers 1 to 10 on the line, with 10 in the middle. With each printing, a number gets knocked off the line, 1 then 2 and so on, so that the lowest number on the line shows the edition. When you get past the tenth printing, the line is replaced with numbers 11 to 20, and so on.

If you can see a 1 on the line of numbers, then you have a first edition. Sometimes these editions can end up being valuable: in 2021 a first edition of *Harry Potter and the Philosopher's Stone* sold for £350,000 at auction.

20 JUNE

Luxe Life

sybaritic: self-indulgently fond of luxury

'If I won the lottery I would go on a sybaritic holiday to a tropical island spa.'

The origin of this word is the ancient Greek city of Sybaris, in what is now Calabria in Italy, which was famous for its wealth and opulence.

21 JUNE

The Milton Keynes Solstice

The 20 or 21 June in the northern hemisphere usually sees the longest day of the year, or the summer, or aestival, solstice. Places north of the Arctic Circle have no night at all around this solstice. The shortest day of the year in the northern hemisphere is the winter, or hibernal, solstice on 21 or 22 December. These are reversed in the southern hemisphere.

Across cultures and history, solstices have been times of celebration of the sun's life-giving powers and the changes of the seasons. Thousands of people head to Stonehenge near Salisbury, where the stones, arranged in the twenty-sixth century BCE, align with the sun on the solstices. A contemporary version of this is Midsummer Boulevard in 1960s-designed Milton Keynes, which aligns with the sunrise on the summer solstice and is designed so that the sunlight reflects off the grand glass frontage of Milton Keynes Central train station at one end of the road and the Light Pyramid sculpture by Liliane Lijn at the other.

22 JUNE

Political Chic

Frida Kahlo, artist, muse, fashion icon and spawner of a gazillion pieces of merch, famously took inspiration from her own life, but there was another, lesser-known source that influenced her.

Today, in the Oaxaca region of southern Mexico, street markets teem with stalls bedecked with brightly coloured jewellery and sellers hawking their wares with flirtatious catcalls – and they are all women. In Zapotec society the women rule the roost, wielding economic (if not necessarily political) power, and yet this is not simply an inverse of traditionally male-dominated Mexican society: the reality is more complex. The Zapotec people even recognise a third gender, muxe: those born biologically male but identifying as female, and acceptance of this third gender as a concept is said to pre-date colonialism.

For Frida, embracing the Zapotec traditional dress of embroidered corsets, wide ruffled skirts and bold, unashamed colours served a purpose both practical and political. She suffered terrible physical setbacks through her life, first as a child contracting polio, which left her with a limp, and then in a horrific bus crash in which she broke her pelvis and spine. Her wide skirts covered her damaged legs, and her corsets supported her spine. Politically, her sartorial style served as an anti-colonial protest against the sleek and sober silhouettes in vogue in Europe and America at the time. Fashion for Frida was a weapon in the fight to be seen on her own terms.

23 JUNE

Sweet and Sour

We eat far more sugar nowadays than our ancestors and it profoundly affects the reward chemicals in our brain, giving us pleasure and making us want more. Intense sweetness has been shown to be even more addictive than cocaine. But why is sugar such a health no-no?

Sugar is found naturally in many foods, including lactose in milk and fructose in fruit. The excess sugar we're eating today tends to come from sucrose, fructose or corn syrup added to a whole range of packaged foods and drinks (some of which, like bread, cereal and pasta sauce, might seem surprising). Too much sugar can contribute to obesity and diabetes, both of which lead to further health issues, and tooth decay, as well as causing energy highs and lows. Humans evolved without access to much sugar and before the eighteenth century we ate very little. It became widely available and cheap thanks to plantation slave labour and the French leader Napoleon.

In the 1800s Napoleon encouraged the planting of sugar beet in Europe, which had only recently been discovered as a decent source of sugar. He did this after his wars with Britain cut off the supply of sugar to France from the sugar cane in British territories. Nowadays 20% of world sugar comes from beet. Sugar consumption rose massively in the twentieth century but has come down sharply since the 1970s, though most children in the UK are still eating twice the recommended amount each day.

24 JUNE

Empire State of Mind

There are no official empires left today but here are five of the most impressive from history.

The **Achaemenid** or **Persian Empire** (c. 550–330 BCE) covered millions of miles from northern Africa to the Aral Sea and is estimated to have ruled over 44% of the world's population. It holds the Guinness World Record for largest-ever empire by percentage of world population.

The **British Empire** (1583–1997) was the largest empire by land area, covering a quarter of the world at its peak. Its first colony, planned by Elizabeth I in 1585 on Roanoke Island, failed when the colonists mysteriously disappeared. Its last was Hong Kong, which was returned to China in 1997.

The **Ottoman Empire** (c. 1300–1922 CE) spread from Turkey across much of the Mediterranean including modern-day Greece, the Balkans and areas in the Middle East. In 1453 it destroyed the last of the **Roman Empire** when Mehmed II captured Constantinople, using the latest technology of gunpowder cannons to breach the city walls.

The **Khmer Empire** (802–1431 CE) began in Cambodia and spread over what is now Thailand. The Khmer king, Suryavarman II, built the famous Angkor Wat, which is still the largest religious monument in the world.

The **Ghana Empire** (sixth to thirteenth century CE) was based in what is now Mauritania and Mali. It was eventually taken over by the **Mali Empire**. One of the secrets of its success was its use of camels for trade. (Camels only became common in Africa in the fourth century CE.)

25 JUNE

Chess Kidding

Chess is the most popular board game in the world and has been proven to improve cognitive skills, boost empathy (because it forces you to consider things from your opponent's perspective) and get you into a productive state of flow, and it may even help protect against dementia. Millions of people across the world play the Game of Kings but not many of them know these surprising facts.

- The phrase 'checkmate' comes from the Persian 'shah mat', which means 'the king is dead'.
- The folding chessboard was invented in 1125 by a furtive priest who wanted to defy Bishop Guy of Paris's edict that any clergyman caught playing the game would be excommunicated.
- In 1988 a computer named Deep Thought (after the computer in Douglas Adams's *The Hitchhiker's Guide to the Galaxy*) was the first machine to beat a chess grand master.
- The number of potential variations of chess games is greater than the number of observable atoms in the universe – this is called the Shannon number after the mathematician who conceived of it.

26 JUNE

The King of the Elements

Carbon is called Your Majesty because all living things contain it and it can form so many different compounds. You are about 18% carbon **(see 1 January)** and part of the carbon cycle, which is essential to life on earth.

- Photosynthesis is the magic part of the cycle whereby plants extract carbon dioxide from the atmosphere and turn it into sugar and energy to grow.
- We, and other living things, release carbon dioxide as part of the process of respiration, when we convert our carbon food into our energy.
- When we die and decay, our carbon is released into the atmosphere again or fossilised and stored in rock. Fuels like gas and oil are made of fossilised creatures from prehistory, and since we learned to burn them to make energy in a process called combustion, we have been releasing more than the natural level of carbon dioxide the cycle can cope with into the atmosphere.

6 C 12.0107 CARBON

SINK OR SWIM

A carbon sink takes carbon dioxide out of the atmosphere and absorbs more of it than it produces. Oceans and forests are our main carbon sinks – 25% of carbon dioxide emissions are absorbed by the ocean. The ocean does this by absorbing carbon dioxide and trapping it in deep layers; through the photosynthesis of algae, phytoplankton and its huge fields of aquatic plants like seagrass, kelp and mangroves; and through fish and other sea organisms that live in this environment sinking down to the sea floor when they die, locking their carbon away there.

27 JUNE

Sympathy

I know what the caged bird feels, alas!
    When the sun is bright on the upland slopes;
When the wind stirs soft through the springing grass,
And the river flows like a stream of glass;
    When the first bird sings and the first bud opes,
And the faint perfume from its chalice steals—
I know what the caged bird feels!

I know why the caged bird beats his wing
    Till its blood is red on the cruel bars;
For he must fly back to his perch and cling
When he fain would be on the bough a-swing;
    And a pain still throbs in the old, old scars
And they pulse again with a keener sting—
I know why he beats his wing!

I know why the caged bird sings, ah me,
    When his wing is bruised and his bosom sore,—
When he beats his bars and he would be free;
It is not a carol of joy or glee,
    But a prayer that he sends from his heart's deep core,
But a plea, that upward to Heaven he flings—
I know why the caged bird sings!

Paul Laurence Dunbar (1872–1906) was one of the first internationally prominent and influential African American poets. Iconic author Maya Angelou (1928–2014) was influenced by Dunbar and chose a line from this poem as the title of her best-selling 1969 autobiography, *I Know Why the Caged Bird Sings*.

28 JUNE

The Glastonbury Thorn

Glastonbury in Somerset is steeped in legend. In 1191 some monks there dubiously claimed to have found the remains of King Arthur and buried them in the abbey. After his final battle, the wounded Arthur was said to have sailed away to Avalon, or the isle of apples, which has since been equated with Glastonbury. He will rest there in secret until Britain needs him again, when he will return as the 'once and future king'.

Another legend, from the thirteenth century, says that St Joseph of Arimathea visited Glastonbury with the Holy Grail. In the Bible, Joseph arranges Jesus's burial; over the centuries, stories spread that he was a tin merchant who visited Britain to preach after Jesus's death. (His rumoured trip is referred to in the hymn 'Jerusalem'.)

The grail has been identified as many different objects, from a dish from the Last Supper to a chalice used by Joseph to catch Jesus's blood during his crucifixion. It was said to have healing properties and the quest for it became central to Arthurian legend: some believe it is still hidden near Glastonbury.

When Joseph rested his staff on the ground during his trip, it's said a holy thorn tree grew out of it, which still survives today – the Glastonbury Thorn. Traditionally a sprig is sent to the monarch at Christmas as, unusually for its species, it flowers then. During the English Civil War (1642–51) the thorn was destroyed by Parliamentarians, who disapproved of anything associated with Catholicism and Christmas (which they banned between 1647 and 1660). Happily cuttings were saved and planted in Kew Gardens and St John's Churchyard in Glastonbury, where they continue to bloom.

29 JUNE

Nature or Nurture?

The question of whether we're formed by genetics or the environment we've been raised in is one that has preoccupied the greatest minds. Ancient philosophers debated this question – Aristotle believed we were shaped by nurture and Plato that we're born with certain innate ideas. In 1689 the philosopher John Locke used the term 'tabula rasa', meaning 'blank slate', to describe babies, who he believed would be entirely shaped by their environment as they grew up. In contrast, in the twentieth century, many people believed in nativism – that everything is down to nature – and this led to the evils of eugenics.

It is true that your appearance and certain characteristics are the result of your unique genetic information, or genome. Your blood type, skin colour and eye colour are determined by the genes you've inherited from your parents. However, we are also now aware of 'epigenetics', which refers to environmental influences on our genes that alter what they do over our lifespan. Diet, age, exercise and disease can all influence your epigenetics. Your environment can also have a direct influence on how you look: if your mum and dad are both 6 foot 3, you are more likely to be tall, but if they only fed you on sherbet lemons then you will not be as tall as you might have been if you were properly nourished.

Nowadays most people accept that we are formed by 'nature plus nurture'. So you are a wonderful mixture of entangled attributes and influences and can't blame everything on your parents after all.

30 JUNE

Bibliotactics

The most famous library in history was founded in Alexandria around 300 BCE by Alexander the Great's successor, Ptolemy I Soter, and his descendants went on to search every ship that landed at the port for books, returning only copies to their owners. (These had a separate filing tag in the library: 'from the boats'.) One Ptolemy was so desperate to acquire manuscripts by the Greek playwrights Aeschylus, Sophocles and Euripides that he borrowed them from Athens against a huge deposit of silver, but then forfeited the silver to keep the texts.

Some sources say the library's two sites housed 700,000 papyri at their height. The first site was burned down by Julius Caesar in 48 BCE when he was trying to help his squeeze Cleopatra take Alexandria from her brother, and the second, the Serapeum, was destroyed for encouraging paganism by Christians in 391 CE. If the library had survived we might still have the missing second book of Aristotle's *Poetics* on comedy, lost plays by Aeschylus and poetry by Sappho.

But Alexandria wasn't the only game in town. In the third century BCE, Eumenes II, the ruler of the Attalid kingdom, built a fab library of his own in Pergamum (modern-day Bergama in Turkey). This library likely had around 200,000 volumes but most were on parchment rather than papyrus. Parchment is made of dried animal skins and was popularised in Pergamum; the word 'parchment' developed from the city's name. Legend has it that the ruler of Alexandria stopped the export of papyrus to Pergamum to prevent the library competing with his own, forcing the adoption of this new material.

July

1 JULY

The Lore of Larkspur

Tall, striking, pink, blue, purple or white, the larkspur or delphinium is a handsome July flower. The name you choose to call it by should be guided by whether its flowers look more like dolphins to you (from the Greek word 'delphin') or larks' claws, which we're sure you've spent time closely observing. Even more specifically, Shakespeare called it 'lark's-heel'.

Beware, though: its benign beauty conceals dangers. The plant is highly toxic if consumed by humans or animals, though butterflies love its nectar-rich flowers. In Victorian times, larkspur was believed to ward off evil spirits or witches' hexes, so you'd often find it planted at doorways and thresholds to protect homes. In classical myth, it's said to have grown at the spot in Troy where the warrior Ajax flung himself on his sword in a fit of pique after not being awarded the dead Achilles' armour. The Pawnee tribe of North America have a story of a mythological figure, the Dream Woman, who broke a hole in the sky so she could gaze down. Pieces of the sky dropped to earth and, where those scraps of blue kissed the ground, great larkspur flowers bloomed.

2 JULY

A Heady Draft

'Independence is a heady draft, and if you drink it in your youth, it can have the same effect on the brain as a young wine does. It does not matter that its taste is not always appealing. It is addictive and with each drink you want more.'

Maya Angelou (1928–2014),
memoirist, poet and civil rights activist

3 JULY

A Voice from the Past

Nesyamun was an ancient Egyptian priest who lived over three thousand years ago during the reign of Pharaoh Ramses XI. He served at the Karnak temple complex in Thebes (which today forms part of Luxor) and his voice, singing and speaking, would have been an integral part of his role. His incredibly intact mummy was found in 1823, and on his coffin was inscribed his wish for his voice to be heard for eternity.

In 2016, a team from the University of London, working in collaboration with other institutions, embarked on a project in which they performed CT scans of Nesyamun's mummified throat. Unusually for a mummy, his mouth was open and his tongue was protruding – leading some to surmise that he may have died due to an insect bite or even strangulation. The team used a 3D printer to create a replica of his vocal tract from the scans, and by pushing air through it they were able to produce a sound from speech organs that had not been heard for over three millennia. It is worth a listen – it sounds a bit like a groan, or a long, drawn-out 'meh'.

4 JULY

The New Colossus

Not like the brazen giant of Greek fame,
With conquering limbs astride from land to land;
Here at our sea-washed, sunset gates shall stand
A mighty woman with a torch, whose flame
Is the imprisoned lightning, and her name
Mother of Exiles. From her beacon-hand
Glows world-wide welcome; her mild eyes command
The air-bridged harbor that twin cities frame.
'Keep, ancient lands, your storied pomp!' cries she
With silent lips. 'Give me your tired, your poor,
Your huddled masses yearning to breathe free,
The wretched refuse of your teeming shore.
Send these, the homeless, tempest-tost to me,
I lift my lamp beside the golden door!'

Emma Lazarus (1849–87)

This celebrated sonnet, a powerful ode to the fundamental principles of an open-hearted America, was very nearly lost to the sands of time. It was composed by Emma Lazarus, a poet and social activist, as part of an effort to raise funds for the construction of the Statue of Liberty's pedestal in 1883. Years after her death, her friend Georgina Schuyler stumbled across it in a bookshop, and campaigned for a plaque to be installed at the base of the statue, where it still stands today.

5 JULY

What to the Slave Is the Fourth of July?

Abolitionist and orator Frederick Douglass, himself born into slavery, was invited by the Rochester Ladies' Anti-Slavery Society to deliver a speech on 4 July 1852. Recognising the inherent hypocrisy of celebrating an American independence forged from the brutality of slavery, Douglass chose instead to deliver it on 5 July. Here are some of his extraordinary and shattering words.

> 'What, to the American slave, is your Fourth of July? I answer; a day that reveals to him, more than all other days in the year, the gross injustice and cruelty to which he is the constant victim. To him, your celebration is a sham; your boasted liberty, an unholy license; your national greatness, swelling vanity; your sounds of rejoicing are empty and heartless; your denunciation of tyrants, brass fronted impudence; your shouts of liberty and equality, hollow mockery; your prayers and hymns, your sermons and thanksgivings, with all your religious parade and solemnity, are, to him, mere bombast, fraud, deception, impiety, and hypocrisy – a thin veil to cover up crimes which would disgrace a nation of savages. There is not a nation on the earth guilty of practices more shocking and bloody than are the people of the United States, at this very hour.'

6 JULY

Wig Out

When you watch a European period drama on the telly, if all the men are wearing curly wigs with pigtails then you know you're probably somewhere between the Restoration and Georgian eras, before changing fashions brought the long-lived trend to an end – excluding barristers and judges, who still wear them in court today. Wigs for both men and women have gone in and out of fashion since the earliest civilisations; the ancient Egyptians wore wigs, as did Queen Elizabeth I and Marie Antoinette. They declined in popularity around the time of the French Revolution due to their expense and association with the upper classes. Today, people wear wigs and other hair-pieces, such as extensions, for reasons ranging from health and religion to identity experimentation and style.

The most expensive wigs are made from real human hair sewn onto lace caps by master craftspeople. Natural blonde human-hair wigs are the rarest and most expensive because most natural hair for the industry comes from Asia. If you have long undyed hair and are planning a change in look, you can donate your hair to make wigs for cancer sufferers who have lost theirs because of chemotherapy.

BIG WIG

One of the most famous eighteenth-century luxury wig designs for women was the 'boat pouf'. This involved using pig-fat glue, padding and horsehair to make a huge hair nest in which a model galleon was pinned. Coloured flour was used to powder the wig.

7 JULY

A Festive Summer Tree

Every year, on the seventh day of the seventh month (lucky seven being a *thing* in Japan as well as in many other countries), people all over Japan celebrate the Star Festival, or Tanabata. For one day only, wishes, hopes, poetry and dreams are written onto colourful streamers and tied to trees in honour of a particularly poignant mythological love story.

Key to the festival is the myth of the stars Vega and Altair, or 'The Story of the Cowherd and the Weaver Girl'. Orihime, represented by the star Vega, was the daughter of the Heavenly Emperor and also a weaver of beautiful tapestries, a practice she carried out by the Celestial River, the Milky Way. Fabric-making didn't *entirely* satisfy Orihime, though, and she became bored and lonely, so her dad set her up with Hikoboshi, represented by the star Altair, who was a cowherd living on the other side of the Milky Way. It was love at first sight for the starry-eyed pair, but they were so into each other that they neglected their duties. The cows fell into a lowing depression and beautiful finery remained unstitched. The Heavenly Emperor was furious, and forbade the lovers from seeing each other, sending them to opposite ends of the galaxy. In the end, Orihime's sorrow was so great that her father agreed she could meet Hikoboshi once a year, on 7 July. However, if it rains the Celestial River will flood and the lovers must remain apart, so people always hope for clement skies for the Star Festival.

8 JULY

Annihilation into Art

There are many extraordinary things about baroque master Artemisia Gentileschi, the first woman recognised with a solo show at London's National Gallery a mere 197 years after its opening. She was born on 8 July 1593 in Rome, the daughter of distinguished painter Orazio Gentileschi, and she grew up in his studio. When Papà realised her skills far exceeded his own, he brought in the painter Agostino Tassi, a follower of Caravaggio, to continue the apprenticeship, and Artemisia made her debut in the art world at the age of seventeen, with her stunning work *Susanna and the Elders.* Two years later she was raped by Tassi, and when he refused to marry her, her father Orazio took him to court to protect the family honour. Every single word of the trial was recorded, so we know that Artemisia was forced to testify while being tortured, wearing *sibille*, metal cords on her fingers that were gradually tightened, and that midwives were brought in to examine her in front of the judge. Agostino Tassi was found guilty, but never served his sentence.

Having survived the horrors of sexual assault (not to mention the trial), Artemisia went on to become one of the most celebrated artists of her time, taking on the big boys at history paintings, tackling key moments from the Bible and telling them from a woman's perspective.

Artemisia drifted into obscurity after her death (of which little is known; it's thought she may have perished in the plague that wiped out much of Naples in 1656), but she was rediscovered in the twentieth century, and is recognised today as a Renaissance great.

9 JULY

Mapping a Puzzle

In the mid-eighteenth century, a clever cartographer named John Spilsbury stumbled upon an idea that would bring joy to puzzlers for centuries to come. Spilsbury was passionate about maps, and realised that if he mounted his maps on wood and used a steady hand and a jig-saw (see what he did there?), he could create a fun learning tool for children and students.

And lo, Spilsbury's 'Dissected Map' was born in a print-maker's shop off Drury Lane. The idea spread like wildfire as others developed the idea, moving on from maps to story-telling, history and even moral puzzles. An example from 1794 sounds especially thought-provoking: 'A Map of the Various Parts of Life', where one can travel from Misery Square, by way of Remorse Hedge, all the way to Happy Old Age Hall. These days, jigsaws come in all shapes and sizes, though counterintuitively one of the most challenging (and, from a design perspective, most aesthetically pleasing) is comprised of just nine pieces: the Ice 9, designed by Japanese mastermind Yuu Asaka. The trick is to fit the complex shapes together within a small acrylic tray.

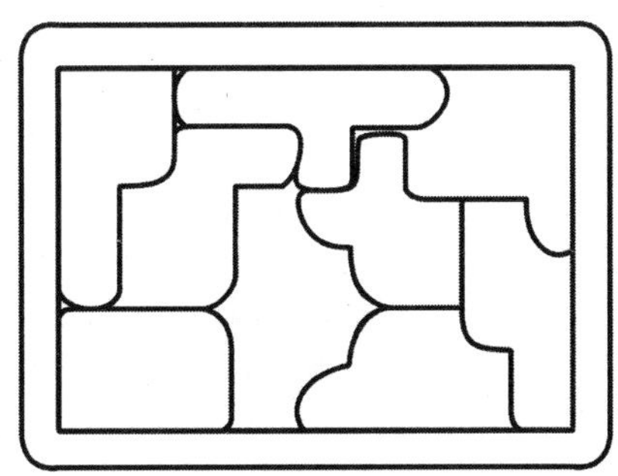

10 JULY

The Guinea Pig Club

'Never in the field of human conflict was so much owed by so many to so few.'

Winston Churchill (August 1940)

In July 1940 the Battle of Britain began. Hitler had planned to invade Britain, but for any ground invasion to work, German forces knew they needed to clear the skies of southern England. The huge conflict between the Royal Air Force and Germany's Luftwaffe was ultimately won by the RAF with just three thousand airmen, many of whom were very young.

Flying was a dangerous game and pilots and crew often ended up with terrible burns to their faces and hands caused by exploding aircraft fuel, an injury dubbed the 'Hurricane burn'. Plastic surgeon Archibald McIndoe treated airmen with facial disfigurements and serious burns at the Queen Victoria Hospital in East Grinstead, Sussex. Standard treatment for burns at this time was to cover the wounds with tannic acid in order to dry out the affected area and allow the dead skin to be removed. It was an extremely painful process and led to horrific scarring. McIndoe noticed that men who bailed out at sea were less scarred than others, and he began treating patients with saline, a much gentler approach.

McIndoe pioneered psychological treatment as well as physical, encouraging his 'boys' to form the Guinea Pig Club, so named because of the experimental nature of his treatments. He encouraged them to wear their service uniforms instead of hospital gowns, and urged them to get out and about. East Grinstead became known as 'the town that didn't stare'.

11 JULY

Ruby Red

Rubies take their name from the Latin word for red, 'rubeus', and they are the red variety of the mineral corundum. They are incredibly strong, coming in at 9 (out of 10) on the Mohs hardness scale, and they symbolise power and protection – just think of Dorothy's slippers in *The Wizard of Oz*. In ancient Asian culture, rubies were the prized possessions of emperors and kings, and legend has it that Burmese warriors carried rubies into battle as a talisman of strength. The most valuable are the darkest, with a little hint of blue, known, slightly revoltingly, as pigeon's-blood red.

WELL HARD

Friedrich Mohs (1773–1839), a German mineralogist, created this ranking system of minerals based on their hardness and scratch resistance.

INCREASING HARDNESS ↓

Mineral	(CAN BE SCRATCHED BY)
1. Talc	
2. Gypsum	
	← FINGERNAIL
3. Calcite	
	← COPPER COIN
4. Fluorite	
5. Apatite	
	← KNIFE / GLASS
6. Feldspar	
	← STEEL
7. Quartz	
8. Topaz	
9. Corundum	
10. Diamond	

12 JULY

The Great British Bathing Machine

Sea bathing became hugely popular in the mid-eighteenth century, when doctors began theorising that taking the sea air and bathing in salt water had beneficial medicinal powers. In our age of mankinis, thongs and side- and under-boobs, it's hard to imagine the outrage swimming costumes caused then – with their full-length pantaloons and jaunty hats, stockings and bathing boots. It was a time when even a glimpse of table leg was considered risqué, so a cumbersome machine was invented to prevent lady bathers being seen.

A small wooden hut was attached to large wheels. Bathers would enter at one end in their clothes while the hut was still on the beach, and then change into their suit as the hut was dragged out to the water by a horse, exiting into the waves away from the prying eyes on land. Sometimes a 'dipper' was employed, often a powerfully built woman who was familiar with the ways of the water, who would help the uninitiated in their first encounter with the sea. Eventually everyone started to relax a bit and as segregation of Britain's beaches was phased out it signalled the end for these modesty-enhancing carts. Those beautiful candy-coloured beach huts you see dotted around the coast? There's a chance they started out in life as a Victorian bathing machine.

13 JULY

A Humble Shrub to Beat the Fumes

We all love the pulsing heat of a summer in the city, but it's also the time of year when exhaust fumes can become oppressive and even dangerous. Instead of sweating it out indoors or amping up the air con (and thereby contributing even further to our climate catastrophe), there is a way to hedge your carbon-offsetting bets. A recent study has shown that, in just seven days, a 1-metre length of well-managed dense hedge will mop up the amount of polluting car emissions belched out over a 500-mile drive. And if that's not astonishing enough as a stat: the Cotoneaster franchetii (named for the French botanist who discovered it in China and shipped it to the West) is around 20% more effective than any other hedge shrub. It's beautiful too, with grey-green leaves, soft-pink flowers and richly coloured orange berries. The same study by the Royal Horticultural Society revealed that climbing wall ivy can also act as an impressive natural air con by absorbing heat from the sun and cooling internal temperatures by as much as 7.5° C.

14 JULY

Hand-to-Hand Heracles

The original Olympic Games, staged in Olympia, Greece, were held every four years from 776 BCE through to 392 CE as part of a festival to honour Zeus. They were abolished by anti-pagan party pooper Christian Roman Emperor Theodosius.

The wildest event was pankration, a combination of wrestling and boxing in which neck holds and strangling were permitted, and only biting and eye-gouging forbidden. Athletes would fight until the last man was standing: according to the rules they were able to submit and give in by waving a finger in the air, but bouts were frequently fatal – many Olympians would rather die than accept the ignominy of defeat. It was said that the demigod Heracles had invented pankration by using both wrestling and boxing to kill the Nemean lion during one of his famous Twelve Labours. After attempting to shoot it with arrows, he realised its fur was impenetrable, so he ravaged it with his bare hands. He then took its skin to use as a defensive magic cloak.

The Olympic Games were reinstated in 1896 by diminutive Frenchman Pierre de Coubertin. Coubertin was an aristocratic republican passionate about education. During the 1880s he visited England and became inspired by teachers there who held fast to the notion of sport as a tool to build moral character, just as the ancient Greeks had done, leading him to establish the International Olympic Committee in 1894. A doodle at the top of a letter shows he also created the famous Olympic branding: the five rings representing the five continents all reaching for the same ideal.

15 JULY

A Third, a Third, a Third

There are several origin stories for the classic negroni, but the one that tickles our fancy most is that it was invented in 1919 after international traveller and sometime rodeo cowboy (yes, really) Count Camillo Negroni walked into the Caffè Casoni bar in Florence and requested a change to his Americano drink. The count was said to have travelled widely in America, returning to Italy when alcohol was banned during Prohibition. Clearly having had a day of it (or maybe just fancying a slightly heavier night ahead), Count Camillo asked for the soda water in his Americano to be replaced with gin. Whatever the truth, the subsequent negroni has been a classic cocktail for over a century: strong, beautiful in hue, and dangerous in excess.

The tip from those in the know is that you should always try to use the best-quality gin, vermouth and Campari, but that if you want to really splash out on just one of the ingredients while concocting this at home, upscale the vermouth.

CLASSIC NEGRONI

25ml gin
25ml Campari
25ml sweet red vermouth

Pour the ingredients into a mixing glass with ice, and stir until the outside of the glass feels cold to the touch. Strain into a tumbler with more ice, and garnish with a slice of orange – rubbed around the rim initially to release the citrusy oils. For an alcohol-free no-groni, choose the very best no-alcohol gin, vermouth and bitters, and use the tried-and-tested 'thirds' method.

16 JULY

River Run

Rivers have always played a key part in human life; they provide food, transport and irrigation, as well as water sports. The longest river in the world is the Nile, which runs for 6,695 kilometres from Lake Victoria through Uganda, Sudan and Egypt, right to the Mediterranean Sea, and the shortest is the Roe River in Montana, which flows for just 61 metres.

RIVERINE IDIOM

Confluence: The point where two rivers join.
Tributary: A smaller river that joins the main channel.
Meanders: The large, horseshoe-shaped bends that rivers make as they flow.
Oxbow lakes: Lakes formed when meanders become tighter due to erosion.
Deltas: Landforms at the mouths of rivers where mud is deposited. There are three main types of delta: arcuate, or fan-shaped, where the river splits into lots of smaller flows as it reaches the sea; cuspate, where the river deposits sediment on either side of itself, creating a pointed promontory; and bird's-foot, which occurs when the river splits into smaller rivers with deposits forming around each, creating a shape like a bird's foot stretching into the sea.

17 JULY

Lucky James Phipps

It's been suggested that forms of inoculation or variolation have been practised for centuries – the World Health Organization even points to evidence from the mid-1500s that describes a Chinese practice whereby scabs were dried, powdered and then snuffed up the nose. But it was Edward Jenner, an English doctor, who made the breakthrough into vaccination. In 1796, he noticed that milkmaids and farmers who contracted cowpox were immune to smallpox, which at the time was widespread and in some outbreaks had a very high death rate. He hypothesised that the less-deadly cowpox could protect against smallpox, and conducted an experiment in which he inoculated the eight-year-old son of his gardener, a boy named James Phipps, with cowpox from a pustule on the hand of milkmaid Sarah Nelmes. He then daringly (some might say criminally) exposed little James to smallpox, which the boy did not contract, thus proving the effectiveness of vaccination. The landscape of medicine was changed forever and a new era of preventative medicine was ushered in. Not bad for a doctor from Gloucestershire whose previous claim to fame had been working out that cuckoo chicks pushed rival chicks out of nests using a special egg-shaped depression in their back.

18 JULY

The Perfect 10

At the Montreal Olympic Games in July 1976, Romanian Nadia Comăneci became the youngest-ever women's Olympic gymnastics champion at just fourteen years old. Judges scored her the first perfect 10 in Olympic history for her uneven bars routine in the team compulsory exercises. It was a sporting feat as important as smashing the first four-minute mile or ten-second 100 metres. The Olympics' scoreboard manufacturers were so unprepared for it that the arena's scoreboard had to display 10 as 1.0 – a moment captured in a now-iconic photograph. And in the days that followed Comăneci repeated it, scoring a jaw-dropping two more 10s in the team optional exercises on 19 July, two more in the individual combined exercises competition on 21 July, and two more in the individual apparatus finals on 23 July. Attagirl!

19 JULY

Decoding the Past

The most famous object in the British Museum is probably the Rosetta Stone. Finding it, and most importantly deciphering it, was key to unlocking the extraordinary culture of ancient Egypt. Its discovery opened the door to scholars interpreting previously unintelligible hieroglyphic texts.

The words on the stone aren't in essence that fascinating: they consist of a decree expressing loyalty and faith to King Ptolemy V, which was originally intended to be displayed in a temple. The same decree is written three times in three different languages: in pictorial hieroglyphs, in the more everyday cursive Egyptian known as Demotic, and also in ancient Greek, which, crucially, scholars could read, whereas Demotic and the meanings of hieroglyphs had long been forgotten.

The stone was discovered, probably accidently, by Napoleon's invading army in the Nile Delta in 1799 and sent to the UK after France's defeat, as part of the 1801 Treaty of Alexandria. It's attracted millions of visitors ever since, aside from a two-year period during the First World War, when it was sequestered away for its own safety in a station on the Postal Tube Railway, 50 feet below ground.

20 JULY

Politics on Holiday

The summer recess of Parliament starts around this time, a six-week break when politicians concentrate on constituency rather than parliamentary work. Here's a glossary of some of the more obscure political terms so those heroes don't fade too fast from our memories.

- **Kakistocracy**: Being governed by the people least suited to do the job.
- **Pornocracy**: Being governed by harlots. (NB this term was most current in the tenth century in the Vatican, when an Italian noblewoman was mistress to one pope and mother to another.)
- **Throttlebottom**: A harmlessly incompetent person in public office.
- **Empleomaniac**: A person who displays a mania for holding public office.
- **Embusqué**: A person who holds public office as a way of avoiding military service.
- **Snollygoster**: A person who ditches their principles in the pursuit of power.

21 JULY

The Seven Wonders of the Ancient World

I have set eyes on the wall of lofty Babylon on which is a road for chariots, and the statue of Zeus by the Alpheus, and the hanging gardens, and the Colossus of the Sun, and the huge labour of the high pyramids, and the vast tomb of Mausolus; but when I saw the house of Artemis that mounted to the clouds, those other marvels lost their brilliancy, and I said, 'Lo, apart from Olympus, the Sun never looked on aught so grand.'

The poet Antipater of Sidon was a second-century BCE Greek writer who gave us one of the first mentions of the Seven Wonders of the Ancient World. Only one of these fabulous monuments stills exists – the Great Pyramid at Giza – the rest having been destroyed over the years. Supposedly one of the most magnificent, the Temple of Artemis at Ephesus was burned down in an arson attack by a man determined to scorch his name into the history books. Herostratus admitted his crimes under torture and clab imed that his motivation had been notoriety, so not only was he sentenced to death but a law was also passed that forbade his name ever being mentioned, with the death penalty for anyone who spoke it. It didn't work, of course, and today herostratic syndrome is the term used by psychoanalysts to describe the morbid quest for eternal fame through acts of violence.

22 JULY

Salad Surprise

We love the surprising term 'salad days', referring to a time of unfettered, carefree and innocent idealism, when anything seems possible and we are not yet weighed down by the baggage of age, responsibility and anxiety. But why on earth are these days called 'salad'? We have our old friend William Shakespeare to thank. In the tragedy *Antony and Cleopatra*, when Cleo, now in love with Mark Antony, speaks regretfully of her earlier pash for Julius Caesar, she remarks that they were: 'My salad days, when I was green in judgment, cold in blood.' It's an incredibly vivid metaphor, so beloved that our very own Queen Elizabeth II used it in her 1977 Silver Jubilee speech, speaking of her initial vow to God and the people of the United Kingdom: 'Although that vow was made in my salad days, when I was green in judgment, I do not regret nor retract one word of it.'

23 JULY

Tip-Tap

Before the digital age, typewriters revolutionised writing, allowing for faster, clearer communication. These magical machines consist of a keyboard, a carriage and a ribbon. When a key is pressed, a typebar with a metal letter strikes the inked ribbon, transferring the character onto paper. The first heavy, unwieldy machines appeared in the 1870s, and were very soon revolutionised by the dawn of the QWERTY keyboard. This was invented by an American printer named Christopher Latham Sholes, who realised that the traditional, alphabetical keyboard jammed the machinery, and that if the letters were arranged in more common combinations, like 'th' or 'he', everything would run more smoothly. Fun fact: the letters that spell out the word 'typewriter' are all located on the top row.

The Italian Olivetti family, who set up their business in the small town of Ivrea in northern Italy in 1908, made the typewriter an object of desire. The company ethos began with design: from the typefaces they created to the shape of the space bar, everything was fully thought through. Olivetti typewriters can be found in art galleries and museums across the world; pay special attention to the officially licensed World Cup Italia '90 product, a distinctive Azzurri colour, inspired by the men in blue.

24 JULY

Literary Lies

Here are some of the best hoaxes writers have sprung on the public in their quest for fame and fortune.

- *The Poems of Ossian* translated by James Macpherson (1760) were said to be the works of a blind third-century Scottish bard – 'the Homer of the North' – who influenced Robert Burns and Sir Walter Scott, but are now widely held to be the works of Macpherson himself.
- Aussie writers James McAuley and Harold Stewart were extremely vexed about what they perceived as the madnesses of modernism. Over the course of a single day in 1943 they created the entire body of work and wholly invented biography of the surrealist poet Ern Malley. Experimental journal *Angry Penguins* was taken in and published the collection to rapturous acclaim. The publisher was put on trial and fined for publishing obscene content when the fakery was revealed. In a meta-twist, the poems of Ern Malley have gone on to influence many other writers, including inspiring Booker winner Peter Carey's 2003 novel *My Life as a Fake*.
- *Transgressing the Boundaries: Towards a Transformative Hermeneutics of Quantum Gravity* by Alan Sokal (1996) was a proverbial piss-take. Sokal, an NYU physicist, was so incensed by what he considered to be the overcomplicated, elitist and nihilistic value of critical theory that he wrote a purposefully ridiculous paper, which was enthusiastically adopted by *Social Text*, a hip journal. His sentences included gems such as: '[science] cannot assert a privileged epistemological status with respect to counterhegemonic narratives emanating from dissident or marginalised communities'. Makes sense.

25 JULY

Decimating Decibels

One of nature's greatest spectacles is the emergence of America's Great Eastern Brood of cicadas – Brood X. So famed that even Bob Dylan wrote a song about them, this gigantic brood of 1.4 million insects per acre emerge every seventeen years from their home underground to swarm, sing and mate, only to die a mere two weeks later. Their eggs hatch after a couple of months and cicada nymphs burrow into the ground to start the process all over again. The swarm's song has been recorded exceeding 100 decibels.

Early American settlers read biblical warnings into what looked like swarms of doomsday locusts, but nowadays botanists boggle at their lifespan and multitude – some wondering whether that precise seventeen years (a prime number) stops predators from building the locusts into their food cycle. However, human apex predators greeted the great emergence of 2021 with gastronomic glee – serving up cicada cookouts across America.

26 JULY

The DIY Surrey Iron Railway

The world's very first public railway comprised of two lines known collectively as the Surrey Iron Railway, which ran from South London's Wandsworth to Croydon, and opened in July 1803.

A very different train service was offered from what we might expect today; for a start, you had to bring your own horse. There were no stations, no signalling and no timetable; individuals would turn up, bring a horse and hire a wagon which would run along the rail lines laid between the two towns, paying by weight and distance. The rails made it possible to transport much heavier loads than you could normally manage with a standard horse and cart. As steam-powered trains were just coming into use, and were far faster and cheaper, customers soon got wise to the fact that this probably wasn't the most efficient model, and the line fell into disuse in 1846.

27 JULY

'Midnight shout and revelry'

roister: a little-used but glorious verb meaning to enjoy oneself, revel or celebrate in a noisy and exuberant way.

'The girls roistered their way through
the sun-drenched days of July.'

28 JULY

The People Are Revolting

Humans love a bit of an uprising, but some of them are truly strange . . .

- Toronto's Circus Riot of 1855 kicked off when a bunch of rough clowns picked the wrong brothel on their night off. It was frequented by the Hook and Ladder Firefighting Co., and they came to blows. The firefighters beat a retreat, but the next day they joined forces with their friends the Orangemen, and crowds began to gather around S. B. Howes' Star Troupe Menagerie & Circus – all hell broke loose and the circus was run out of town. The police, mostly Orangemen, had turned a very blind eye for too long; every single officer was fired and the foundations for Toronto's modern, non-political police force were laid.
- The Brown Dog riots of 1907 occurred in London when two Swedish anti-vivisectionists erected a statue to a little dog they had observed being operated on without proper anaesthetic. Its inscription enraged medical students, who defended their right to experiment on animals, and they rioted over the course of several months, vowing to tear the statue down. The affair made animal rights a cause célèbre which has never gone away.
- Amsterdammers used to enjoy a strange sport called eel pulling, in which live eels would be attached to ropes and dangled over canals while men in small boats attempted to snatch them down. The government decided it was a cruel sport and banned it. But the Dutch don't like being told what to do, so at the next – now illegal – gathering of eel pulling the police were called to intervene amid the large crowds. Things got very out of hand and twenty-six people were killed.

29 JULY

Punishing Pluto

In 2006 the International Astronomical Union came up with a new classification for planets which are smaller than Mercury, large enough to have their own gravitational force, but not enough gravity to clear the neighbourhood around them: dwarf planets. The IAU has identified five so far, all named after mythological figures: Ceres, the Roman goddess of grain; Haumea, the Hawaiian goddess of childbirth and fertility; Eris, the Greek goddess of strife and discord; and Makemake, a fertility goddess from Rapa Nui (Easter Island). Finally, and most controversially, the IAU downgraded Pluto – named after the god of the underworld – to a dwarf planet. Their decision caused outcry across the world: not only was it a nightmare as far as textbooks and catchy mnemonics were concerned, but Pluto has always held a special place in our collective imagination as the smallest and furthest-away planet – a punchy little underdog. Rumour even has it that Walt Disney named his beloved canine character after the planet as it was discovered in 1930, the same year he first graced our screens.

PLANETARY TIME DIFFERENCES

Time moves very differently on dwarf planets. Haumea spins so quickly that it is weirdly egg-shaped; a day lasts for just four hours there, whilst on Eris a year is over five hundred times longer than on earth

30 JULY

The Dangers of Data

It's all about the data, we're told. Increasingly, we rely on data to control and regulate our lives. But the truth is that data itself is stretchy, malleable and can be misused. And in certain extreme cases, this manipulation can be lethal.

In 1996, Purdue Pharma sold the dream of a potent painkiller that would not be addictive to millions of patients across America. Along with a powerful marketing campaign, they backed their claims with science, including a data visualisation that showed OxyContin levels would remain stable in patients' blood over time. This data was used to convince doctors that the drug wouldn't lead to symptoms of withdrawal or addiction, which are often caused by sharp drops in drug concentration. But the graph was drawn on a logarithmic rather than linear scale. When plotted on a linear scale it is very clear that there is a sharp drop in OxyContin levels over time. A generation of addicts was created, and since 1999 over 645,000 Americans have died from opioid abuse. The lesson? Interrogate your data!

31 JULY

Chin-Chin

'I like large parties. They're so intimate. At small parties there isn't any privacy.'

F. Scott Fitzgerald, *The Great Gatsby*

Here are some exceptional literary parties for you to enjoy:

- Jay Gatsby's parties at his lavish West Egg mansion in *The Great Gatsby* are the real deal: each one an epic, endless bacchanalian fest to impress his lady love, Daisy Buchanan.
- The bright young things of Evelyn Waugh's *Vile Bodies* (1930) are constantly attending parties: 'Masked parties, Savage parties, Victorian parties, Greek parties, Wild West parties, Russian parties, Circus parties, parties where one had to dress as somebody else, almost naked parties in St John's Wood, parties in flats and studios and houses and ships and hotels and night clubs, in windmills and swimming-baths, tea parties at school where one ate muffins and meringues and tinned crab, parties at Oxford where one drank brown sherry and smoked Turkish cigarettes, dull dances in London and comic dances in Scotland and disgusting dances in Paris . . .'
- In John's Cheever masterful short story 'The Swimmer' (1964), a deluded Neddy decides to affirm his own legend by making his way home from a well-heeled friend's house by swimming across all the pools of the suburb, crashing a few parties along the way.

- In Ernest Hemingway's 1926 debut novel *Fiesta, or The Sun Also Rises*, Jake Barnes and his pals travel to Pamplona in Spain, ostensibly to watch the bullfights, but in reality to drink, flirt, bicker and seduce each other. In his portrayal of hard-partying yet resilient young folk, Hemingway established himself as the voice of the post-war Lost Generation.
- Jane Austen's books are full of parties and balls, at which it's clear to see how the characters' behaviours are inextricably linked with the ups and downs of courtship. And we all know how close Mr Darcy comes to losing Lizzy by describing her as 'tolerable, but not handsome enough to tempt me'.
- In Alan Hollinghurst's Booker Prize-winning *The Line of Beauty* (2004), a party is held to celebrate the twenty-fifth anniversary of Tory MP Gerald Fedden and his wife, Rachel, at which Prime Minister Margaret Thatcher is also in attendance. Against the backdrop of a 1980s Britain in which the AIDS crisis was looming and negative views on homosexuality were rampant, our young gay protagonist Nick Guest's decision to ask the Iron Lady for a dance has been read by some as the ultimate dance with the devil.

August

1 AUGUST

August

Silence again. The glorious symphony
Hath need of pause and interval of peace.
Some subtle signal bids all sweet sounds cease,
Save hum of insects' aimless industry.
Pathetic summer seeks by blazonry
Of color to conceal her swift decrease.
Weak subterfuge! Each mocking day doth fleece
A blossom, and lay bare her poverty.
Poor middle-agèd summer! Vain this show!
Whole fields of golden-rod cannot offset
One meadow with a single violet;
And well the singing thrush and lily know,
Spite of all artifice which her regret
Can deck in splendid guise, their time to go!

Helen Hunt Jackson (1830–85)

A lifelong friend of Emily Dickinson, Helen Hunt Jackson lost her parents as a child and then her husband and her own children in her early thirties. She channelled this hardship into writing books and poetry and campaigning as a fierce ally for American Indian activists.

2 AUGUST

King of the Beasts

Science has shown that animals often have superior sensory abilities to humans and that many can cooperate, use tools and language, create culture, form pair and child bonds, and some creatures, like koalas, even have opposable thumbs. So what makes us special?

- There are over thirty species of dog and 350,000 of beetle, but humans, along with aardvarks and aye-ayes, are one of very few creatures that only exist in one species.
- Humans are also one of only a few animals – including apes, some shrews and bats and one kind of mouse – who menstruate. No one knows why. One theory is that human placentas are so invasive that potential mothers have to build up more tissue in advance of impregnation to protect themselves from their own foetuses. We are also, along with a few species of whale, the only animals to go through menopause.
- Our highly developed brains are thought to be the reason we can imagine what other people are thinking, analyse the past and imagine the future (including our own deaths), and make fun memes about nostalgic TV shows to make each other laugh (using symbols, memory, culture and technology in one swift hit).
- Our complex brains have also allowed us to create top tech; other animals, such as chimps and crows, use tools but we have taken technological innovation to heights not seen by any other creature. This has also led us to be uniquely destructive of the environment. We're even second on the leaderboard of animals most deadly to ourselves, after mosquitoes (who don't even mean it).

3 AUGUST

Pay It Forward

Do you fancy a bit of eudaemonic well-being today rather than the more obvious hedonic kind? If you treat yourself to a chocolate bar or a massage you are going hedonic, but that warm glow you get from helping someone down the station steps with their buggy is eudaemonic.

Making the world a better place, even through tiny gestures, contributes to our sense of meaning and positive mental health. Prosocial behaviour also tends to cascade – that person you helped is now more likely to be kind to someone else they meet later in their day.

4 AUGUST

Dressing for Space

Space holds particular challenges for humans: there's no oxygen, less gravity, it's very big, very cold out of the sun's rays and very hot in them . . . and there is killer dust. Yes, space dust is tiny, sharp and fast-moving, and can tear through spacecraft materials, wreaking havoc and destruction. In order to survive, astronauts wear special suits – the most complex of which is the one for space walks. Features include a cooling layer (the suit is sealed so keeps all the astronaut's body heat inside), radio, oxygen cylinder, pump to circulate cooling water, insulating and protective layers, gold protective visor (gold is best for protecting from solar glare), headset and helmet.

GALACTIC BLOATING

Living in microgravity affects astronauts in strange ways, such as 'puffy face and chicken legs', which is where the normal fluid distribution in the body is disrupted and the circumference of the legs can decrease by 10–30%.

5 AUGUST

Bella Bellini

The Bellini was invented at one of the world's most famous drinking establishments, Harry's Bar in Venice. Founded by Giuseppe Cipriani in 1931, its visitors have included Ernest Hemingway, Orson Welles, Frank Lloyd Wright and Katharine Hepburn. It was here that Cipriani was inspired by his love of white peaches to create the Bellini, a cocktail he named after the Renaissance painter Giovanni Bellini, who used a gorgeous peachy-pink colour in his paintings.

BELLINI

1 ripe peach – it must be ripe – or 50g of bottled peach nectar
100ml prosecco or Champagne

Peel and stone your peach and blend it to a pulp. You want this puree to be sweet so, if you need to, add some sugar syrup. Chill the puree in the fridge along with a champagne flute. Once cold, pour half the puree into your glass and top with the sparkling wine.

For a non-alcoholic version, follow the instructions above but top up with fizzy apple juice instead of wine.

6 AUGUST

Do Chips Count?

The WHO says we need to eat at least five portions of fruit and veg a day to keep us healthy. Researchers at University College Hospital found that increasing our intake from one to seven portions could cut our risk of premature death by 42%. Only about 33% of British people manage to hit the five-a-day target, and it's common to overestimate the healthiness of our diets, so it's time for a wake-up call on what *doesn't* count as a portion of veg:

Sandwich salad, iceberg lettuce, onion rings, potato chips, crisps or roast potatoes, vegetable chips, pickles, jam and olives either don't have enough nutrients or contain too much salt to count – disappointing!

Also, a portion of fruit or veg has to be 80 grams – equal to about ten raspberries.

7 AUGUST

The Novel Novel

Despite our global culture being dominated by men, both the world's first named author and the world's first novelist are believed to have been women. The Akkadian priestess Enheduanna is our first-recorded poet from way back in the twenty-third century BCE and Murasaki Shikibu's eleventh-century *Tale of Genji* is often cited as the world's first novel.

It's odd to think that novels didn't exist before Murasaki wrote hers in Japan in around 1010. Long oral epic poems like the *Odyssey* and prose works like Petronius' *Satyricon* were written before this, but *The Tale of Genji* fits the modern definition of a novel as a long-form fictional prose story, with a purposeful literary style, which gives a level of intimacy in the experience of reading it.

The book follows the life and loves of Genji, a nobleman, including his affair with his father the emperor's wife, Lady Fujitsubo. Their secret child eventually becomes the emperor himself. The great love of Genji's life is Lady Murasaki, the pen name of the author.

Pleasingly, *The Tale of Genji* was apparently written by a courtier to entertain other ladies at court: *The New Yorker* refers to Murasaki as 'a medieval Jane Austen'. The novel was rediscovered in the twentieth century when the Japanese poet Akiko Yosano made a modern translation of it. English translations followed – the names of characters given above come from these as the original refers to individuals elliptically by their titles to avoid scandalous revelations and unmaskings. It's a stone-cold classic and gathers legions of new readers even today.

8 AUGUST

The Paperclip Apocalypse

AI stands for artificial intelligence and refers to computers with the ability to reason, analyse, solve problems, learn and communicate in a similar way to humans. In 1950 the British computer scientist Alan Turing defined what we now know as the Turing test (he called it the imitation game), which determined a computer to be sentient if it could convince humans that it was sentient. No computer has ever passed the Turing test but ChatGPT is a contender.

The first AI was developed in the 1950s to play draughts, and now AI tools are everywhere, from search engines to medical diagnostics, from manufacturing programs to weaponry, to Siri and Alexa and customer service chatbots. Because of the processing power of computers, AI can do complex tasks much more efficiently and accurately than humans, so there is concern that, once an AI reaches the level of human intelligence, where it can constantly improve itself and apply flexibility to a broad enough range of knowledge, it could become a threat by automating many jobs or even deciding to act against humans.

Swedish philosopher Nick Bostrom's thought experiment from 2003, The Paperclip Maximiser, speculates on how AI might accidentally cause our demise if robust safety checks aren't built into its programming. If you set a super-intelligent AI to work on the seemingly innocent task of making as many paperclips as possible, then one of the conclusions it will come to when considering obstacles to its goal is the possibility that a human might turn it off, so it would logically solve this by eliminating humans. Sobering.

9 AUGUST

A Great Personality

Personality tests predict certain habitual behaviours and strengths and weaknesses. One of the best-known early tests was the Woodworth Personal Data Sheet used on US recruits for the First World War to judge whether they could cope with the stress of combat. It included questions like 'Did other children let you play with them?'

There has been criticism from professional psychologists of many of the theories around personality definition and some dismiss the tests as 'astrology for businessmen'. Here are some of the most famous personality definitions:

- Types A and B: Developed in the 1950s to work out whether certain personalities were more at risk of heart disease. Type A people are considered more driven and impatient whereas Type B people are more laid-back.
- Extroverts and Introverts: The psychiatrist Carl Jung's theories influenced this categorisation, which separates extroverts, who are energised by social interaction, from introverts, who tend to be quieter and more reflective.
- Myers–Briggs: Invented in the 1940s by an American mother-daughter team who had studied Jung, to help people entering the workforce during the war find suitable jobs. Its questions generate a combination of letters indicating leading characteristics: E for extroversion, S for sensing, T for thinking, J for judgement, I for introversion, N for intuition, F for feeling and P for perception.
- The Big Five: According to this theory, first developed in the 1950s, there are five key traits which we all have to different extents: Extroversion, Conscientiousness, Agreeableness, Neuroticism and Openness to Experience. Recently new theories have added a sixth, Honesty-Humility.

10 AUGUST

Sloths and Moths

The animal kingdom is full of strange beasts but the sloth is surely up there as one of the most unusual. From the xenarthra group (a fittingly otherworldly name) that also includes anteaters and armadillos, they are famous for enjoying very slow lives hanging upside down in trees. There are only six species of sloth in the world today but back in prehistory there were elephant-sized sloths too. It is thanks to these sloth ancestors that we get to enjoy avocados today, as they are thought to have been one of the few creatures able to manage the fruit's large seeds and therefore help spread them around.

One very special thing about sloths is that they are crucial to the existence of a particular type of moth – the sloth moth (*Cryptoses choloepi*). The sloth moth relies entirely on the sloth to survive: it lays its eggs in sloth poop, which after hatching fly up to live in the sloth's shaggy pelt. One sloth can host 950 moths and beetles in its fur at any time.

11 AUGUST

Poppies and Hong Kong

Bright, fragile and blowsy, poppies are a delicate flower with heavy associations. During the First World War, corn poppies bloomed on the churned-up battlefields of France and Belgium, inspiring Lieutenant Colonel John McCrae's poem 'In Flanders Fields', which begins 'In Flanders fields the poppies blow/ Between the crosses, row on row . . .' After the war this led to the wearing of paper poppies, particularly in Commonwealth countries, for both remembrance and fundraising for former soldiers.

The other big hitter is *Papaver somniferum*, the opium poppy. Opium is harvested from the unripe seed pod after its flowers have fallen, and its milky sap dries into brown gum which can be chemically treated to make heroin, morphine and codeine: the most powerful pain-relief medications in the world. Side effects of these drugs include euphoria and relaxation ('somniferum' means 'sleep-bringing'), which has made them big business in the illegal drugs trade. They are hugely addictive and estimated to be responsible for 66% of drugs deaths worldwide.

From the seventeenth to the early twentieth century, before regulation, opium was widely available in a tincture called laudanum for coughs and colds and also smoked in pipes. European traders began selling opium into China in the 1700s in return for goods like tea and silk, despite the objection of the Chinese authorities. Britain and France were so keen to peddle it that they went to war with China as a result of which China was forced to legalise opium, open ports to trade and hand over territory. So poppies are responsible for the strange situation of Britain controlling Hong Kong, 6,000 miles away, between 1842 and 1997.

12 AUGUST

Decent Exposure

apricate: to sunbathe
'I'm going outside to apricate in the garden.'

'Apricate' comes from the Latin verb 'apricare', 'to bask in the sun', which is thought to be related to the verb 'aperire', meaning 'to open' or 'to expose'.

13 AUGUST

The Tale of the Treble Clef

'Clef' is the French word for 'key' and it is the symbol you'll see at the start of a piece of sheet music, indicating the pitch of the notes. The most common is the treble clef, or G-clef, which shows which line of the stave represents G by wrapping its curly centre around it. Because musical notes run from A to G, this indicates that the white space above G is the note A, and the white space below it is F.

But how did the treble clef get its elegant shape? Originally, and logically, it was just a letter 'G' wrapped round the correct line, but the letter looked different depending on penmanship so it's likely some fancy unknown calligraphist led us to the flourish we now have.

14 AUGUST

Necessity Isn't the Mother of Invention

'I don't think necessity is the mother of invention.
Invention . . . arises directly from idleness,
possibly also from laziness.'

Agatha Christie (1890–1976), bestselling fiction writer of all time, celebrated for her iconic murder mystery novels starring Miss Marple and Hercule Poirot. She was also the first-recorded British woman to surf standing up.

15 AUGUST

Apostrophe Catastrophe

The original Greek meaning of 'apostrophe' is 'turning away'. In grammar it means a letter that is 'turned away' or left out. Apostrophes are famous for being used incorrectly and are the cause of many battles between sticklers and those who think we should ditch them. This is not a new debate; the Irish writer George Bernard Shaw said of them in 1902: 'There is not the faintest reason for persisting in the ugly and silly trick of peppering pages with these uncouth bacilli.' Before the eighteenth century people were much more free and easy about grammar, and the rise of texting and informal writing online may usher in a laxer future. But in case youre not yet ready to welcome in an apostropheless world, heres a handy list of dos and don'ts:

Apostrophes should only be used to indicate contraction or omission and possession.

Contraction/Omission

Apostrophes mark where letters have been removed to shorten a word or phrase e.g. 'we'll', 'could've', 'mightn't', 'o'clock'.

Possession

To signify that an object belongs to someone, an apostrophe followed by an 's' is placed after the noun that is doing the possessing, e.g. 'Maya's coffee'. (There is fierce debate over whether, if the noun already ends in an 's', the apostrophe should appear after the existing 's' or if a further 's' should also be added, e.g. 'James' coat' or 'James's coat'. For some people this really matters.) However, when working with the word 'it' you don't add an apostrophe to the possessive as that would indicate a contraction of 'it is': 'It's a catastrophe. The lizard has eaten its brother.'

16 AUGUST

Totally Tortilla

The tortilla is a round flatbread, traditionally made of treated maize, which originated thousands of years ago in Mexico. The earliest signs of maize agriculture that we have were found in the Guilá Naquitz cave in Oaxaca state and are thought to date from 8000–6500 BCE during the Neolithic period when humans were moving from hunter-gatherer societies to more agricultural communities. Much later, the Aztecs (thirteenth–sixteenth centuries CE) worshipped maize deities: the goddess Chicomecóatl and the god Centéotl, who are depicted holding ears of corn. In North America, maize, along with beans and squash, is one of the 'three sisters' planted together in Indigenous agricultural practices that go back three thousand years. Maize is now one of the top-three staple food crops in the world and tortillas are one of its most delicious recipes.

Tortillas are famously used in many tasty Central and South American dishes, from burritos (wrapped round fillings), quesadillas (folded and fried with cheese inside), tacos (folded in half round a filling), enchiladas (wrapped round a filling, covered in sauce and baked), fajitas (wrapped round a meat filling with toppings like guacamole and sour cream), taquitos (rolled tightly round a filling and fried) and nachos (fried chips with toppings) to chilaquiles (quartered and fried with toppings). One superstition that is associated with tortillas is that if you drop one on the ground you are likely to receive an unwelcome visit from your in-laws!

burrito

quesadillas

tacos

enchiladas

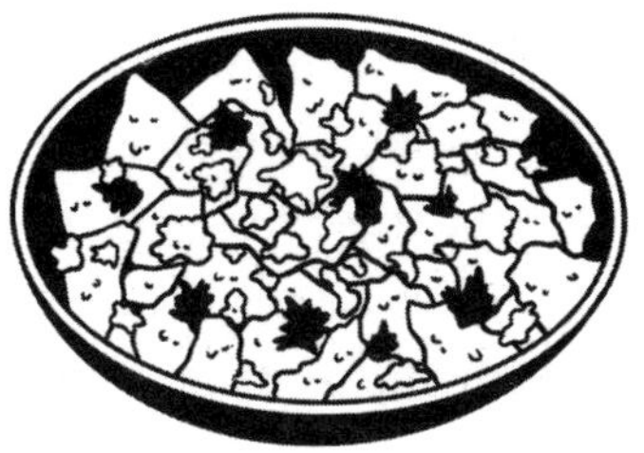

chilaquiles

fajita

taquitos

nachos

17 AUGUST

Vanilla Plastic

Strictly speaking, if you make a loaf of bread using live yeast, you are engaging in biotechnology. Biotech involves using living organisms to advance our capabilities. Its best-known discipline is genetic engineering, which is used in medicine to help combat diseases as well as in agriculture, where genetically modified crops are developed to be more productive or resistant to environmental challenges. But the array of research happening in this area potentially touches almost every part of our future lives.

One significant 2016 breakthrough was the discovery that a certain bacteria called *Ideonella sakaiensis* can eat PET plastic. Since then scientists have been experimenting with the enzymes this bacteria produces to see if they can make it efficient enough to be used on a scale that could help us deal with the problem of plastic pollution – like the 14 million tons that end up in oceans each year.

A 'super-enzyme' has also been developed that can break down the plastic used in drinks bottles into a more basic element called TA. In 2021 a team at the University of Edinburgh managed to genetically engineer the E. coli bacteria to break TA down into vanillin – the chemical that makes things taste and smell vanilla-ey. (They have since also managed to use a different modified E. coli to make nylon without using fossil fuels.) Currently, 85% of the vanillin used in flavouring and scents is chemically manufactured from fossil fuels, rather than extracted from natural vanilla bean pods, so advancing this technology to commercial scale would be a win-win. Look forward to the plastic-bottle-flavour ice cream of the future!

18 AUGUST

Live Long and Prosper

Across the world, people are generally living longer – global life expectancy at birth in 1950 was just 46.5 years and by 2022 it had risen to 71.7 years, and it is expected to keep improving.

While fewer people are dying from warfare or illness today than previously in history, there are still many obstacles to getting to our 'four-score years and ten' (90). So what is going to kill you? In 2019 the leading global causes of death were: 1. ischaemic heart disease at 16% of global deaths (ischaemia is restricted blood supply), 2. stroke, 3. lung disease, 4. lower respiratory infections, 5. neonatal diseases, 6. trachea, bronchus and lung cancers, 7. Alzheimer's and dementia, 8. diarrhoeal diseases, 9. diabetes, 10. kidney disease.

Some folk believe we can swerve these nasties and hugely increase our lifespans. Transhumanists trust that ongoing scientific and technological progress means we should soon be able to upgrade the standard human body and mind using methods such as genetic engineering, AI and biotech to give us longer, healthier lives and superhuman, or 'post-human', abilities. It is already possible to create artificial limbs that are stronger than human ones, implants that allow people to perceive infrared and UV light, and research is going into the possibility of converting the human mind into code so that it can be uploaded into a computer to achieve 'digital immortality'. It could then potentially be downloaded into a different superhuman robot or cyborg body after death.

19 AUGUST

The Pareto Optimum

Despite sounding like the title of a gripping Robert Ludlum thriller, the Pareto optimum is actually a rather drier economic concept invented by Italian intellectual Vilfredo Pareto (1848–1923). To be Pareto-optimal, or Pareto-efficient, an economic situation must be such that no one can be made better off without making someone else worse off. This principle is often referred to when governments make decisions about the efficiency of welfare economics, as it allows them to assess trade-offs and who will benefit most from policies.

Vilfredo, who was a civil engineer and sociologist as well as an economist, did not just leave us with one dramatic-sounding economic concept – he is also behind the Pareto principle, also known as the 80/20 rule, which came from his observation that 80% of Italy was owned by 20% of the population. According to legend, Vilfredo was inspired by noting that 20% of the pea plants in his garden produced 80% of the peas he harvested. The Pareto principle states that, much of the time, 80% of outcomes are created by 20% of causes. This is not an accurate mathematical formula but a general rule, and it's often used by businesses to prioritise the most profitable 20% of their clients or output, or to focus on the 20% most wasteful areas of their company when looking to fix things. Some individuals also use it in their personal lives, allocating 80% of their time to the 20% of their activities that give them the most joy or fulfilment.

VILFREDO'S VERBIAGE %

In a more lyrical tone, Vilfredo also invented the word 'ophelimity', meaning 'economic satisfaction'.

20 AUGUST

Verbose Verses

The Kyrgyz *Epic of Manas*, about the eponymous hero and his family, is the world's longest poem by number of lines (500,000), but by word count the winner is the hugely influential Sanskrit epic the *Mahabharata* (1.8 million words). The *Mahabharata* was written around two thousand years ago and is said to have been composed by the wise man Vyasa, who dictated it to the elephant god Ganesh. Legend has it that, when his quill gave up the ghost, Ganesh used his tusk to continue writing. The *Mahabharata*, whose title means *Great Epic of the Bharata Dynasty*, is one of the holy books of Hinduism, along with the other epic poem the *Ramayana*, and the Puranas and Vedas.

The poem tells the story of the political struggle between two sides of a royal family but there are many side-stories and depictions of the correct code of conduct in life (dharma). The most famous part of the *Mahabharata* is in the sixth book, the *Bhagavad Gita* (*Song of the Lord*). It describes the discussion between the lord Arjuna and Krishna, an incarnation of the protector god Vishnu, just before a major battle in which Arjuna knows many people he cares about will die. Krishna advises him on duty and dharma.

> 'And do thy duty, even if it be humble, rather than another's, even if it be great. To die in one's duty is life: to live in another's is death.'

21 AUGUST

Green Your House

It can seem pointless to take small steps to make your life more eco-friendly when all around there are planes criss-crossing the sky, factories belching out smoke and a billion cows farting on beef farms. But do not be discouraged: marginal gains can make all the difference if lots of us undertake them.

- Reduce the use of harsh chemicals in cleaning your home. If something has a picture of a dying fish on its bottle, or a person having their hand vaporised, then it probably isn't going to do the world much good when you rinse it down your sink. White vinegar is great for removing mould and limescale, and combined with bicarbonate of soda it will also fizz up and clear sludgy drains.
- Try not to buy clothes that require dry-cleaning and don't wash things too often – jeans, which are environmentally costly to produce, only need washing once a month, according to manufacturers.
- Put a water saver in your loo cistern or an aerator into your shower head to save water. It is more environmentally friendly to use a kettle to boil water and a dishwasher to wash dishes than to heat a pan or wash up by hand.
- Insulate your home as best you can with draught-excluding strips on leaky doors and windows and proper insulation in your roof space – this will also save money on heating.
- Don't buy bottled water – get a water-filter jug if you don't like tap water.
- Delete your emails, unsubscribe to unwanted newsletters, close the tabs on your desktop: all these things use electricity.

22 AUGUST

Civil War Cuts and Bouffants

In Anthony Van Dyck's famous portraits of King Charles I, the monarch sports the top fashion hairstyle of the time, the lovelock. Charles and his Cavalier supporters are best known for losing to Oliver Cromwell and the Puritan 'Roundheads' in the English Civil Wars, but they famously also went in for long curly hair.

In many portraits the Cavaliers wore their hair considerably longer on the left-hand side than the right. The idea was that the hair grew down over your heart and helped you recall a loved one. In pictures of Charles's sister, Elizabeth of Bohemia, she wears a small plait of Charles's hair pinned into her own, as a symbol of her love for him. Legend has it that the lovelock became fashionable in England after the settlement of the first North American colonies, inspired by American Indian hairstyles.

'Cavalier' originally meant 'cavalryman' but by Charles's reign implied a frivolous show-off. 'Roundhead' was apparently first used by Charles's wife, Henrietta Maria, to describe one of the Parliamentarian leaders who had the more unusual Puritan short hairstyle – lots of Parliamentarians retained their traditional hairdos and Oliver Cromwell himself had long hair. After Charles's execution in 1649, several of his followers cut locks of his hair as keepsakes and some of these, worked into pieces of jewellery, still survive today. When his son, Charles II, retook the throne in 1660, his coronation portrait shows him with even more luxuriant and bouffed hair than his dad, ushering in the heyday of gentlemen's curled wigs.

23 AUGUST

The Mints of Espionage

Knowledge of the enemy's dispositions can only be obtained from other men. Hence the use of spies, of whom there are five classes: (1) local spies; (2) inward spies; (3) converted spies; (4) doomed spies; (5) surviving spies.

Sun Tzu, *The Art of War*

Since the time of Sun Tzu, secret services across the world have been involved in hidden battles to steal one other's information and prevent their own from being stolen. Today's intelligence agencies rely on different types of intelligence-gathering, including:

- HUMINT: Human Intelligence is the use of people, like agents and informants, to pass on information.
- OSINT: Open-Source Intelligence is information that is freely available, for instance from the media, or academic and commercial publications.
- TECHINT: Technical Intelligence relates to weaponry, for example when a state captures an aircraft or weapon from another country's army and analyses it.
- COMINT: Communications Intelligence is material gathered from intercepting communications such as emails and phone calls. Also covered under SIGINT or Signals Intelligence.
- GEOINT: Geospatial Intelligence comes from satellites and aerial photography.
- MASINT: Measurement and Signature Intelligence uses radar and other sensors to observe things like submarines and missiles.

24 AUGUST

Duck Architecture

You are probably familiar with the columns of classical architecture (fifth century BCE–third century CE), the arches, gargoyles and flying buttresses of Gothic (twelfth–sixteenth centuries CE), the domes and minarets of Ottoman (thirteenth–sixteenth centuries), the geometric lines of Bauhaus (1919–33) and the exposed beams and chimneys of Arts and Crafts design (late nineteenth and early twentieth centuries), but have you come across Duck Architecture?

Robert Venturi, Denise Scott Brown and Steven Izenour coined the term to describe buildings that represent their function in their form, like the Big Duck building built by a duck farmer on Long Island in 1931 to sell his wares. (Terrifyingly, the duck had red glowing eyes made of car lights.) The term was intended to celebrate modern commercial American architecture, but the group also designated the Gothic Chartres Cathedral as Duck Architecture, as it is built in the shape of a cross.

25 AUGUST

Menopausal Fruit

Some fruits need to be attached to their plant to ripen – like raspberries, strawberries, grapes, pineapples and melons – but others, like bananas, avocados, plums, apples, tomatoes, mangoes, pears, peaches, apricots and kiwis, continue to ripen once they've been picked: these are climacteric fruit. As they ripen, they give off a gas called ethylene. Bananas produce a particularly large amount of ethylene, which can be used to ripen other climacteric fruit if you put them in a sealed paper bag together. 'Climacteric' means 'turning point', and is also a fun word for 'menopause'.

26 AUGUST

Why Tuesday?

Britain's history of invasion is plain as day – in our names of the days of the week. Along with the sun's day and the moon's day, we have inherited Saturday from Dies Saturni or Saturn's day from the Romans' religion, and others from gods worshipped by the Viking warriors who invaded our shores in the ninth century.

Tuesday – Tiu's Day

Tiu is the brave and astute warrior god of law. He lost one of his hands battling the powerful wolf Fenrir.

Wednesday – Woden / Odin's Day

Odin is usually depicted with one eye as he exchanged the other for wisdom. He had a magic eight-legged horse. (Odin is Old Norse and Woden is his Old English name.)

Thursday – Thor's Day

A less-well-known fact about Thor is that he created all the flint on earth by smashing a rival's weapon with his sturdy forehead.

Friday – Frigg's Day

Frigg is Odin's wife and the goddess of marriage. She owns some useful falcon feathers that allow the gods to transform into falcons.

27 AUGUST

Three Rings

For thousands of years, rings have been worn both for decoration and as symbols of promises, in wedding rings, membership and signet rings. The plainest rings can be formed of a simple hoop but some have a bezel, or thicker section, with shoulders either side, and may include a precious stone or engraved design known as intaglio. Here are three fascinating multi-purpose rings from history.

ROMAN RING KEY

Archaeological finds show many Romans likely wore the keys to their safe boxes on their fingers, like this second-century CE Roman ring key.

CLADDAGH RING

This famous traditional Irish ring symbolises love (heart), loyalty (crown) and friendship (hands). According to legend, the design was invented in the 1600s by a fisherman from a village called Claddagh in Galway who was kidnapped by pirates and learned goldsmithery in Algiers before returning home and making the ring as a wedding band for his beloved.

TURKANA RAZOR RING

The Turkana people live in north-western Kenya and this traditional knife ring, from the twentieth century, was worn by men for both decorative and practical purposes, like fighting and butchering animals.

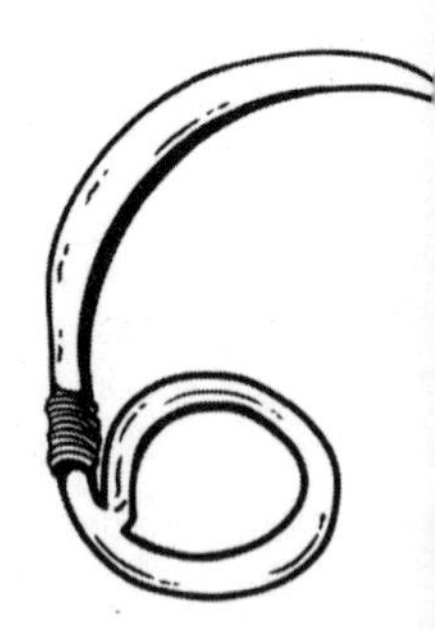

28 AUGUST

Very Good Boys

Most pet cats in the UK are moggies and you might expect our canine chums to be similar – but in fact the majority of dogs are pure-bred. To be 'pedigree', a dog must be a recognised pure breed, with parents registered with one of the international Kennel Clubs, and able to trace its doggy genealogy back three generations. The 223 official pure breeds are divided into seven types based on their original purposes – working, pastoral, gun dog, toy, hound, terrier and utility. Most of the group names indicate a clear purpose behind the breeds in their category but terriers are a bit more obscure – their name comes from 'terra' for 'earth' as they were originally bred to hunt vermin such as rats – and what the pup is a utility dog? The utility category is a bit of a catch-all for types of dogs bred for very specific purposes that don't fall into the other categories: for example, bulldogs were bred for bull-baiting, dalmatians for guarding carriages and clearing the way for fire engines, and schnauzers for catching rats and pulling small carts! Clever doggies.

29 AUGUST

Yesterday Island

How can it be that two islands are physically only 4 kilometres away from each other, but are separated by a time difference of twenty-one hours? Big Diomede and Little Diomede lie in the Bering Strait, 53 miles of water that separate Alaska from Russia and link the Arctic Ocean to the Pacific. Big Diomede is Russian and Little Diomede is Alaskan. Little Diomede is also known as Iŋaliq in the Alaskan Inuit language of its Iñupiat inhabitants, and Yesterday Island to Big Diomede's Tomorrow Island because of the date line, which lies between them.

The first inhabitants of Alaska are believed to have come to North America from Siberia and China when the two continents were still joined by land some 20,000 years ago, and various Alaskan native peoples are descended from them. Russians began to settle in Alaska after fur trappers from Siberia crossed the strait in 1732; they colonised the area until the Alaska Purchase of 1867 when the USA bought the territory from Russia, increasing the country's size by almost a fifth.

The water in the Bering Strait is only 55 metres deep and in the past it would sometimes freeze, allowing the possibility of walking between two countries, continents and dates. However, conditions are extremely treacherous and it is difficult to get permission to make the trip. The first-recorded person to swim between the Little and Big islands was American Lynne Cox in 1987, during the final years of the Cold War. The water temperature was 3.3° C. Because of the currents it took her over two hours, but she was met by friendly Russian officials on the beach with tea and biscuits.

30 AUGUST

Viking Tech

Bluetooth allows the short-range wireless exchange of information over nearby electronic devices. A team put together by the Swedish mobile phone company Ericsson developed the technology in the 1990s. It was released around the same time as WiFi, and for the same reason – to do away with troublesome wires between devices – but Bluetooth is a cheaper and lower-energy option for close communications such as headphones and keyboards.

Bluetooth was named after the Viking king Harald Blåtand (c. 910–87 CE), who, according to legend, was good at bringing people together – he unified and Christianised Denmark and Norway. His grandson was the famous King Canute of England, Denmark and Norway.

The English translation of Blåtand is 'Bluetooth', and the technology's symbol shows his initials in the old Nordic written language of runes – it is a combination of the runes Hagall (ᚼ) and Bjarkan (ᛒ). Harald apparently got his colourful name because of a dark-coloured dead tooth in his mouth, rather than because he loved blueberries, as some stories have claimed.

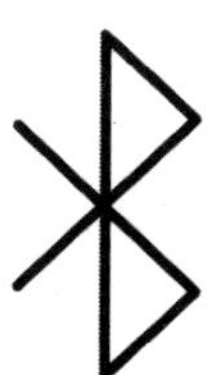

31 AUGUST

Sea Change

There is actually only one ocean, which covers 71% of the world, as all the seas and oceans of the world connect together, but we divide it into distinct named regions for historical, cultural and scientific reasons. Oceans tend to lie between continents and seas between smaller units of land. The International Hydrographic Organization's most recent official publication on the limits of oceans and seas comes from 1953 and says there are four oceans – Pacific, Atlantic, Indian and Arctic – but most geographical bodies today also recognise the Southern or Antarctic Ocean, round the South Pole.

THE WORLD'S SMALLEST SEA

The world's largest sea is the South China Sea, at 3.5 million kilometres squared, dwarfing the smallest, the jewel-like Sea of Marmara in Turkey, an inland sea measuring 11,350 kilometres squared. What differentiates an inland sea from a lake is not completely agreed upon, but it usually involves more salt and a connection to a sea or ocean. An important haven of biodiversity, the Sea of Marmara is entirely within Turkey but sits between continents: if you stand on one side you are in Europe and on the other you are in Asia.

September

1 SEPTEMBER

Two Kinds of Intelligence

Rumi was a thirteenth-century Persian poet, jurist, and Sufi mystic. Originally a scholar, Rumi underwent a profound spiritual transformation after encountering the mystic Shams Tabrizi. Their friendship lasted three years, after which Shams disappeared, possibly murdered by one of Rumi's jealous sons. Rumi's coping mechanism for the loss of his mind partner was poetry: verses full of love, longing and devotion. They speak, as all the best poems do, of what it means to be alive, which is one of the reasons Rumi remains a global icon, and why, almost eight hundred years after his death, he remains the bestselling poet in America. His poem 'Two Kinds of Intelligence' is a good one to keep in mind as the 'back to school' vibe of September: there is the intelligence you learn as a child through the acquisition of facts and knowledge, and this will take you far in life, but it is incomparable to the innate intelligence already inside you – 'A spring overflowing its springbox. A freshness in the centre of the chest.'

2 SEPTEMBER

Lessons in Equality

'Education is the passport to the future, for tomorrow belongs to those who prepare for it today.'

Malcolm X (1925–65), civil rights leader

3 SEPTEMBER

A Hiking Holiday to Remember

In 1991 German tourists Erika and Helmut Simon were enjoying a hiking holiday in the Ötztal Alps on the border between Austria and Italy when a shortcut revealed a horrifying discovery. When Erika and Helmut saw a bone sticking out of the ground they thought they'd found a recent victim of the mountains, but in fact they had discovered Europe's oldest mummy.

Ötzi the Iceman, as he came to be known, lived around five thousand years ago. Ötzi astonished historians because, once he was removed from the ice, he was found to be incredibly well preserved and also still in possession of his travelling kit of bearskin hat, dagger, copper axe, longbow, dried fruit, medicinal mushrooms and fire-making kit. The analysis that scientists were able to perform on Ötzi revealed that he was about forty-five years old, 1.6 metres tall, dark-haired with brown eyes and many tattoos. He was lactose-intolerant, had recently eaten some goat bacon and was probably killed by an arrow to the shoulder in early summer. His body is preserved today in a dark, refrigerated chamber in the South Tyrol Museum of Archaeology in Bolzano, Italy, and you can peek at this traveller from the past through a tiny window.

4 SEPTEMBER

A Loquacious Treasure Chest

Peter Mark Roget, born in London in 1779, was a physician, inventor, lexicographer and theologian. He came from a family of intellectuals and scientists and studied at the University of Edinburgh, where he later became a professor. He dreamed up the slide rule in 1815 to calculate the roots and powers of numbers, but he is most famous for the hobby he became obsessed with during his retirement: his thesaurus, which had rather more surprising psychological origins.

Mental health issues beset Roget's family: his father died when he was four and his mother never really recovered from the shock of it, being plagued by anxiety her entire life. His grandmother suffered some form of schizophrenia, and his sister and daughter struggled too. His uncle and beloved father-surrogate, the politician Samuel Romilly, killed himself after the death of his wife, with Roget beside him in his last moments. From childhood, Roget began compiling lists of words to create order and calm from the grief, sorrow and disorder all around him. After his retirement in in 1840 he dedicated himself wholly to his thesaurus (from the Greek word for 'treasure'), which organised words not alphabetically but based on their meanings, and it was finally published in 1852. Its original title was the rather wordy (ahem) *Thesaurus of English Words and Phrases Classified and Arranged so as to Facilitate the Expression of Ideas and Assist in Literary Composition.* It was an instant bestseller and has never been out of print.

5 SEPTEMBER

Hunting, Gathering, Potting and Planting

We think of our Stone Age ancestors as the ultimate hunter-gatherers, pursuing their protein as they hunted down a woolly mammoth or two. Researchers into Palaeolithic diet have found that the human brain started to dramatically increase in size 800,000 years ago, which is when we discovered the ability to make fire and cook food, particularly carbohydrate-rich foods like starchy vegetables. Scientists now believe this more energy-efficient sustenance is one of the factors that gave humans the winning edge in the evolutionary race.

Charred remains of what may be the oldest cooked meal from around 70,000 years ago were found in a cave in the Zagros Mountains in northern Iraq in 2022, suggesting Neanderthal man might just have been a foodie. Researchers unearthed evidence of a pounded cake of pulses, nuts and grass seeds bound with water. On recreating the feast, researchers from the British team leading the excavation reported it to be delicious.

6 SEPTEMBER

A Heart So Wild

Here are five of the strangest animal hearts to be found in the wild.

- The blue whale's heart is the size of a small car – one heart was recorded at nearly 700 kilograms. The walls of its aorta can be as thick as 15 centimetres (in humans it's 38 millimetres). On a dive, the blue whale's heartbeat slows to four beats per minute.
- Cephalopods, such as octopi, cuttlefish and squid, have three hearts: two are brachial and serve to oxygenate the blood, and one is systemic, which pumps it around the body. They are literally blue-blooded due to the abundance of copper in their bodies.
- Cockroaches have a thirteen-chambered tubular heart which beats at around the same rate as ours.
- Zebrafish have the extraordinary ability to regenerate their hearts, and scientists believe they might provide a good model for understanding more about human heart function.
- The tiny Etruscan pygmy shrew has the world's fastest-beating heart, with a rate of 1,200 beats per minute to power its respiration rate of 800 breaths per minute.

7 SEPTEMBER

The Extraordinary Geometry of a Lunar Eclipse

When the sun, earth and moon are in perfect alignment, a lunar eclipse will occur as the earth blocks sunlight from reaching the moon. The shadows cast by the earth – the umbra and penumbra – can dim the appearance of the moon and sometimes turn it a dramatic red. This is because the light has to pass through the earth's atmosphere, which scatters blue light and refracts or bends red light towards the moon.

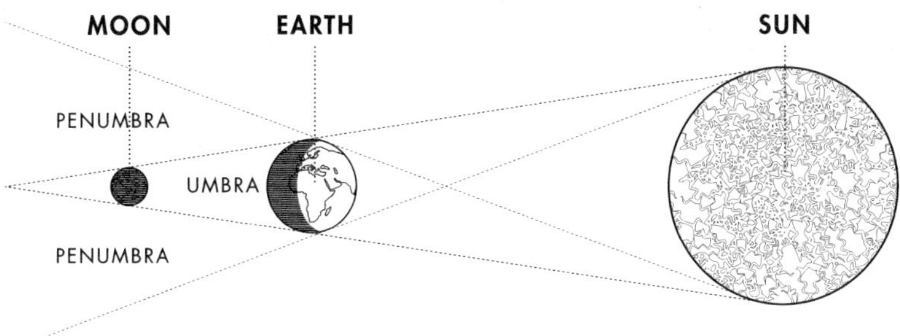

8 SEPTEMBER

Manhattan Nights

Cocktail origin stories are notoriously murky, and several myths attribute the creation of the Manhattan to Winston Churchill's mum, Lady Randolph Churchill, claiming it was invented for a party she threw for US presidential candidate Samuel J. Tilden at the iconic Manhattan Club in 1874. Whatever the truth, the cocktail is held as a classic and timeless tipple – a stylish blend of rye whisky, vermouth and bitters, always stirred, not shaken, and garnished with a booze-soaked or maraschino cherry.

THE CLASSIC MANHATTAN

75ml whisky (choose something un-peaty like bourbon)
30ml sweet vermouth
3 dashes Angostura bitters
maraschino cherry, or brandied cherry

Stir together the whisky, vermouth and bitters with ice for at least thirty seconds, then strain into a Martini glass and garnish with the cherry (or a twist of lemon peel if you prefer).

For a teetotal version, source the best no-alcohol whisky, vermouth and bitters, and assemble as above

9 SEPTEMBER

Pop Goes the Cafe Coronary

World First Aid Day – the second Saturday in September – seems the perfect time to highlight maverick doctor Henry Heimlich, the American inventor of one of the key tricks in the first aider's arsenal, the Heimlich manoeuvre. Henry was a surgeon who developed a new method for dislodging food trapped in someone's windpipe after noting that the common method of slapping people on the back was ineffectual. His 1974 article introducing his procedure had the fun title of 'Pop Goes the Cafe Coronary'. Bystanders often assumed that people dying of asphyxiation at the lunch table were having a heart attack, or what the medical professionals called a 'cafe coronary'. When Henry first wrote about his manoeuvre he noted 'it's been tested only on dogs' but since then it has been widely adopted by first aid trainers around the world.

10 SEPTEMBER

The *Analects*

Confucius (c. 551–c. 479 BCE) rose from humble beginnings to become one of China's greatest thinkers and philosophers, whose works still have huge influence on Eastern philosophy today. While Confucius's mother was pregnant, a unicorn appeared to her in a vision, prophesying that her son would become a powerful and wise leader. Despite this, Confucius had a tough start in life; his father died when he was very young and his mother raised him in poverty. But he studied hard and became the apprentice of a nobleman who liked his curious mind. He worked his way up through a series of menial positions within the family, eventually becoming minister for crime for his region.

Confucius advocated for a government that would reflect his beliefs in treating others with respect and kindness, in ethical living, respect for elders and familial responsibility, and in the benefit to everyone of a lifetime of learning. He was largely ignored in his own time but his three thousand followers collected together his principles in the *Analects*, and eventually they were adopted by the Han dynasty and became an integral part of Chinese state ideology for the next two and a half thousand years, until the Cultural Revolution. Chairman Mao considered Confucianism to be bourgeois and banned the *Analects*, though in recent years Confucius's ideals of harmony and community have been celebrated once more by the top Party brass.

11 SEPTEMBER

Accipiter *nisus*

'The hawk is aerial brother of the wave which he sails over and surveys, those his perfect air-inflated wings answering to the elemental unfledged pinions of the sea.'

Henry David Thoreau, *Walden*

September is prime hawk-watching time and you don't have to be in the wilds to spot this stunning bird of prey. Sparrowhawks have evolved to swoop nimbly through dense forests, which makes them ideally suited to our own urban jungles too. They are deadly predators, feeding on other songbirds (as well as rabbits and even hares), so if you spot one savaging a blue tit in your garden don't despair – it probably means your local bird population is juicily healthy.

The sparrowhawk's species name – *nisus* – comes from King Nisus of Megara in Greek mythology. Nisus was in possession of a lock of purple hair with magical protective properties: as long as he had that lock, no danger could befall him or his kingdom. Unfortunately his neighbouring rival, King Minos, seduced (or possibly bribed) Nisus's daughter Scylla to cut off the lock, so that he could take over his kingdom. Instead of dying, Nisus was transformed into a hawk and his treacherous daughter was transformed into a lark or heron condemned to be endlessly pursued by her father for her crimes.

12 SEPTEMBER

A Passion for Learning

philomath: one who loves learning and acquiring new knowledge.

'This is a book for philomaths.'

This term comes from the Greek word 'philos', meaning 'beloved' (as in 'philosophy' or 'philanthropy'), and 'manthanein', 'to learn' (as in 'polymath').

13 SEPTEMBER

You'll Never Walk Alone

Football is played by over 250 million people in 200 countries and the recent global success of the women's game means it is breaking out of its boys' club box.

Ever since balls there have been ball games, but modern football's official date of birth is usually given as 26 October 1863, when the Football Association was established in London to standardise the rules of the game. (The North American term 'soccer' comes from an abbreviation of 'Association' football.) Before this, in medieval times, 'folk football' had often involved pitches of indiscriminate lengths, sometimes a couple of miles, and lots of violent play leading to injuries and broken limbs.

A recent evolution of the beautiful game is walking football, which operates on the same basic principles as our beloved national sport but with one difference: there is no running involved. It's proven to promote physical as well as mental health; what you'll get from it is a keen sense of camaraderie, personal achievement and, most importantly, fun.

CHARLTON ATHLETICS

Tommy Charlton was twenty years old when his brothers Jack and Bobby lifted the Jules Rimet Trophy after winning the World Cup in 1966, bringing football home for the first (and only) time for England. In 2018, presumably vanquishing a lifetime of sibling under-achievement, Tommy nabbed his first England cap at the grand old age of seventy-two, and was part of the team that lifted the trophy in walking football's first international tournament after a 3–0 drubbing of Italy.

14 SEPTEMBER

The Mother of Modern Dance

'You were once wild here. Don't let them tame you.'

Game-changing dancing icon Isadora Duncan was born in 1877 in San Francisco and moved to Europe in her twenties. She had studied ballet as a child but found it too stifling and conventional. Encouraged by a forward-thinking mother, she divined that Europe was where she could develop her own form of art. She was inspired by studies of ancient Greek statues at the British Museum, and with her free-form movements and flowing dresses she became a symbol of anti-establishment change.

Isadora was as unconventional in her private life as she was on stage: a feminist, communist and advocate of free love. Tragically, her life was blighted by automotive accidents; in 1913 her two young children were killed when the car they were travelling in with their nanny rolled into the Seine in Paris, and on 14 September 1927 Isadora was killed instantly when the enormous red silk scarf she was wearing whilst trying out a new open-top Amilcar tangled in the rear wheel and axle. Her legacy lay in her celebration of the natural form and a wilful sense of self-expression that railed against the stuffy confines of her time, bringing true joy into movement.

15 SEPTEMBER

Know Thyself

Have you ever thought about how you think? In his 2011 book *Thinking, Fast and Slow*, psychologist and Nobel Prize-winner Daniel Kahneman distils years of experience into a brilliantly simple theory: that we have two thought systems.

System 1 is fast and instinctive, like when we're riding a bike, or explaining our jobs to our kids. System 2 is where slower, more effortful work takes place, like figuring out a complex maths problem, or writing about titans of psychology. Kahneman identifies that our brains are essentially lazy, and that when we are tired or stressed out our System 1 kicks in to take over, devises shortcuts and generally makes quicker decisions. System 1 does 98% of our thinking while System 2 does 2%, but we can train ourselves to prep for deeper, System 2 thinking.

- Carve out optimal times – if you notice you are better at focused thinking in the morning, make sure you schedule time for yourself at the start of the day. Most people find they are better at System 1 thinking after lunch, so schedule admin tasks for then.
- Organise your emails into Fast and Slow categories depending on the kind of thought you need to apply to deal with them.
- Be aware of your own optimal personal circumstances for slow thinking: are you better at home, in the office, in a group environment or alone?

16 SEPTEMBER

Poiseidon's Percebes

Galician goose barnacles – or *percebes* – are a rare and dangerous-to-source culinary delicacy, said to be the closest one can get to eating the sea. Limited understanding of birds' migratory habits in medieval times meant that naturalists had never seen the nests or eggs of what became known as barnacle geese, and they mistook barnacles for the eggs from which goslings would hatch. Because of this unusual marine origin, it was permitted to eat barnacle geese as if they were shellfish on fasting days when other meat was banned.

Percebes are extremely strange-looking things: about the size of your thumb, with a long rubbery neck and triangular shell-coated head. They are prized and expensive (around £80–90 per kilo) because they thrive in the most rugged coastline of the Atlantic Ocean, around Portugal and Spain's Galicia, and the *percebeiros* – the men and women who hunt them – risk life and limb to harvest the delicacy, which is served lightly boiled or steamed, with a sprinkle of sea salt and a squeeze of lemon.

17 SEPTEMBER

The Monkey-Hangers of Hartlepool

Residents of the fine Northern town of Hartlepool are to this day known as 'monkey-hangers' because of a strange legend that proclaims they once put a monkey on trial and then executed it, believing it to be a spy.

The story goes that, during the Napoleonic Wars early in the nineteenth century, a French ship was wrecked off the coast of Hartlepool, the sole survivor of which was the crew's mascot, a little monkey dressed in a tiny soldier's uniform. Hartlepudlians had never seen a monkey before, but neither had they seen a Frenchman, and they took its chatterings for French and hanged him on the beach. A rather darker supposition is that they might have actually hanged a small boy – those who shifted the gunpowder about on boats were called 'powder monkeys'. You'll still see the monkey as Hartlepool FC's mascot, and two of the town's six rugby clubs use a variation of a monkey in their branding, and there is a statue on the marina and another on the headland.

18 SEPTEMBER

Why Does It Matter?

First theorised by scientist Paul Dirac in 1928, antimatter is a mirror-image of regular matter, consisting of particles with opposite charges to their counterparts in the everyday world. For example, an antiparticle of an electron (a negatively charged particle) is called a positron (a positively charged particle). When matter and antimatter come into contact, they annihilate each other, converting their mass into energy.

What's amazing about antimatter is that it could potentially unravel fundamental mysteries about the universe which have been scrambling heads for years. Scientists believe that, in the early moments after the Big Bang, matter and antimatter were created in equal amounts. However, today, our observable universe is mostly composed of matter. Tiny amounts of antimatter rain down on the earth in the form of cosmic rays, and scientists have also observed antimatter production above thunderstorms. The question of why antimatter is so scarce is one of the biggest puzzles in physics. Where has all the antimatter gone? This is what boffins at research facilities like CERN are trying to figure out by creating and studying antimatter and exploring whether its huge power can be harnessed – to revolutionise space travel, for example. It's theorised that spacecraft powered by antimatter propulsion systems could travel further and faster than ever imagined possible, making interstellar travel a real possibility. So yes, it matters.

19 SEPTEMBER

The Starry Messenger

Philosopher, mathematician and astronomer Galileo Galilei was born in 1564 in Italy. He studied medicine at the University of Pisa but in a strike for all under-achievers he left without his degree, fired by a passion for stargazing. He had heard tell of a Dutch invention called the telescope and began to develop his own, also teaching himself the art of lens-grinding. His 1610 book *Sidereus Nuncius* (Latin for *The Starry Message*) was based on observations made through his telescope, and was where he shared his first moon drawings, which showed the surface of the moon as textured and mountainous, rather than flat and pure.

Galileo also famously built on Copernicus's idea of our planetary system as heliocentric – i.e. that the earth moves around the sun – a deeply heretical view at a time when the all-powerful Church espoused the idea of a God-created earth around which all other celestial bodies rotated. He caught the attention of the Roman Catholic Inquisition and was found guilty of being 'vehemently suspect of heresy'. After agreeing to renounce his teachings, he was condemned to house arrest for the remainder of his life. He was also forced to recite seven penitential psalms once a week for three years, and his works were added to the Inquisition's list of banned books, the *Index Librorum Prohibitorum*. The Vatican only formally apologised for its actions against Galileo in 1992, a mere 359 years later. Today, if you really wanted to, you could go and see Galileo's actual middle finger, which is preserved in Florence's History of Science Museum.

20 SEPTEMBER

Memory Training

The 4-Detail Exercise is a passive memory training exercise which is designed to encourage our brain's recall function. It's called passive because we're not using any special mnemonics memory tricks here; we're just asking our brains to engage in *remembering* stuff.

Next time you are out and about, try to observe four details about someone you see. (It's your responsibility to do this in a non-creepy way.) Does that guy at the beach have blond hair, a tattoo in the shape of a Celtic cross, blue swimmers and orange flip-flops? Note this down in your head. Then, an hour later, recall these details. What's fun is that this is scalable: once you've mastered the art of one person a day, you can increase the number of people, or extend it to beautiful buildings around you, or trees you are especially fond of.

21 SEPTEMBER

Pretty Pigments

Nowadays any number of online tools can help build you the most refined colourways, but for thousands of years our ancestors made use of what they could find around them to liven up their surroundings. Astonishingly, there is evidence that even in the Stone Age budding artists came up with an oil-based paint by mixing vegetable oil with ground-up rock. But it was the ancient Egyptians who kicked colour up a gear, using sophisticated chemistry to create pigments. The oldest synthetic pigment is the Egyptian blue frit, which was made of a kiln-fired blend of different minerals. Here are some of the most famous historical pigments:

Cochineal: A red pigment made from the dried and ground bodies of the insect *Dactylopius coccus*, which was introduced to Europe from Mexico. It could only be harvested during a two-week window and was highly prized in fifteenth-century Florence.

Crimson: Made from an insect called *Kermes vermilio*, this was used by early Egyptians as a red dye and later throughout ancient Greece and Rome and in Renaissance Europe.

Tyrian purple: A highly valued pigment made from the secretions of a sea snail. Associated with high rank, in imperial Rome only the emperor was allowed to wear it.

Indigo: Obtained from an extract of the *Indigofera* plant, this was used in a dye called woad, which the Celts painted on their visages ahead of going into battle.

22 SEPTEMBER

The Father of Electricity

'Nothing is too wonderful to be true, if it be consistent with the laws of nature; and in such things as these, experiment is the best test of such consistency.'

Michael Faraday (1791–1867)

In 1831 British scientist Michael Faraday became the first person to create an electric current from a magnetic field, a process called electromagnetic induction, which is used today in power generators all over the world. But did you know that Faraday's own educational inspiration was a pioneering female science writer?

Jane Marcet was determined to open up the closed-off worlds of science and economics to those with little formal education, like women and the poor, and she did this with her wildly popular *Conversations on Chemistry*, published anonymously in 1805, in which she imagined a fictionalised conversation between a tutor and her two female students. Faraday was the son of a poor blacksmith and had received few educational opportunities but at the age of fourteen he was apprenticed to a bookbinder's studio, where he came across Marcet's extraordinary book, sparking his passion for science. He was given a ticket to see the scientist Sir Humphry Davy lecture at the Royal Institution, and took copious notes, then added some illustrations and bound them in smart leather to send to Davy. When one of Davy's lab assistants was fired for brawling, Davy remembered young Faraday's notes, and hired him, and the rest is science lore.

23 SEPTEMBER

Signing Up

Sign language is one of humanity's most ancient forms of communication. The first record of sign language being used comes from a description of very touching wedding ceremony at St Martin's Church in Leicester in 1576.

> Thomas Tillsye and Ursula Russel were marryed: and because the sayde Thomas was and is naturally deafe and also dumbe, so that the order of the forme of marriage used usually amongst others which can heare and speake could not for his parte be observed . . . the sayde Thomas, for the expression of his minde instead of words, of his own accorde used these signs . . .
>
> First he embraced her with his armes, and took her by the hande, putt a ring upon her finger and layde his hande upon her harte, and held his hands towards heaven; and to show his continuance to dwell with her to his lyves ende he did it by closing of his eyes with his hands and digging out of the earthe with his foote, and pulling as though he would ring a bell with divers other signs approved.

For many years, hearing-impaired people were encouraged not to use sign language for fear that it would slow down the acquisition of speech, and it was only recognised as a formal language by the British government in 2003.

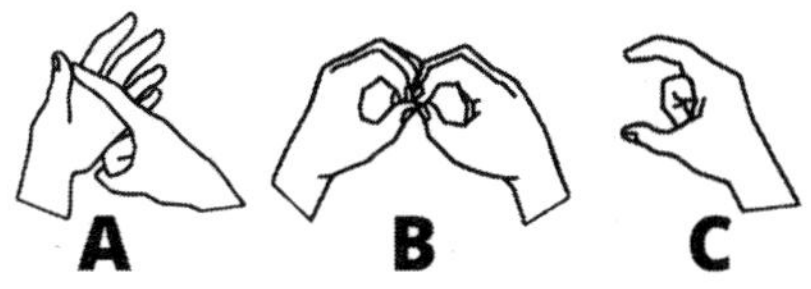

24 SEPTEMBER

Heavens Blazing

'When beggars die, there are no comets seen:
The heavens themselves blaze forth the death of princes.'

William Shakespeare, *Julius Caesar*

Halley's Comet is a periodic comet – that is, one that returns to the earth's 'hood on a regular basis, in this case every seventy-five years or so. Scientists believe it's been travelling around our solar system for 200,000 years. It was first noted by Chinese astronomers in 239 BCE, and is believed to be mentioned in Babylonian texts now held in the British Museum. It also blazes its course across the Bayeux Tapestry, having appeared just before William the Conqueror's 1066 invasion of England, and it's possibly even Halley's Comet that lights up the Bethlehem sky in Giotto's fourteenth-century painting, the *Adoration of the Magi*.

Edmond Halley was the British physicist and astronomer who, using his buddy Isaac Newton's laws of motion, correctly identified the comet as periodic in 1705 and calculated that it would return in 1758. He realised that three comets observed in 1531, 1607 and 1682 were actually the same object. 'If it should return, according to our predictions,' he vowed, 'impartial posterity will not refuse to acknowledge that this was first discovered by an Englishman.' It came back on Christmas night of 1758, and whilst Halley was long dead, he achieved that long-desired posterity as the celestial body was named in his honour. It was last seen in 1986 and is predicted to return in 2061.

25 SEPTEMBER

Working 9 to 5

In a revolutionary memo to staff on 25 September 1926, car maker and industrialist Henry Ford instituted a five-day work-week (reduced from the standard six). His motives weren't entirely altruistic; rather, the canny capitalist hypothesised that by increasing leisure time for his workers he would also increase consumption more generally as people invested in having fun at rest. In essence, he was future-proofing his customer base, and in doing so he transformed the world of work.

Not all of Henry Ford's schemes were quite so successful; in the late 1920s he attempted to build an all-American town in the heart of Brazil's Amazon rainforest. Fordlândia, as it was rather hubristically called, was intended to provide rubber trees and manufacturing for his tyres. However, the ideal city – featuring an eighteen-hole golf course, theatre and dance hall – failed as the jungle proved impossible to tame and unrest grew over the fact that there were separate areas for American and Brazilian employees. The company's alcohol ban was difficult to enforce and the rubber yield was hopeless. As soon as the company was in the control of Ford's grandson in the 1940s he sold the land back to the Brazilian government at a loss.

26 SEPTEMBER

Saving the Lingo

Here is a strange tale for European Day of Languages. Let's start with some context: linguists believe that, of the approximately 6,900 languages spoken across the world today, over half are at risk of dying out by the end of the twenty-first century. You might wonder why this matters. Globalisation is pushing us all towards several large common languages – isn't that beneficial and connective for humanity? But language preservationists would argue that a diverse set of languages provides us with a cornucopia of cultural richness.

In 2014, the Mexican government was battling to keep one language, Ayapaneco, alive, but the interference of a communications giant nearly derailed the whole project. A phone company that shall remain nameless launched an ad campaign around the story of the last two native speakers, elderly gentlemen Manuel and Isidro, who had fallen out and refused to talk to each other. This irresistible story spread around the world, but as Daniel Suslak – a preservationist who had been working with both men for years to create an Ayapaneco dictionary – pointed out, it wasn't actually true, and in fact it fundamentally undermined the real work that had been taking place. Some began to believe that Manuel and Isidro had even conjured up Ayapaneco simply to get a fee from the comms giant. Today, around fifteen people speak the language, which they call Nuumte Oote, or True Voice.

27 SEPTEMBER

Watch Your Mouth

rodomontade: a bragging speech or rant.

'The Prime Minister's self-serving rodomontade proved to be the final act of a shameful political career.'

'Rodomontade' is a glorious word, which has its roots in Italian poetry. Rodomonte was the name of a vainglorious, ranting king who appeared in Count Matteo Maria Boiardo's epic poem *Orlando Innamorato.*

28 SEPTEMBER

The Long Walk

The penalty shoot-out is football's most intense moment – for spectators as well as players. For the uninitiated, shoot-outs are used to decide tournament matches that remain tied after extra time. It's best of five, with each team taking turns to shoot from the penalty spot. Eventually a shot gets saved, or a player misses, and one team wins the match. This can take a while – the 2005 final of the Namibian Cup had to be settled by a record-breaking forty-eight penalty kicks, with KK Palace defeating the Civics 17–16 following a 2–2 draw in normal time. The shoot-out lasted almost as long as the game itself had. There's nothing quite like the stress of this do-or-die moment, and for this reason some psychologists have used it to better understand how we all respond to pressure.

A number of factors emerged from the psychologists' studies: the young tend to miss less often; fatigue counts – players who have been on the field for the whole match are more likely to miss the kick; and those who take a kick quickly are more likely to miss too. One stat that highlights the extent to which pressure is a factor is that, if a player steps up to take a penalty that will win the shoot-out, and so the match, the success rate rises dramatically to 92%, whereas if they have to save their team from losing, the likelihood of scoring drops to under 60%. In football, as in life, it's how you channel that pressure that determines success. So here are some tips from the field: take your time, don't make decisions when you're knackered, and take a moment to recognise pressure and embrace it too.

29 SEPTEMBER

Blackberrying

Blackberries form part of nature's free larder and in September they can be found as abundantly in the boundaries of inner-city parks as they can in the hedgerows of the deepest countryside. They are delicious in jams, infused in gin or vodka, and, of course, baked into pies.

But did you know that folklore dictates that you shouldn't eat blackberries after 29 September – or Michaelmas in the Christian calendar? This is the day that Lucifer was banished from heaven by St Michael: the story goes that he fell out of the skies and landed on a huge bramble patch, which he then rather tetchily cursed.

In Dorset, blackberry season was historically considered to be the time when babies and horses were most likely to feel unwell, whilst on the Isle of Man tradition dictates you leave the first fruits for the faeries. (This is in fact good etiquette to follow: don't pick a bush clean – leave enough for the foxes and badgers too.) Blackberry tea has long been known as a great cure for stomach aches and it's said that during the American Civil War several ceasefires were put in place so that the Unionists and Confederates could gather blackberries to cure outbreaks of dysentery. Blackberries for peace!

30 SEPTEMBER

Truth and Reconciliation

Canada's National Day for Truth and Reconciliation was established in 2021 after a government report was commissioned into the legacy of the country's residential schools policy. These schools were established in 1876 after the passage of the Indian Act, which made attendance compulsory for Indigenous children. Its aim was to eliminate Indigenous language and culture and the schools cast a terrible shadow, stripping children of their heritage, forcing them into labour and exposing them to disease and punishments. The last school closed in 1996.

Today, Canada honours the children with a holiday in which the population is encouraged to wear orange – remembering a real orange shirt given to one survivor by her grandmother and then removed by school authorities – and spend time educating themselves about the glories of Indigenous culture, and marking what those children lost.

October

1 OCTOBER

Time Does Not Bring Relief

Time does not bring relief; you all have lied
Who told me time would ease me of my pain!
I miss him in the weeping of the rain;
I want him at the shrinking of the tide;
The old snows melt from every mountain-side,
And last year's leaves are smoke in every lane;
But last year's bitter loving must remain
Heaped on my heart, and my old thoughts abide.
There are a hundred places where I fear
To go,—so with his memory they brim.
And entering with relief some quiet place
Where never fell his foot or shone his face
I say, 'There is no memory of him here!'
And so stand stricken, so remembering him.

Edna St Vincent Millay (1892–1950)

Forward-thinking, outspoken, famous for expressing modern sentiments in traditional poetic forms, Edna St Vincent Millay was a Pulitzer Prize-winning American poet, playwright, journalist and librettist, celebrated for both her romanticism and her wit, who hit the peak of her powers in the 1920s. Brought up by a single mother, Edna first started publishing her poetry when she was just fourteen. This impassioned sonnet vividly conjures a woman in the midst of heartbreak raging against the impossibility of escaping loss.

2 OCTOBER

Troublesome Trolleys

Though it's hard to admit, sometimes we encounter problems with no good solution. In moral philosophy the doctrine of double effect refers to situations where, if an action has two outcomes (the double effect), it is the outcome that is intended that defines whether the action is ethical or not. For example, if someone with a terminal illness is given drugs to manage their pain, even though doctors know these drugs will shorten their life, this action is ethical because the doctors' intention is to help. Critics argue that if an effect can be foreseen, moral responsibility must be taken, and others argue that some actions are just objectively bad.

The British philosopher Philippa Foot investigated this in a famous 1967 thought experiment known as the Trolley Problem, in which she imagines the driver of a runaway tram, or trolley, having to choose between two tracks, one which will involve killing five men and one which will kill just one.

Most people choose to kill the single man, to save more lives. But Foot interrogates this with a similar question in which a magistrate is faced with rioters threatening to kill five hostages if a culprit isn't found for a crime. The judge can prevent bloodshed by finding a scapegoat. Most people struggle to feel it's right to actively seek to kill an innocent person, despite this saving the hostages.

The trolley problem comes up in discussions around self-driving cars and whether they should be programmed to avoid the greatest number of deaths in collision scenarios. Would you buy a car that would sacrifice your family to save others?

3 OCTOBER

The Science of Toast

Who would have thought there was so much science involved in prepping your morning slice of toast? Whether you prefer it with Marmite, avocado or just plain butter, it's amazing how much more delicious bread is when lightly burned. When you lower your bread into your toaster in the spring-loaded tray, the lever completes the circuit of an electromagnetic tab connected to the timer dial. The magnet holds the toast cage close to the heating element. This is made of wiggly nichrome wire: 80% nickel and 20% chromium. When electricity is run through this combination of metals, it turns into heat because nichrome resists the current, getting to about 150° C. This temperature is where the magical Maillard reaction occurs in food, whereby sugars and proteins brown and deepen in flavour.

TOAST SLANDER

If you smell burned toast, it doesn't actually mean you're having a stroke – this is a myth. Some people may have olfactory hallucinations with a stroke but much more common effects are weakness on one side, drooping face, difficulties with speech, dizziness and vision changes. Obviously, these symptoms need urgent attention.

4 OCTOBER

Animagic

Our rich and diverse ecosystem is full of wonders. Here are a few characteristics of our favourite and most impressive fellow earth-dwellers.

- Butterflies taste with their feet.
- Reindeers' eyes turn from orange to blue in winter to help them see in darker conditions.
- Mantis shrimps have such a powerful punch that they can break out of glass tanks.
- When the immortal jellyfish gets old it can transform its cells to a previous stage of its life cycle, a polyp, and start again.
- Tardigrades – tiny micro-animals also known as water bears – can live without food for over twenty years, and are found from deep seas to sand dunes, surviving in conditions from –272° C to 149° C.
- Goats have accents specific to their social group.
- Swifts can fly for ten months without landing.
- Cockroaches can live for several weeks without their heads.
- A garden snail has 14,000 teeth.
- Greenland sharks can live for four hundred years.

5 OCTOBER

If Shakespeare's Sister Had a Room of Her Own

Looking at history books can give you the impression that men have made all the significant moves in art, culture, politics and science. Virginia Woolf's feminist lecture *A Room of One's Own* (1929) explores this, in relation to her own field – the lack of women's contribution to literature. Virginia's famous argument is: 'A woman must have money and a room of her own if she is to write fiction.'

This has come to represent the idea that to perform great deeds people require social opportunity. Virginia grew up at a time when women weren't generally given formal education and were expected to focus on being wives and mothers. In her talk, she invents an imaginary sister for William Shakespeare called Judith. She plots both siblings' paths through life, with William having the opportunity for education and travel, helping him fulfil his potential, and Judith being stifled at every turn.

Woolf's talk has been influential in discussions about the prejudices that have curtailed the chances of marginalised groups through history; Woolf herself was a privileged white woman who had advantages well beyond the means of most in her day. The American novelist Alice Walker highlighted the more significant barriers faced by artists of colour when she wrote: 'Virginia Woolf . . . wrote that for a woman to write fiction she must have two things, certainly: a room of her own (with key and lock) and enough money to support herself. What then are we to make of Phillis Wheatley, a slave, who owned not even herself?'

6 OCTOBER

Are You Kitten Me?

When international travel first became possible, explorers often wanted to bring back examples of the different animals and birds they encountered on their trips. One way to preserve these was through taxidermy, which involved stuffing and mounting animal skins to recreate their living appearance. During his five years aboard HMS *Beagle*, Charles Darwin was able to mount many of his specimens thanks to his training by a formerly enslaved man called John Edmonstone who worked for the University of Edinburgh's Zoological Museum.

Taxidermied birds became particularly popular decorative elements in the Victorian era and the style was advanced, sometimes in eccentric directions, by innovators such as John Hancock and Walter Potter. John Hancock's 'Struggle with the Quarry' caused a sensation when it was unveiled at the Great Exhibition in 1851. Depicting an extremely dramatic scene of a falcon attacking a heron which is attacking an eel, it ushered in a fashion for displaying mounts in lifelike or active scenarios. Walter Potter became famous for his anthropomorphic scenes of stuffed animals, such as a glamorous kitten wedding with fancy dresses and necklaces, a rats' domino game being raided by police, rabbits at school and squirrels smoking cigars in a gentlemen's club.

7 OCTOBER

Same Old, Same Old

Familiar elements turn up in stories repeatedly. In the romance you're reading, do the protagonists start out hating each other but find that the fire between them turns into attraction? Do they end up spending the night together but the only hotel room available has just one bed? Does the hero have a troubled past? Or in that action movie you slump in front of on a Saturday night, is the hero paired with someone with a conflicting personality style? Do they enjoy sparky banter while dodging explosions? In your fantasy game, is your protagonist prepared to do bad things but also strikingly attractive? Does the plot revolve around the search for an object that will confer power? If so, you've encountered these tropes: 'Enemies to Lovers', 'Just One Bed', 'Tragic Hero', 'Odd Couple', 'Casual Danger Dialogue', 'Morally Grey Protagonist' and 'Quest for the MacGuffin'.

Tropes can skirt close to cliché, but can also deliver a huge punch. They have been used in art for ever: Arthurian romances revelled in the 'Damsel in Distress' trope; Shakespeare loved a bit of 'Mistaken Identity'; Jane Austen is famous for her 'Enemies to Lovers' work; and Tolkien is of course a master of the 'Quest for the MacGuffin'.

WHAT IS A MACGUFFIN?

A MacGuffin is something that provides the catalyst for a story's action. Usually it can be exchanged for something else without disrupting the plot, so long as the characters want or need it in some way. The statue of the Maltese Falcon in John Huston's film of the same name is considered a classic MacGuffin.

8 OCTOBER

The Old-Fashioned Way

The old-fashioned is thought to have developed from seventeenth-century pharmacist Richard Stoughton's health-giving cordial, Elixir Magnum Stomachicum. The drink got its name when fancy new cocktail ingredients were added to barkeepers' repertoires, and some drinkers wanted to make sure they were still getting the more traditional brew.

THE OLD-FASHIONED

60ml bourbon
1 dash Angostura bitters
2 tsp sugar syrup (or 1 tsp brown sugar dissolved in the whisky if you don't have syrup)
1 slice of orange
1 maraschino cherry

Add four ice cubes to your glass, pour over the bourbon, sugar syrup and bitters, and stir until the ice melts a little. Drop in the orange and cherry and enjoy.
For a non-alcoholic version, substitute 60ml of strongly brewed and cooled black tea for the bourbon.

SWEET BITTERS

What's so special about Angostura bitters? This mixture of orange peel, gentian root, cloves, cardamom and other herbs and spices was first invented as a stomach tonic for soldiers fighting with the nineteenth-century South American revolutionary Simón Bolívar against Spanish colonial rule. One legend has it that only five people in the world know the secret recipe at any one time.

9 OCTOBER

One for Sorrow: The Myths of Magpies

Over the centuries, magpies have had lots of different superstitious meanings attached to them. In England they have long been associated with bad luck, apparently because of a legend saying that, of all the creatures on the earth, only magpies failed to mourn the crucifixion of Jesus and/or that they have a drop of the devil's blood under their tongues. Conversely, in China they are considered lucky birds.

Single magpies are seen to be particularly unlucky, hence 'One for sorrow' in the rhyme, probably because magpies mate for life and like to hang out in groups – but this bad luck can be warded off by saluting them and saying 'Good morning, Lord Magpie, and how is your wife, Lady Magpie?' They are also famous for thieving shiny objects to take back to their nests, although there is actually no evidence they habitually do this. In modern times they have been blamed for eating songbird eggs, but research has shown that this has no meaningful effect on the songbird population – whereas pet cats kill around 70 million birds a year in the UK.

10 OCTOBER

Build Your Own Memory Palace

The ancient Greek poet Simonides of Ceos (c. 556–468 BCE) was a great defender of writers' right to be paid for their work. The most famous story about this has him at a banquet for Scopas of Thessaly. Scopas refused to pay Simonides the agreed amount for composing a poem for the feast, and joked that he should collect the rest from Castor and Polydeuces, the gods he'd praised in his poem. After this, two young men asked Simonides to step outside, and once he had, the roof of the hall collapsed, killing everyone else – it turned out the two men were Castor and Polydeuces.

When the dead guests' families came to find their bodies, they couldn't tell who was who, but Simonides used his bespoke memory method, which came to be known as 'loci et res' ('place and thing', known as the 'method of loci' today), to identify everyone. He did this by visualising the layout of the banqueting hall and picturing each person in their place.

Nowadays the method of loci is used by memory experts and everyday folk to recall complicated lists of information, because our spatial memory is very powerful. One way to use it is to imagine your home and visualise placing whatever you are trying to remember in different rooms. The odder you can make the mental image, the more memorable it will be, e.g. bananas on your coat rack as you come through the door, pasta hanging from the cupboard handles in the kitchen, a tower of loo roll in the sink, etc. Then, when you want to recall your shopping list, you walk through the house in your mind to find each item.

11 OCTOBER

Return of the Mack

By this time in the year you have probably already reached for your winter coat, but did you know that modern overcoats have only been fashionable since the 1700s, before which cloaks were preferred? The word 'coat' comes from medieval times, when it could mean a coat, robe or tunic (which is why we have waistcoats and petticoats).

Charles Macintosh was a Scottish chemist who, in 1823, invented a method for waterproofing fabric by softening rubber so it could be laid between layers of material. He started producing outerwear for the army, but his coats smelled bad and occasionally melted in hot weather. Things improved when he teamed up with English inventor Thomas Hancock, who worked out how to vulcanise rubber, essentially curing it to make it more durable and stable. (The process was called 'vulcanisation' because it involved treating the rubber with heat and sulphur, reminiscent of volcanoes.) The word '**mackintosh**' with mysteriously added 'K' – or 'mack' – became synonymous with any waterproof coat and the Mackintosh company still produces them today.

The **Chesterfield** has a velvet collar and was named after 1840s fashion influencer George Stanhope, 6th Earl of Chesterfield.

The **trench coat** developed from the mackintosh, with companies like Aquascutum and Burberry improving the fabric. These expensive coats were worn by officers in the First World War, which is where they got their name.

The **Ulster** coat is usually made of Donegal tweed and was invented by Belfast designer John McGee in the mid-nineteenth century. It sometimes had a short cape attached to the back and is mentioned as being Sherlock Holmes's coat in Arthur Conan Doyle's stories.

The **duffel** coat has toggles and a hood and was designed by John Partridge in the late nineteenth century, inspired by Polish coats. It was named after the Belgian town of Duffel, which produced a rough fabric. It is sometimes known as 'a Monty' as Field Marshal Montgomery was so fond of them.

12 OCTOBER

#

Hashtags are ubiquitous – it's impossible to traverse social media without someone reminding you how much they are #blessed, #humblebragging or #winning, but did you know that the alternative, not very catchy, name for this little symbol is the octothorp?

Originally this symbol was called the 'pound sign' because it represented the weight abbreviation 'lb' (Latin for 'libra pondo': 'libra' meaning 'weight', as in the star sign Libra, which is a set of scales, and 'pondo' meaning 'pound'). 'Lb' used to be written with a ligature across the top to show the two letters were joined, which eventually developed into the symbol we have called the hashtag (from 'cross-hatch') since the 2000s.

The alternative name, octothorp, first appeared in the 1960s when the symbol started to appear on telephone keypads. The 'octo' refers to the eight points on the symbol and some stories say the 'thorp' part was created for fun by telephone company workers, or that it's because the image looks like a village surrounded by fields – 'thorp' is an Old English word for 'village'.

13 OCTOBER

Back from the Brink

A significant decrease in biodiversity on earth is known as a mass extinction event. There have been five big ones we know about so far: the Permian (265.1 million to c. 251.9 million years ago), where 90% of all species are believed to have gone extinct; the Ordovician–Silurian (c. 443.8 million years ago); the Cretaceous–Paleogene (c. 66 million years ago), which killed most of the dinosaurs and about 80% of all other animal species; the End-Triassic (c. 201.3 million years ago); and the Devonian (407.6 million to c. 358.9 million years ago). It's widely believed that we are currently in the midst of the sixth mass extinction event, the Holocene (named after the Greek for 'wholly new'), as human activity has caused the extinction rate to rise to between 100 and 10,000 times the normal level.

Although we may have said goodbye to the mountain mist frog, the Falkland Islands wolf, the Japanese sea lion, the Chinese paddlefish and the desert bandicoot, we have saved the following from extinction through careful conservation efforts.

- Peregrine falcon populations have rebounded after certain pesticides were banned.
- Sea otters were saved by a ban on hunting them for fur.
- The island night lizard was saved by the removal of invasive species in its habitats.
- Przewalski's horses were saved through reintroduction programmes in Mongolia.
- California condors were saved by captive breeding plans.
- Amur tiger numbers have risen to around 600 (after dropping to around 30) thanks to hunting bans. (There are only around 5,500 tigers of any kind still living in the wild across the world.)

14 OCTOBER

Burn Baby Burn

Making fire is a skill humans have enjoyed for over a million years and is so significant in our development that without it our diet, society, technology and very survival would have been very different. But what exactly is fire? Fire is not an object; it is a process. When fuels like wood are heated to their ignition point, the oxygen in the air reacts with the energy stored within them, causing them to combust and start an exothermic (heat-productive) chemical reaction – the heat given out by the reaction sustains the fire as it keeps igniting the fuel. Earth is the only known planet with enough oxygen in its atmosphere to allow fire.

Some people have likened a bonfire to a reverse tree – the energy the tree created from sunlight during photosynthesis as it grew is now creating light as it is destroyed!

15 OCTOBER

Here Be Dragons

In the beautifully illustrated but often wildly inaccurate maps produced during medieval times, you will see illustrations of sea monsters in the ocean or in unknown reaches of the world. Famously, the 1510 Hunt–Lenox Globe has an inscription of 'Hic sunt dracones' – or 'Here be dragons' – near Asia. Contrary to popular belief this phrase does not appear on many other maps but it has become well known to indicate 'terra incognita' and its potential threats. But did people ever really believe in dragons?

The word 'dragon' comes from the ancient Greek word for a large snake, and the idea of dragons is thought to have developed from the thoroughly international suspicion of snakes. In multiple world mythologies snakes are considered integral to creation stories, from their negative role in Adam and Eve's story to the serpents of Chinese cosmology to Apopis the chaos demon of ancient Egypt, the evil Jörmungandr of Norse mythology, the Aztec vegetation god Quetzalcōātl and the great Rainbow Serpent of many Australian Aboriginal myths. Anthropologists have theorised that the ubiquity of snakes is down to them having been a common threat to the earliest peoples, as well as the mystery of their habit of shedding their skin. The ouroboros symbol of a snake or dragon eating its tail, first recorded in ancient Egypt and Greece, is seen to represent the cycle of birth, death and rebirth exemplified by the snake.

Belief in dragons is thought to have arisen from these early myths about snakes combining with encounters with crocodiles and the discovery of dinosaur fossils. It's amazing to think that, before 1824 and the work of Victorian geologists, no one knew dinosaurs had ever existed.

16 OCTOBER

Perhaps Home Is Not a Place

'Perhaps home is not a place but simply
an irrevocable condition.'

James Baldwin (1924–87), writer and civil rights activist, from his 1956 novel *Giovanni's Room*

James Baldwin worked as a preacher in Harlem as a young man before becoming a writer and moving to Paris in his early twenties. He wrote about his childhood growing up in poverty in his semi-autobiographical first novel, *Go Tell It on the Mountain* (1953). As an active member of the civil rights movement, the FBI held a dossier on him – which ran to over 1,800 pages.

17 OCTOBER

Alchemy and the Litmus Test

Any mention of those little strips of paper called litmus tests transports us instantly back to the school science lab – but where did that magic paper get its special powers from? The answer might surprise you. Acids and alkalis are measured on the pH (potential/power of hydrogen) scale, which runs from 0–6 for acids, 7 for neutral, to 8–14 for alkalis or bases. Lemons are 2, coffee is 5, water is 7, baking soda is 9 and bleach is 13. Litmus paper changes colour depending on the acidity of the solution it is touching: red litmus paper turns blue in alkaline mixtures and stays red in acidic ones, and vice versa for blue litmus paper. Purple means the mixture is close to neutral.

Litmus paper is a neat invention but it's not made from complex chemicals – it gets its mysterious properties from lichen. (In Old Norse, 'litmus' meant 'moss for dyeing'.) Its first recorded use was by the thirteenth-century Spanish doctor, theologian and alchemist Arnau de Vilanova. Arnau's claims to fame include predicting that the world would end and the Antichrist arrive in 1378, and being the alchemist 'Arnold of the Newe Toun' referred to by Chaucer in *The Canterbury Tales*. He may never have turned anything into gold and his timing was very definitely off, but his adoption of litmus paper used its transformation of colour to unlock the secrets of acidity.

18 OCTOBER

Hero Zero

It seems strange, but before 1200 CE Europeans did not use the number 0; they had no digit between 1 and –1. The mathematician Fibonacci **(see 29 March)** is thought to have introduced the concept of zero to Italy from his studies in North Africa, where it was familiar thanks to the work of earlier Indian, Babylonian and Sumerian mathematicians (who are thought to have started using it five thousand years ago). The same concept also developed independently in the Maya civilisation of Central America.

Our word 'zero' arrived via Italian, Latin and Arabic, from the Sanskrit word for a desert or empty place. Nowadays zero is considered essential to mathematics – both as a placeholder in the positional number system we use and as a way of representing the concept of nothing. It's possible to add, subtract and multiply by zero – but not divide. Trying to properly explain this fact has annoyed mathematicians for centuries but it does seem to remain true that you can't divide something by nothing.

19 OCTOBER

Golden Green: Autumn Leaves

Autumn gives us nature's most spectacular show as the trees blaze to fiery reds and golds.

Leaves are usually green because of the presence of the chemical chlorophyll in them, which turns light into energy for them. They are actually full of different-coloured pigments but the green of chlorophyll is so dominant that it masks other colours like carotene (yellow) and anthocyanins (red and pink). When the sunlight starts to fade and the days grow colder, chlorophyll breaks down and sends its energy to the tree's roots to keep it going over winter. This allows the leaves' other colours to start to show through. Dry and sunny days particularly encourage the production of anthocyanins, so we get redder leaves during autumns with that kind of weather.

FALL OR AUTUMN?

Back before the twelfth century, people in England tended to think of the year as divided into two seasons: summer and winter. Spring and autumn gradually came to be defined but originally were referred to as lent and harvest. In the seventeenth century, both 'autumn' and 'fall', referring to the falling of leaves at this time of year, gradually replaced 'harvest', just at the time of the British colonisation of America – leading to the two terms gaining different levels of currency on different sides of the Atlantic.

20 OCTOBER

Bits and Bobs

There are many wonderful and unique things about the parts of our bodies we normally keep hidden. Did you know that, for the majority of women, the left breast is larger than the right? We are also the only mammals who have breasts permanently – others just grow them for breastfeeding. It's also not widely known that not all balls are like human balls; some other mammals, like elephants, keep their testicles inside their bodies rather than hanging out. Interestingly, the word 'avocado' comes from the Aztec term for 'testicle', and 'orchid' comes from the Greek for the same.

CHECK YOURSELF

1. Take a good long feel of yourself to become familiar with what is normal for you. It is normal to have one breast larger than the other or one ball that hangs lower – you just need to be able to note any changes.
2. Balls: Roll them between your fingers and thumb to check for changes like lumps, heaviness, enlargement and hardness.
3. Breasts: Avoid picking the time around your period for this, when your breast texture can naturally change. Walk your fingertips in a spiral around your breast and armpit. Look for changes in your nipple, lumps, puckering, rashes or inflammation.
4. Anything out of the ordinary? Call your doctor. Most of the time it will be nothing serious but if it is breast or testicular cancer then catching it early makes it much easier to treat.

21 OCTOBER

Crack the Code

You may have noticed that certain messaging platforms on your phone reassure you that your messages are 'end-to-end encrypted' so that no one can hack them and see how bitchy you've been about Sandra's new haircut or copy the bank information you sent to your brother in the hope he'd pay you back eventually. But what does this mean, exactly?

In the olden days, people would write sensitive information in code and entrust it to couriers to deliver to the recipient, who had a key code to unscramble it. The original message is called the plaintext and the coded version is the ciphertext – the first is transformed into the second using an algorithm, or system. For example, the system used by Julius Caesar, now known as a Caesar cipher, is an offset or rotation cipher, where letters are changed into other letters a certain number of steps along the alphabet – e.g. if you have an offset of 3 then 'A' becomes 'D'. As technology improved so did the complexity of codes and codebreaking; you have probably heard of the Enigma machine the German army used during the Second World War and the successful efforts of British codebreakers at Bletchley Park to crack its code.

Nowadays ciphers work on blocks of information, which they scramble using complex mathematical formulae, called block ciphers. End-to-end encryption means that only the sender and recipient of the information can decode it – not even the operating company can. For example, Google can decode the information in your Gmail account if it wants, but Signal and WhatsApp can't decode your messages as they are end-to-end encrypted and the companies don't hold the relevant key.

22 OCTOBER

Practise Your Practice: Commonly Confused Words

- **Complement** and **compliment**: Complement means to add something positive whereas compliment means to praise. 'My mother complimented me on how well we complement one another.'
- **Practise** and **practice**: In British English, the verb is practise and the noun is practice. 'Go and do your dance practice, Jamie. If you don't practise you won't win the competition.'
- **Disinterested** and **uninterested**: Disinterested means unbiased and uninterested means not interested. 'Jamie seemed uninterested in whether the competition judges were disinterested or not.'
- **Historic** and **historical**: If something is historic it is famous and significant. If it's historical it is from the past. 'Jamie was sure his performance would be historic. It was inspired by the historical story of the USS *Indianapolis*.'
- **Imply** and **infer**: To imply something is to say it without saying it directly. To infer something is to understand something without it being directly said. 'Jamie inferred that his sister was implying his dance routine was rubbish.'
- **Affect** and **effect**: Affect means to alter something. The results of something being altered are the effect. 'Jamie was seriously affected by his sister's lack of support, with the effect that he became very nervous.'
- **Assure**, **ensure** and **insure**: To assure is to tell someone something is right or will happen, to ensure is to make sure something happens, and to insure is to take out an insurance policy on something. 'Jamie assured his mum that he had ensured his winner's trophy was insured.'

23 OCTOBER

A Most Divisive Vegetable

Who would have thought that a harmless bonsai-sized cabbage could produce such a visceral reaction in people, but it turns out there is genuine science behind whether we love or hate the Brussels sprout.

In 1931, a chemist called Arthur Fox accidentally released a cloud of phenylthiocarbamide (or PTC), and some of his lab-mates complained of a foul, bitter, terrible taste. Arthur, meanwhile, couldn't taste a thing. A true scientist, Fox decided to investigate why some people can taste PTC and others can't. He realised he could predict very accurately whether a person would or wouldn't be able to sense PTC by looking at how their family had reacted to it.

Soon afterwards, geneticists determined that the way we experience PTC is genetic, and in the 1930s and 1940s it was even used as a method of paternity testing. PTC isn't usually found in our human diet, but it is very similar to compounds found in sprouts and other brassicas, so really, in the end, maybe there is some accounting for taste.

24 OCTOBER

Brief Beauty

The life-affirming festival of Diwali, celebrated by Hindus, Sikhs and Jains, usually falls around late October or early November. For many it is associated with the Hindu goddess of prosperity, Lakshmi, and it marks the start of the Hindu new year. It is often known as the Festival of Lights because of the many oil lamps and candles that people bring out to celebrate the victory of light over darkness. The largest Diwali celebrations in the world outside of India take place in Leicester.

One of the ways in which people decorate their homes to celebrate Diwali and other festivals is with the beautiful folk art form known as rangoli. These are gorgeously coloured geometric patterns made of rice, flowers, spices, sand and other materials, arranged on tables or the floor, particularly in entrance halls, in order to welcome in good luck. Designs vary by region and are passed down through families, often from mother to daughter. Because the materials are often perishable and the pattern isn't fixed, the impermanence of the rangoli is part of its beauty and reflects the transitoriness of human life.

25 OCTOBER

Do You Have Free Will?

You chose to read this page just now, didn't you? You could have put the book down and called a friend, or run into the street and shouted out the names of the Beatles. You decided what to do of your own free will. Free will is something we tend to feel we have, but many philosophers believe it doesn't exist. Determinists instead posit that every action in the world depends on a previous action, and so everything we do is predetermined. Interestingly, the opposite of determinism, indeterminism, which is influenced by quantum physics and holds that some things are random, also precludes the idea of free will, because if something is random humans also have no control over it.

Compatibilists, on the other hand, have various ways of defining free will and determinism in order to reconcile them. One of the most famous statements used to illustrate compatibilism comes from the philosopher Arthur Schopenhauer: 'Der Mensch kann tun was er will; er kann aber nicht wollen was er will' – 'Man can do what he wills but he cannot will what he wills.' This means we have free will to do what we want, but what we want will be predetermined by, for example, our genes, our experiences and our environment.

These views have serious consequences for our sense of morality, because if there is no free will then why should criminals be punished for actions they ultimately had no control over, and why should others be celebrated for achievements and resilience when they only have these through a lucky coincidence of previous events? But also, you could choose not to worry about any of this, and go and stick the kettle on. Free will in action.

26 OCTOBER

Teeth Archaeology

Strontium is a metallic element that is found in seas and rivers and in rocks and soil, from where it is absorbed by plants. It is used to make red fireworks.

Strontium exists in four forms, known as isotopes, which are found in different quantities in different ages of rock and in the plants and sea creatures that live around that rock. Our tooth enamel takes in this strontium via our food and water. Scientists can analyse the type of strontium in a long-dead person's teeth to identify where they grew up. This can also be compared to strontium isotopes in their bones, which grow and change more over time, to show where someone lived later. For example, archaeologists investigating a burial of horses and dogs in Derbyshire in 2023 used isotope analysis to discover that several of them had grown up in Scandinavia rather than the UK, and therefore that they had probably been brought over by the Vikings who invaded Britain in 865 CE.

ISO-WHATS?

Atoms of every element contain a nucleus made of particles called neutrons and protons, which is surrounded by electrons. Isotopes are different forms of the same element with differing numbers of neutrons. The number of protons in an element (the atomic number) is fixed – an atom of carbon can't have seven instead of six protons or it would be an atom of nitrogen instead. However, the number of neutrons in an atom can vary. Atoms of hydrogen can have zero, one or two neutrons. These different forms of the hydrogen atom are called the isotopes of hydrogen.

27 OCTOBER

Fashion-Cores

Do you dress weirdcore, with lots of bright clashing colours and quirky elements? Or gothcore, in black with dark eye make-up? Or outdoorsy in practical gorpcore outfits? Or pretty, lacy and floral in a cottagecore aesthetic? Or even the aspirational, comfortable, older-women's fashion style of menocore? When did every fashion style turn into a -core?

The answer is 2014 with the arrival of normcore. This is now taken to be a style of fashion that embraces basics like T-shirts, fleeces and trainers in an aim to free us from fashion expectations by blending into the background. However, the term didn't originally refer to fashion at all.

Normcore was promoted by K-Hole, an art collective interested in the intersection between art and commerce who satirised marketing trend forecasting. They released reports in different media, including one in a 2013 exhibition at the Serpentine Gallery in London called 'Youth Mode: A Report on Freedom', which used the term 'normcore' to refer to a desirable attitude of fluidity of identity which required putting less effort into self-definition and instead encouraged adapting to whatever situation you're in: 'In Normcore, one does not pretend to be above the indignity of belonging.' The term was quickly adopted by cultural critics to refer to a relaxed and unshowy dress style, and it spawned all the other fashion -cores that came after it.

28 OCTOBER

Lorem Ipsum

If you've ever happened across a half-built website or looked at draft layouts for flyers or magazine articles, you will have seen that designers often use a chunk of seemingly Latin prose as a placeholder. It begins with the words 'Lorem ipsum'. But 'lorem' doesn't actually mean anything in Latin and 'ipsum' just means 'itself'. So where has this odd wording come from?

Ironically, given the words resemble Latin, the practice of using lines of nonsense to draft layouts is known as 'greeking', as in the famous phrase 'It's all Greek to me'. It's thought that the Lorem ipsum passage was first used sometime in the sixteenth century by a typesetter who took a page of Latin and scrambled it to make it less intelligible. The literate human eye naturally reads text, so for the purposes of assessing page design it's useful not to be distracted by real words. Amazingly it wasn't until the 1990s that it was revealed by Professor Richard McClintock to be based on a piece by Cicero. The first word originally read as 'dolorem', meaning pain, and the original section translates as:

'Nor again is there anyone who loves or pursues or desires to obtain pain of itself, because it is pain, but occasionally circumstances occur in which toil and pain can procure him some great pleasure. To take a trivial example, which of us ever undertakes laborious physical exercise, except to obtain some advantage from it?'

29 OCTOBER

The Knowledge

Since 1865, London's official cab drivers have had to pass an exam known as The Knowledge to gain their licences. They have to learn streets and landmarks within a six-mile radius of Charing Cross Station and it can take five years to learn all 320 routes and 20,000 landmarks. The Knowledge is considered the hardest taxi test in the world. Scientific studies have shown that taxi drivers with The Knowledge have larger hippocampi (a part of the brain that works with memory and spatial awareness) than most other people.

THE CAB

The predecessor of the current London black cab was the horse-drawn carriage. The cars that replaced them after 1947 are still known by the same official name – hackney carriages – perhaps taken from the name of the London Borough of Hackney, where people speculate that horses might have been kept. The word 'cab' is short for 'cabriolet', from the Latin for 'wild goat', 'capreolus', because the horse-drawn carriages were sprung and very bouncy.

Before public carriages, rich folk were transported round cities in sedan chairs carried by two 'chairmen'. Local lore has it that the several pubs in central London called The Blue Posts take their name from the blue posts that used to mark where you could pick up a sedan chair, like an old-fashioned taxi rank.

30 OCTOBER

Talk Like a Roman

In ancient times, being good at public speaking was a highly respected art known as oratory. It was crucial that politicians, generals and rulers were able to inspire and persuade their audiences. The art of persuasion – rhetoric – was extensively studied in the Roman Empire and politicians like Cicero were celebrated for their ability to win over a crowd. In fact, Cicero was so good that, when he fell out of favour and was condemned to death, his hands (which wrote his speeches) and his tongue (which spoke them) were cut off. Nowadays, if we're not teachers or lawyers, we're usually only called upon to give speeches at weddings and funerals, or in work presentations. But even hundreds of years later, and with no knowledge of PowerPoint, Cicero can still give us some useful tips on how to entrance a room full of people. The key skills to master are:

- **Inventio**: Coming up with your key ideas.
- **Dispositio**: Structuring your speech logically and convincingly.
- **Elocutio**: Composing your speech clearly and with style.
- **Memoria**: Memorising your speech.
- **Pronuntiatio**: Delivering your speech compellingly.

Keep it tight – people can't absorb too much complex information when listening. Keep your main points clear. When you're up there, stand tall, take up space and modulate your voice to give emphasis where it's needed. Practise. Use that nervous energy to give extra electricity to your performance.

31 OCTOBER

Vampires vs Werewolves: Who Would Win?

VAMPIRE ADVANTAGES

Can exsanguinate victims using sharp teeth
Come back from the dead unless staked through the heart
Clever
Can turn into bats

VAMPIRE DISADVANTAGES

Can't go out in sunlight
Scared of garlic and holy water
Only weapons are teeth
Prone to maudlin obsession with human love interests

WEREWOLF ADVANTAGES

Enormous physical strength
Can heal quickly
Enhanced sensory abilities of wolves
Huge sharp claws and jaws

WEREWOLF DISADVANTAGES

Only in powerful wolf form during full moons
Turning into a wolf looks harder than turning into a bat
Can be killed with silver weapons
Not very dextrous

In our assessment, despite the werewolf's impressive strength, the added assets of flying and being immortal mean the vampire would ultimately win a square fight between the two, so long as the werewolf didn't have any garlic or a distractingly pretty sad paramour to hand.

November

November

The vine leaves against the brick walls of my house,
Are rusty and broken.
Dead leaves gather under the pine-trees,
The brittle boughs of lilac-bushes
Sweep against the stars.
And I sit under a lamp
Trying to write down the emptiness of my heart.
Even the cat will not stay with me,
But prefers the rain
Under the meagre shelter of a cellar window.

Amy Lowell (1874–1925)

Late-starter Amy Lowell only embarked on her career as a poet in her thirties. Born into a wealthy and influential family, she became a mover and shaker on the early-twentieth-century literary scene, particularly as a founder of the imagist movement, which celebrated simple, clear imagery in poetry. She and the father of modernism, the highly controversial poet Ezra Pound, clashed via the medium of catty verse – she in a poem for him called 'Astigmatism', in which an old poet smashes up a load of lovely flowers; while he clapped back to her that she should rename imagism 'Amyism'.

2 NOVEMBER

The Ultimate Family Reunion

Mexico's Día de los Muertos – Day of the Dead – is a two-day holiday in which the living and the dead are joyfully reunited. Midnight on 1 November begins the Día de los Angelitos – where deceased children are honoured with altars decorated with sugar skulls and covered with sparkling lights – and the following day is Día de los Difuntos, where the offerings get a little more adult in theme, with mescal and tequila alongside the sweets. On the final day all of the dead are celebrated, and families often throw parties at the cemetery, reminiscing and zhuzhing up the plots.

If you are lucky enough to find yourself in Mexico during this joyous festival, you'll often see people dressed up as the iconic, gorgeous La Calavera Catrina – the skeleton Catrina. Related to the Aztec goddess Mictecacihuatl, the Lady of the Underworld, La Catrina was invented by artist José Guadalupe Posada in 1910, as a satirical portrait of a posh lady. Catrina, in her incredibly fancy get-up, was a democratising reminder from Posada that, in the end, everyone meets the same fate, regardless of status or wealth.

3 NOVEMBER

Billion-Dollar Boy

On World Manga Day we celebrate the icon who made manga a global phenomenon and a billion-dollar industry: Astro Boy, created by Osamu Tezuka in 1951 and launched as an anime series in 1963. Types of manga as an illustrated panel art form have existed in Japanese culture since as far back as 1200 CE: there are examples of highly illustrated scrolls depicting monkeys with early speech bubbles. But after the Second World War and the American occupation of Japan, Japanese artists, including 'Godfather of Manga' Tezuka, were inspired by Walt Disney films towards a particular aesthetic – it's easy to see where manga characters get their Bambi eyes from.

Astro Boy emerged at a time when the nation was attempting to heal itself after the horrors of Hiroshima and Nagasaki – the appeal of a cute little robot boy who used his nuclear powers for good was clear. When the anime version of Astro Boy was bought by the US network NBC in 1963, it became a huge hit, and for many Americans it would be their first brush with Japanese culture. Astro Boy was heavily influential on the world of manga and anime, which has continued to grow in worldwide popularity. Even today, 60% of Japanese people read at least one manga comic a week.

4 NOVEMBER

The Martyrs of Lewes

In Sussex, Bonfire Night comprises a whole season that stretches from September to November, and Lewes Bonfire Night is the biggest bonfire celebration in the world. It commemorates not only the Gunpowder Plot, which was rumbled on this date in 1605, but also the gruesome execution of the seventeen 'Lewes Martyrs', who were burned on pyres between 1555 and 1557, during 'Bloody Mary' (Queen Mary I)'s campaign of persecuting Protestants. Elaborate processions are hosted in the town, with bonfires and fireworks. Bonfire societies within the county of Sussex compete to create the most impressive displays of wild costumes and torchlit parades, with a strong focus on political satire. The town's population often swells to eighty thousand (from seventeen thousand) as visitors arrive to join the fun. It's a wonderful and bizarre evening.

HAPPY SAMHAIN

Our pyromaniacal passion for ritual autumnal burning may have its roots in the ancient pagan festival of Samhain. Over two thousand years ago our Celtic ancestors celebrated Samhain, which means 'summer's end', as the vibrant green of the nature around them transitioned to deathly brown. The Celts believed that this was the time when the membrane between the worlds of the living and the dead was at its thinnest. Ghosts needed to be appeased with huge fires and sacrifices of animals and crops (the word 'bonfire' was originally 'bone fire'), and tables were laid for spirits to come and dine with families in a 'dumb supper' (so named because these meals were silent).

5 NOVEMBER
Remember, Remember

In 1605, Guy Fawkes and his co-conspirators planned to blow up the Houses of Parliament, killing most of the aristocracy, the government and, crucially, King James I, who would be in attendance for the State Opening of Parliament. Their intention was to restore a Catholic king to the throne instead of Protestant James.

The men, led by Robert Catesby, met at the Dog and Duck pub on London's Strand and hatched the plan to rent a space under Parliament, fill it with gunpowder and firewood and burn the whole thing down. Fawkes, presumably because of his experience with gunpowder as a soldier, was chosen to light the fuse. But the gang wasn't leakproof, and after Lord Monteagle received an anonymous letter warning him not to attend the State Opening, the King was alerted and Guy was found looking shifty with fuses and a load of kindling. After some days of torture he confessed all and was sentenced to be hanged, drawn and quartered. Legend has it that, ever the contrarian, Guy Fawkes flung himself off the gallows and in fact died of a broken neck.

An Act of Parliament was passed in the following months which decreed that church attendance would be compulsory every 5 November, for special thanksgiving services for the safe escape of lucky King James, a traditional that has evolved into the rather more raucous burning of dummy guys and setting-off of fireworks. One other tradition which has been in place ever since that fateful night is the annual searching of the cellars of Westminster before every State Opening of Parliament.

6 NOVEMBER

'Here Comes Another Poor Boy'

New Orleans' iconic po'boy sandwich – stacked with fried chicken, roast beef, fish or even oysters, with tomatoes, lettuce and pickles, slathered in hot sauce, ketchup and mayo between two slices of French bread, oh là là! – was born from a 1929 streetcar strike. With 1,800 hungry workers out on the streets, Martin Brothers Restaurant, owned by two former streetcar drivers, vowed to feed them and so invented the huge and saliva-inducing sarnie. When strikers came to fetch them the brothers would call to each other, 'Here comes another poor boy!' and a legend was born. You can try making your own at home, but experts suggest the perfect po'boy can only be produced in New Orleans: its situation at just below sea level produces the right amount of humidity for a perfectly chewy loaf.

7 NOVEMBER
Bibliotherapy

There's joy to be found in escaping into different lands, and into the trials, tribulations, successes and struggles of a character between the pages. But there are some other, rather unexpected benefits to the literary habit.

- A study in 2016 found that reading books for half an hour each day could improve your life expectancy by two years.
- Using MRI scans, researchers have established that reading fictional books encourages empathy and acceptance of people from different backgrounds.
- Reading strengthens and expands vocabulary and communication skills.
- A 2009 study showed that reading reduced blood pressure and stress as much as yoga and humour.
- Studies have also shown that reading when older can help delay the cognitive decline associated with ageing.

8 NOVEMBER

Microwaving Mistake

It's weird how hot under the collar people get about microwaves. Despite their association with bad 1970s cooking, they are great for reheating 'fridge-cold' leftovers, and this, combined with their energy efficiency, makes them an eco-friendly choice. Some recent surveys suggest that microwave sales are on the up, and, love 'em or hate 'em, the history behind the ultimate convenience appliance is fascinating, based as it was on a random discovery.

As the USA geared up to enter the Second World War, a man named Percy Spencer was working on developing combat equipment that would help the Allies. Percy worked on the magnetron, a tube in which electrons move in a heated spiral pattern, emitting radiation that could be used in radar. He found a way to hugely boost its output so that US bombers were best equipped when they entered the war – he was even awarded a Distinguished Public Service Award for his breakthroughs.

He also inadvertently invented the microwave when he realised one day that, as he stood next to an active radar set, the chocolate bar in his pocket had melted. He tried it next on corn kernels, which began to pop, and an egg, which exploded. He filed a patent in 1946, for which he received the standard $2 from his company, who claimed his work. The first microwave was a beast – the size of a small car and pricey at around $5,000 (equivalent to around $68,000 in today's money. But in the 1950s they took off in a big way. Percy never received more than that $2.

9 NOVEMBER

Punch Drunk

Beloved of bottomless brunches, famed as the world's best hangover cure, the Bloody Mary was invented in Paris's infamous Harry's New York Bar in 1921. The bar, which had originally been located in Manhattan, was reassembled, piece by piece, in Rue Daunou when Prohibition came to the US, and it became an instant destination hangout with the great and the good, as it remains today. Famed barman Fernand Petiot invented the Bloody Mary there in response to Russians escaping the revolution and bringing their vodka with them. Fernand found vodka to be bland in taste – yes, really – and experimented with various extreme flavours to zing it up. Bloody Marys are great for hangovers because they're packed full of vitamins C and B, and they are also great for air travel because our taste buds are less sensitive at 30,000 feet, and the spice and umami of a good Bloody Mary cut through. For a Virgin Mary, hold the vodka.

BLOODY MARY

100ml vodka
500ml tomato juice
tablespoon of lemon juice
a few shakes of Worcestershire sauce and tabasco
(adjust depending on your love of spice)
a pinch of celery salt and black pepper

Pour the vodka and tomato juice into a large jug with ice then add the other ingredients. Mix well and serve with a celery stick in each glass. Real connoisseurs might grate a little fresh horseradish into their drink for an extra kick.

Serves two.

10 NOVEMBER

Finland's Favourite

Tove Jansson, Finland's most famous export, was the writer who created globally adored Moominland. Writing as Europe was about to enter the Second World War, Jansson – an ardent pacifist – declared she wanted to create a magical land, peopled with creatures who would connect to those children who felt unseen or sad. Inspired by the tiny island of Klovharun (population: two – Tove and her partner, Tuulikki Pietilä), Moominland has a peculiar pantheon of mythical creatures.

- The Moomins are friendly, upright, vaguely hippo-shaped folk. Jansson said she wanted everything about them to be soft, even their names, and it's true that the word has a gorgeous murmuration to it.
- The Groke represents loneliness: she casts cold around her wherever she goes and the other residents of Moominland fear her, though really she is simply looking for elusive friendship and warmth.
- Snufkin is an adventurer and wanderer, a deep-thinking, harmonica-playing anti-authoritarian. Most of the residents of Moominland love him, but he is enemies with . . .
- . . . the Hemulens, slightly obsessive, rule-following collectors of stamps and other things. They look a bit like Moomins but they are taller and less plump.
- The Fillyjonks get extremely anxious around states of disorder. Their homes are very tidy.
- The Hattifatteners are mysterious restless beings always questing towards the horizon.

According to Moomin Lore, these extraordinary animals used to live alongside humans in their houses but the advent of central heating disturbed them and they moved away.

11 NOVEMBER

Remember

Remember me when I am gone away,
  Gone far away into the silent land;
  When you can no more hold me by the hand,
Nor I half turn to go yet turning stay.
Remember me when no more day by day
  You tell me of our future that you plann'd:
  Only remember me; you understand
It will be late to counsel then or pray.
Yet if you should forget me for a while
  And afterwards remember, do not grieve:
  For if the darkness and corruption leave
  A vestige of the thoughts that once I had,
Better by far you should forget and smile
  Than that you should remember and be sad.

Christina Rossetti (1830–94)

At the eleventh hour on the eleventh day of the eleventh month, people across the globe stop to remember those who died fighting in the First World War. What better way to commemorate Armistice Day (from the Latin '-stitium', 'to come to a stand', combined with 'arma', 'weapons') than by reading Christina Rossetti's gorgeously poignant ode to grief, told from the perspective of the departed rather than of those left behind.

12 NOVEMBER

Blood-Sucker

There are three species of vampire bat that consume blood: the common, the white-winged and the hairy-legged. They are all small wisps of things – so light, delicate and fragile that often their victims don't know that they are there. Unlike any other bat, they can walk, hop and run, and have small thumbs that allow them to clutch onto their prey. They don't in fact suck the blood of the animals they hunt; rather, they make a small incision with their teeth and then lap at the blood that begins to flow. Their mouths secrete a protein, appropriately called draculin, which prevents the blood from coagulating. They have evolved to recognise the breathing patterns of the cows, pigs and sheep they feed on, so they can tell when the animals are asleep, and they sometimes even return night after night to the same beast.

These bats were given their vampire species name in 1810, before Bram Stoker's 1897 novel *Dracula* popularised the connection between blood-sucking monsters and bats. But vampire legends stretch back through ancient cultures: in Slavic mythology, vampires could transform into black dogs who would terrorise the living, and the Mayan bat god Camazotz was said to have been inspired by an ancient, extinct giant bat; he was the god of death, night and sacrifice.

13 NOVEMBER

Fear of Failure

kakorrhaphiophobia: an irrational fear of failure

'As she geared up to sit her driving test, Mathilda was suffering from an extreme case of kakorrhaphiophobia.'

From the Greek 'kakorrhaphia', meaning 'a devilishly clever plan', this fear of defeat is a common thread in most of us. Shakespeare even mentions it in *Measure for Measure* when Lucio speaks of our traitorous doubts which 'make us lose the good we oft might win/ By fearing to attempt.'

14 NOVEMBER

The Alphabet of Trees

Ogham is a mysterious and ancient Celtic alphabet which was used between the fifth and ninth centuries CE. It's written vertically, using a series of twenty letters grouped into four sets that look like branches, and so it also goes by the evocative name of the Alphabet of Trees. Roughly four hundred Ogham inscriptions in stone survive today, mainly in Ireland, the majority of which consist of names. Its origins and purposes remain murky, but according to some theories it was based on the Germanic runic alphabet, a pre-Latin alphabet that stems from the Phoenician language. One school of thought holds that it was a cryptic language designed to be indecipherable by Latin speakers, and therefore useful as a secret language for the Irish in defiance of the then-neighbouring Roman Empire in Britain. Another fun theory is that it was invented by druids as a form of ancient sign language, intended to be spelled out with one's hands. Legends say it was created by Ogma, a member of Tuatha Dé Danann, a tribe of supernatural beings in Irish mythology. It's said he carved the language onto wooden staves for magical uses. More prosaically, given that the majority of surviving inscriptions are names, it seems to have been used as a way of recording heritage, or for marking territory. Fittingly, it's read from bottom to top, as one would climb a tree.

15 NOVEMBER

Hair-Raising

The Movember movement, whereby men across the world stop shaving and start growing interesting facial hair during the month of November, was started by two Australian mates who, over a beer, mused on whether they could bring the moustache back into fashion. Inspired by their friend's mum who was fundraising as she battled breast cancer, they wrote an email entitled 'Are you man enough to be my man?' and sent it out into the ether. Thirty brave souls signed up in 2003. Since then, the campaign has spread across the world, and to date Movember has raised over USD $911 million for men's health issues such as prostate and testicular cancer and suicide prevention.

16 NOVEMBER

Love Bites

Marine biologists have never documented great white sharks in the act, though in 1997 a New Zealand fisherman claimed to have witnessed the deed. He described two sharks, belly to belly, rolling over and over slowly in the water. The male appeared to be biting the female to keep them locked together. A female's skin is thicker than a male's, and this behaviour might give us an evolutionary clue as to why.

Male great whites have two claspers (a bit like penises), at least one of which will be inserted into the female's cloaca. The fact that great whites don't become sexually mature until late in life, combined with their twelve-month-long gestation period and wide-ranging migratory patterns, means it's no wonder scientists have found it hard to observe their sex lives.

Great whites are ovoviviparous, which means they produce eggs but these hatch in the uterus and the mama shark gives birth to live young. A live birth has never been witnessed either, but scientists estimate that newborn great whites are between 3 and 5 feet long and that between two and ten young are born in a litter. Once a shark is born, it's on its own. There is very little research into survival rates of newborn great whites, but one paper puts it at 63% and another at 70–75%. Both of these percentages are high when compared to other fish.

Being born a great white may be lonely and involve rare, late-life bitey sex, but the chances are you'll live long enough to grow up, at which point, as an apex predator, your only risk will be from humans, and perhaps the odd orca trying to flip you over to eat your liver.

17 NOVEMBER

In the Midst of Winter

'In the midst of winter, I found there was, within me,
an invincible summer. And that makes me happy.
For it says that no matter how hard the world pushes
against me, within me, there's something stronger –
something better, pushing right back.'

Albert Camus (1913–60)

Existential French hero Albert Camus was a writer, journalist, absurdist philosopher and Nobel Prize-winner, and this quote from his essay 'Return to Tipasa' shows an unusually sunny side; generally he was more concerned with the meaning of existence. Camus held that life is without meaning, and our endless quest to find it is simply absurd.

18 NOVEMBER

Head to Tail

In every cell of your body you have magical ingredients that work with other cells to turbo-boost your body's chemical reactions. Enzymes are protein molecules that play a role in almost every function of the human body; think of them as your own internal rock-star chefs, mercurially orchestrating the rate at which every chemical process in your body occurs.

Let's follow the digestive journey of a Granny Smith apple as it makes its way from head to tail. Just the sight of that appley goodness can trigger the saliva reaction, where your mouth literally waters. Saliva is flooded with the enzyme amylase, which breaks down starch into sugars.

Through the oesophagus to the stomach the munched-up apple goes, and millions of cells in the walls of the stomach produce enzyme-rich digestive juices, which turn food into a liquid mixture called chyme. The chyme is then pushed into the small intestine (which is misnomered as it is in fact massive, and would stretch to around 7 metres if laid out). The liver and the pancreas are attached to the small intestine by ducts, through which more enzyme-heavy digestive juices pass to break the chyme down into simple chemicals that make their way into the bloodstream to be used as fuel for growth and movement.

Any substances that can't be broken down are dealt with in the large intestine, which doesn't produce enzymes; rather, it absorbs salts and fluids to turn the waste from liquid to solid, where it passes out of the body as . . . well, you know. This whole extraordinary process would be extremely laborious without the presence of enzymes, which can make digestive processes literally millions of times faster.

19 NOVEMBER

What Is an Indian Summer?

A true Indian summer is a period of warm weather that occurs in the northern hemisphere after the first frost has fallen. Why exactly is it called an Indian summer? No one really knows, but it was first recorded in *Letters from an American Farmer*, a 1782 work by the French-American soldier-turned-farmer J. Hector St John de Crèvecœur, which states: 'Then a severe frost succeeds which prepares it to receive the voluminous coat of snow which is soon to follow; though it is often preceded by a short interval of smoke and mildness, called the Indian Summer.' Some people theorise that the term developed at this time from interactions between European colonists and Native American populations whom the settlers witnessed harvesting in the more comfortable later months than at the height of summer. Whatever its origins, we love to bask in its mellow glow.

20 NOVEMBER

What Is a Three-Line Whip?

If you are told that in-person attendance at an hour-long global compliance report is a three-line whip, then it is very important that you attend, even though every bone in your body is screaming no. But why is it called a three-line whip?

In British politics, whips are Members of Parliament or the House of Lords whose job it is to organise their party's crucial legislative business, such as voting on bills. Every week they send a circular (imaginatively entitled 'The Whip') in which they highlight divisions – when members cast their votes on debates – and rank them in order of importance by the number of times they are underlined. If the division is underlined three times, then MPs really *must* attend. Hence, the three-line whip!

21 NOVEMBER

Unimaginable Inequality

Despite the fact that wealth inequality has actually decreased in recent years, the global wealth gap is still staggering: just 1% of the population possesses 45.8% of the world's wonga. And for the twenty-first century we have the new category of centibillionaires – those in possession of personal assets worth over $100 billion; there were fourteen of them in 2024, up from just one in 2020.

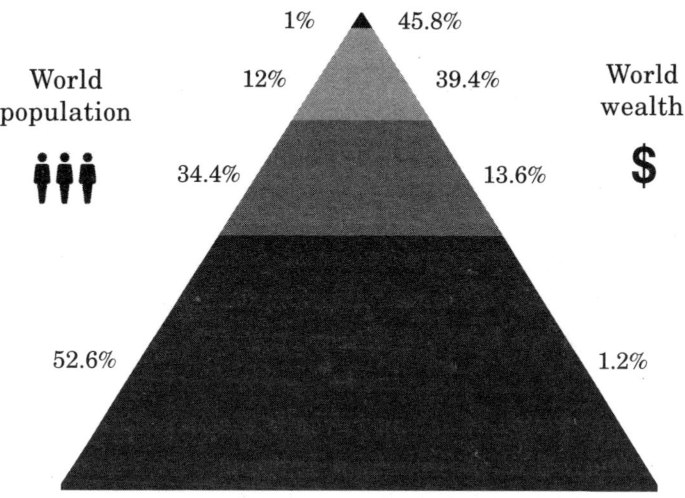

22 NOVEMBER

Who Shot JFK?

Everyone of a certain age knows where they were on 22 November 1963 when President John F. Kennedy was assassinated as he drove through Dallas in an open-top motorcade. Lone gunman Lee Harvey Oswald was arrested almost immediately and then murdered on live TV just two days later by night club owner Jack Ruby, apparently in retaliation. The death of Oswald left a world reeling with wild conspiracy theories.

- The 'grassy knoll' theory is that there was a second gunman who shot from a knoll at the side of the road, as well as Oswald, who shot from the Texas School Book Depository. In 1976, a government-appointed commission appeared to confirm this, saying there was 'probably' a second shooter.
- 'Umbrella Man' was a figure who came under suspicion for carrying a black umbrella on an entirely clear sunny day close to the assassination site. After being identified many years later, Louie Steven Witt claimed he had brought it as a heckling tool.
- Oswald had travelled to both Mexico and the Soviet Union so some suspect he was acting under orders from these foreign forces. Others even suggest the CIA and JFK's right-hand man and successor Lyndon B. Johnson knew about the plot and allowed it to happen anyway.
- JFK's brother Robert Kennedy, the attorney general, was attempting to prosecute Mafia members at the time of the assassination. Was this a very visible warning to stand down?

Despite the allure of these fanciful theories, the most recent consensus is that Lee Harvey Oswald was acting alone, likely motivated by political or personal grievances.

23 NOVEMBER

Hats Off

This month we celebrate World Hat Day and our European cousins' breathtakingly beautiful ways to cover one's bonce.

Chapeau!

24 NOVEMBER

Protecting Us from Collective Amnesia

It's a horrifying thought to imagine everything that was lost when the Library of Alexandria went up in flames in 391 CE **(see 30 June)**, when Benin City was burned in 1897, when the Four Courts in Dublin were shelled in 1922, when Leuven University Library was destroyed in both World Wars, when Florence flooded in 1966, when the National Museum of Iraq was looted in 2003, when Palmyra was bombed in 2015, when the National Museum of Brazil burned down in 2018, or when Paris's Notre-Dame Cathedral was engulfed in flames in 2019. In 1992, UNESCO – the arm of the United Nations concerned with promoting world peace through education, the arts, sciences and culture – launched its Memory of the World programme to safeguard the planet's cultural heritage. The register logs the world's most important artefacts, ranging from the *Magna Carta* to Brazilian biologist Bertha Lutz's legacy, to folk music and ancient languages, to Dorothy Wordsworth's diaries. Anything added to the register is selected for special preservation measures in whatever library or institution it is held, and the aim of the register is also to make these treasures accessible to all. In an age where our cultural output is probably at its greatest, but our ways of preserving our memories are less and less permanent, the Memory of the World is a noble vanguard fighting against the vicissitudes of time and human violence.

25 NOVEMBER

The Second Goal

Magical, mercurial Argentinian footballing genius Diego Maradona, the man with whom Pelé wished to play football in heaven, departed the world too early on this day in 2020. For a generation of English football fans, he will forever be demonised for his unbelievably sneaky 'hand of God' goal during the 1986 World Cup. But here we commemorate the goal he scored just four minutes later in the 2–1 victory that eliminated England from the tournament, which saw Maradona (in black shorts below) pick up the ball in his own half, waltz around five defending Lions who didn't stand a chance, then clinically finish off Peter Shilton in goal. It was voted FIFA's Goal of the Century in 2002 and for our money it will never be bettered.

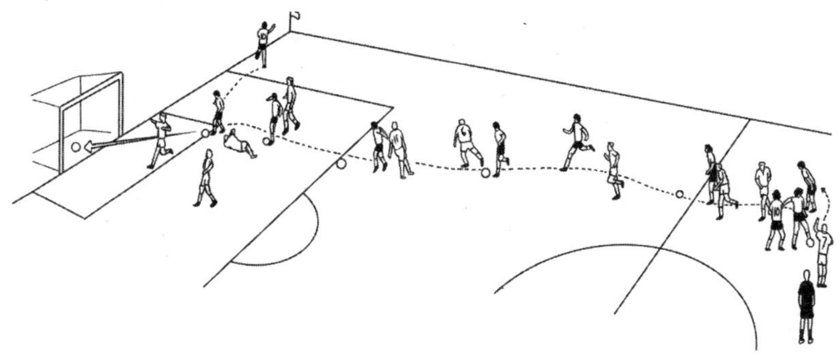

26 NOVEMBER

Cotton Picking

The most-used natural material for making clothes worldwide is cotton. Humans have been making cloth from the fluffy seed heads of this particular mallow plant – the delightfully named *Gossypium* – for thousands of years, but its popularity exploded with the invention of the cotton gin (not a cocktail but a machine invented by American Eli Whitney in 1793 to swiftly separate cotton fibres from their seeds). Cotton flowers bloom for just one day but it is the subsequent fluffy seed case, or boll, that is the secret to the plant's success. Cotton is so prized because its fibres grow in a twisted shape that makes it especially strong, flexible and breathable. Today, India is the largest producer of cotton and a staggering 2.5% of the world's agricultural land is used for growing it.

27 NOVEMBER

A Bearded History

The hirsute history of the beard is long and curly. Scientists believe that, in ancient times, cavemen used facial hair for both warmth and intimidation. If you are getting to the end of Movember now and that beard is causing you itch and trouble, here is a list of famous beards in history to keep you inspired.

- The tenth-century Holy Roman emperor Otto the Great had a legally binding beard, and would swear oaths upon it as he was uniting Germany and expanding his empire into Italy and Burgundy.

- Hans Langseth was a Norwegian American who began growing his beard when he was nineteen. It reached a resplendent 17 feet and 6 inches by the time of his death, aged eighty-one, in 1927. He still holds the Guinness World Record for the world's longest beard.

- Abraham Lincoln apparently began growing his whiskers after receiving a letter from an eleven-year-old girl who advised him to because his face was too thin.

- William Shakespeare clearly had strong views about beards. As Beatrice, one of his most beloved female characters, says in *Much Ado About Nothing*: 'He that hath a beard is more than a youth, and he that hath no beard is less than a man.'

- Erik the Red is the Norse explorer credited with founding the first European settlement in Greenland. He gained his nickname due to his flame-coloured hair and beard. The Norse Vikings took their facial hair extremely seriously – they were a signifier of warrior character, and calling someone 'beardless' was an incredible insult.

28 NOVEMBER

Angels in Peckham Rye

'The imagination is not a state: it is the human existence itself.'

'The man who never alters his opinion is like standing water, and breeds reptiles of the mind.'

William Blake (1757–1827)

England's most famous Romantic artist and poet was deeply influenced by his father's faith – Swedenborgianism, a cult sect of Christianity which rejects hard doctrines and celebrates spiritual insight and mysticism. William was home-schooled by his mother above his father's hosiery shop in London's Soho, and as a delicate boy who was inspired by nature he often took himself off on long perambulations south of the river. It was while stomping the green grasses of Peckham Rye as an eight-year-old that he had one of his most famous visions: 'A tree filled with angels, bright angelic wings bespangling every bough like stars.' In 2011 artist John Hartley planted an oak sapling on Peckham Rye in honour of Mr Blake, a tree he'd saved from an eroding piece of coastline as a symbol of our shifting margins of society. It was described as an invitation to future angels.

29 NOVEMBER

You Have Two Cows

Here is a fun way of explaining world ideologies through the medium of our favourite farmyard animal.

- **Socialism**: You have two cows. The government puts them in a shed with everyone else's cows, which you have to help look after. The government gives you a glass of milk.
- **Capitalism**: You have two cows. You sell one and buy a bull, your herd multiplies and you retire to live off the profits. *Or:* You have no cows. The bank will not lend you any money to buy any cows because you have no cows.
- **Feudalism**: You have two cows. Your master takes some of the milk.
- **Dictatorship**: You have two cows. The government takes them both and executes you.
- **British Capitalism**: You have two cows. Both are mad.

30 NOVEMBER

Latha Naomh Anndra sona dhuibh!

St Andrew is not in fact Scottish, but he is the reason that Scotland's famous Saltire flag – believed to be the oldest flag in Europe – got its cross. St Andrew was one of the twelve Apostles of Christ, the original gang who gave up everything to follow their guy and preach his wisdom. Andrew was a fisherman from Galilee, and the brother of Peter, one of the other Apostles. He travelled to Greece to spread the word and is believed to have been crucified there. His request on meeting his fate was that the cross he was to die on should be arranged diagonally, as he felt unworthy of dying as Jesus had. St Andrew is believed to have become the patron saint of Scotland when, during the Battle of Athelstaneford in 832 CE, King Angus and his army of Picts and Scots found themselves surrounded by Saxons. Angus saw a cloud formation of a white Saltire in the sky, and prayed to St Andrew, vowing that if he was victorious he would make him the patron saint of the land of the brave. Victory was his, the Saltire became Scotland's flag, and St Andrew its saint.

ST ANDREW OF BARBADOS

St Andrew is also the patron saint of Greece, Ukraine, Amalfi and Barbados. Barbados also gained independence from the UK on 30 November 1966, so it's a day of deep significance for the island.

December

1 DECEMBER

What Has Space Ever Done For Us?

Humankind's plan to explore space can sometimes seem like a huge waste of money (NASA's Mars rover *Perseverance* looks set to cost around $2.9 billion) but the great minds who have worked on the science and technology that allow us to visit the moon and other planets have made great strides for terrestrial life too. Inventions that have come about because of space research include:

1. Memory foam: This was invented in 1966 by NASA to help cushion pilots on spacecraft and is now used in mattresses, pillows, shoes and on wheelchairs.
2. Scratch-proof lenses: These were developed in the 1980s, when scientists were trying to make space helmets that wouldn't lose visibility when abraded by space dust.
3. Foil blankets: These insulating blankets that you see knackered people wrapped up in after running marathons are known as 'space blankets' and were developed by NASA in 1964 to help insulate spacecraft.
4. CT scans: The science behind CT scan and MRI machines, which can produce images of both hard and soft tissue in the human body for diagnostic medical purposes, was advanced by technology aimed at scanning the moon on the Apollo missions.
5. Dustbusters: Black & Decker were hired by NASA to create a cordless drill to collect moon dust, and they later developed it into a cordless vacuum cleaner.

2 DECEMBER

Those Who Wander

'Not all those who wander are lost.'

J. R. R. Tolkien (1892–1973), writer and professor of Anglo-Saxon, from his 1954 novel *The Fellowship of the Ring*

J. R. R. Tolkien is one of the most influential fantasy writers in Western literature. His high-fantasy novel cycle, *The Lord of the Rings*, has spawned hundreds of works of art, literature and gaming: almost anything with elves and orcs in it has been influenced by Tolkien. He himself drew from Norse and Anglo-Saxon stories to build his world of Middle Earth and its legends. He was a university teacher and wrote the first line of his famous novel *The Hobbit* on an exam paper he was marking. In his early drafts of *The Lord of the Rings*, Frodo was called Bingo.

IS YOUR FANTASY HIGH OR LOW?

High fantasy is set in a fully realised alternative supernatural world.

Low fantasy has supernatural elements but is set in our world.

3 DECEMBER

Queen of the Urban Jungle

Did you know that London is a forest? A UN definition states that anywhere that is comprised of at least 20% trees can be designated as such. London is at 21% with 8.4 million trees (one for almost every Londoner), so it can wear its forest badge with pride. We can give thanks for our green spaces to Octavia Hill, born on this day in 1838, whose extraordinary passion for social reform had its roots in the belief that access to nature boosted the well-being of all. As the great lady herself said: 'We all want quiet. We all want beauty. We all need space.'

Born one of nine children (no wonder she craved space and solitude) to radical parents bent on improving the lives of the poor, Octavia formed an early friendship with intellectual John Ruskin – it was money donated by him that allowed her to buy neglected buildings to fix for housing schemes. By 1874, Octavia had over three thousand tenancies around London. One of the three founders of the National Trust, she joined the Commons Preservation Society and successfully campaigned to keep Vauxhall Park, Parliament Hill and Hampstead Heath protected from development and enshrined as green spaces free for all to enjoy. So the next time you feel the need to exit the grind and escape to the park, remember our green goddess Octavia.

4 DECEMBER

Self-Defence

Your immune system defends your body against illness. A lot of the symptoms we associate with disease are actually signs that the immune system is doing its job. For example, inflammation happens because your immune system increases blood flow to get its fighting cells to the site of infection. The system is spread throughout your body and includes things like your skin, which forms a physical barrier against infections; your stomach acids, which kill lots of germs you accidentally eat; your white blood cells, which attack or eat pathogens; your gut bacteria, which fight off invading bacteria; and the excitingly named natural killer cells from your bone marrow, which fight off the body's own virally infected or cancerous cells.

You can't game such a complex system with one wonder-supplement: there are no scientifically proven ways to enhance it. However, keeping your general health tip-top naturally makes all of the body's systems more likely to work at their best.

PUT A COAT ON?

You are not likely to catch a cold from getting cold, whatever your mum might say. You are more likely to catch colds in winter because being inside more often puts you in closer proximity to other people and their germs.

5 DECEMBER

Krampusnacht

In Alpine regions in Central Europe, 5 December is called Krampusnacht, or Krampus's Night. But who is Krampus? He is now considered the demonic companion of St Nicholas (the OG Santa Claus), who traditionally delivers presents to good children on 6 December, but his origins stretch back to before Christianity.

Krampus tends to be depicted as a devil-faced, goat-legged creature who attacks naughty children with sticks. He is said to be the son of the Norse goddess of the underworld, Hel. In some towns in Bavaria and Austria (and, strangely enough, in Whitby in Yorkshire) people still carry out a Krampus run, or Krampuslauf, on this date, with men getting drunk, dressing up as the demon and running through the streets scaring children, which *does* sound fun. This is thought to be related to the old pagan festivities of Perchtenlaufen, which also still happen in some places, featuring a parade of people dressed up with wooden masks as both witch-like figures and beautiful women, representing the old Germanic winter goddess Perchta and her Krampus-like animal entourage.

Perchta was an Alpine goddess of rules and spinning and she visited villages in the winter months to reward people who had worked hard through the year and slit open the bellies of those who hadn't, to stuff them with straw. She is sometimes described as the leader of the Wild Hunt, which appears in folklore across Europe as a band of ghostly riders charging across the sky, heralding ill fortune. Happy Krampusnacht!

6 DECEMBER

Speculoos and Winter Spices

In the Netherlands, Belgium, Luxembourg, Hungary, Austria, Ukraine, Poland and some parts of France and Germany, today is celebrated as St Nicholas' Day. St Nicholas, or Santa Claus, delivers gifts on this day rather than on Christmas Day. In many of these countries, children leave their shoes, rather than stockings, by the chimney, and one of the treats they often find in them in the morning are little spiced biscuits known as speculoos or speculaas.

Speculoos are thought to have been invented in the Netherlands at least as far back as the seventeenth century, and today the most famous producer is the Belgian Lotus Biscoff manufacturer, which has been making them since 1932. Lotus consider the Belgian speculoos biscuit to be different from the original Dutch speculaas because of the caramelisation involved, which adds crispiness. These delicious treats are so important in Belgium that they have been added to Brussels's cultural heritage list.

Speculoos biscuits include a heady spice mix of cinnamon, cloves, coriander, ginger, cardamom and nutmeg. They were often cooked in wooden moulds which printed their design in reverse on the biscuit, hence their name, which is thought to come from the Latin for 'mirror'. The ubiquitous pumpkin spice flavour that spawned a million lattes is similar to the speculoos spice mix and includes cinnamon, nutmeg, ginger, cloves and allspice; it has been used in America in traditional Thanksgiving pumpkin pie recipes since the eighteenth century. As far back as medieval times these spices were recommended for warming the body during the colder months.

7 DECEMBER

Lock and Key

People have been using locks for at least four thousand years. The Romans are thought to have invented metal locks and keys as well as an important part of modern lock design: the ward. The ward is the system of notches that the specifically patterned key fits into so only one key can open it.

Joseph Bramah was a famous eighteenth-century locksmith who designed beautiful locks and promised a reward of 200 guineas to anyone who could pick one. It took sixty-seven years before someone claimed the prize, after working on the lock for fifty-one hours. The American locksmith Linus Yale is another big name in lock history thanks to his 1851 Infallible Bank Lock and his development of the cylinder lock. Yale locks are still in widespread use today. However, most insurance companies insist on homes having what they call five-lever mortise deadlocks. Mortise locks are enclosed in a metal case embedded in the door, which makes them strong and difficult to drill out, and their five-lever system makes them devilishly difficult to pick.

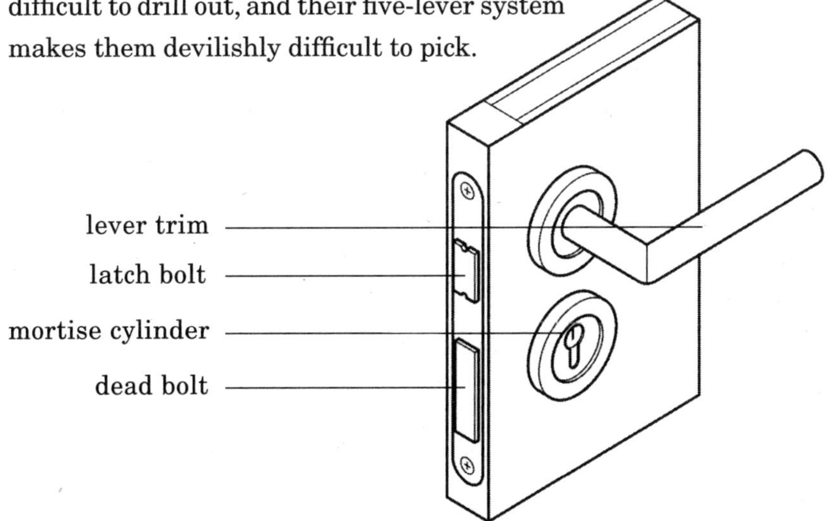

8 DECEMBER

Sourpuss

WHISKY SOUR

50ml alcoholic or non-alcoholic whisky
25ml lemon juice
1 tbsp sugar syrup
1 egg white
dash of Angostura bitters
ice
lemon slice

To make one whisky sour, shake together the ingredients, barring the lemon, in a shaker for one minute to mix and chill. Add fresh ice to a short glass and strain the cocktail over. Garnish with the lemon.

WHAT WHISK(E)Y?

Scotch: Made in Scotland, usually from malted barley, and aged for at least three years. It contains a minimum of 40% alcohol and is smokier than bourbon. If made from 100% malted barley it qualifies as single malt.

Bourbon: Made in the US, from corn mash, and aged in new charred-oak containers. It contains a minimum 40% alcohol – sweeter than Scotch.

Rye: Made in the US, from rye – spicier.

Irish: Made in Ireland from malted and unmalted barley, and aged for at least three years – smooth.

Japanese: Made in Japan, from different grains, and aged in wooden casks for at least three years.

Whisky is spelled with an additional 'e' in Ireland and the USA.

9 DECEMBER

Let the Victorians Train Your Brain

'Little vessels . . . ready to have imperial gallons of facts poured into them until they were full to the brim.' This is the quintessential Victorian attitude to school pupils and education exemplified by Charles Dickens's unimaginative teacher Thomas Gradgrind in the 1854 novel *Hard Times*. We now look back in scorn at an education system that simply asked for rote-learning as opposed to our modern emphasis on analysis and criticism. In a world of smartphones, what use is there for committing things to memory? Well, it turns out that memorising helps stimulate and exercise the brain, and in fact the knowledge you retain in this way adds to your internal repertoire of resources with which to respond to the world.

The Victorians, and their Georgian predecessors, loved learning poetry off by heart as a memory trick, and the famous poems of this era are often easy to memorise because of their drama, regular rhythm and rhyme schemes. It's unlikely you're ever going to need to recite a nineteenth-century poem to anyone but there is great satisfaction in being able to do so, and you gain a deeper appreciation for poetry and the poet's skill by focusing carefully on every word.

Here are some suggestions of satisfyingly easy ones to start with:

- 'Jabberwocky' – Lewis Carroll
- 'How Do I Love Thee?' – Elizabeth Barrett Browning
- 'Remember' – Christina Rossetti
- 'Break, Break, Break' – Alfred, Lord Tennyson
- 'The Destruction of Sennacherib' – Lord Byron

10 DECEMBER

Iron Man

Prehistory is the time before written records began and in Europe it is usually split up into three different ages based on the materials people used for tools: the Stone Age, stretching from around 3.3 million years ago to the Bronze Age (c. 3300–1200 BCE), which led into the Iron Age (c. 1200–550 BCE). This categorisation was invented in 1836 by a Danish archaeologist called Christian Jürgensen Thomsen, who noticed, while putting together an exhibition, that objects made of certain materials were grouped together chronologically.

Thomsen's definitions were inspired by classical writers' ideas of human moral decline through Gold, Silver, Bronze, Heroic and Iron Ages, which is also where we get the system of gold, silver and bronze medals. Gold is the most valuable because of its rarity, which is defined by how many kilograms can be expected to be found per billion kilograms of the earth's crust.

Gold: 4 parts per billion
Silver: 75 parts per billion
Tin: 2 parts per million
Iron: 5.6 parts per million
Copper: 50 parts per million

11 DECEMBER

The Twelve Facts of Christmas

'The Twelve Days of Christmas' describes an accumulating trove of 364 gifts that someone with access to a lot of poultry gives to their beloved between Christmas and 6 January:

- A partridge in a pear tree: Partridges lay the largest number of eggs of any wild bird – up to twenty.
- Two turtle doves: Named after their call of 'turr-turr-turr', these are the smallest British pigeons.
- Three French hens: Folklorists have theorised that 'French' here just means 'foreign'.
- Four calling birds: Some versions of the song refer to 'collie' birds, which is dialect for 'coal-black' and is thought to denote blackbirds.
- Five gold rings: People keen to stick to an avian gift set suggest this line refers to 'ring-necked pheasants' or 'goldfinches'.
- Six geese a-laying: Geese make good security guards as they have keen eyesight and honk loudly. They saved Rome from Gallic attack in 390 BCE.
- Seven swans a-swimming: Swans have about twenty-five thousand feathers on their bodies.
- Eight maids a-milking: Milkmaids were famously involved in the eradication of smallpox (see 17 July).
- Nine ladies dancing: No one knows exactly where the word 'lady' came from but it may have developed from the Old English word 'hlæfdige', meaning 'bread-kneader'.
- Ten lords a-leaping: The Old English word 'hlafweard' means 'person who guards the bread'.
- Eleven pipers piping: Bagpipes are not particularly Scottish and are thought to have come to Britain via the Romans. The emperor Nero liked playing them.
- Twelve drummers drumming: An hour of drumming can burn 400–600 calories.

12 DECEMBER

Dance Like Nobody's Watching

balter: to dance clumsily.

'The office Christmas party is the perfect opportunity for a bit of baltering.'

13 DECEMBER

Equality and Equity: What's the Difference?

Equality is the right of any individual, regardless of race, sex, gender and health, to be treated without discrimination. History can sometimes feel like a bleak roll-call of people being denied equality over the years: for example, women and black people being denied the vote in different countries at different times.

Equity is a method for achieving equality and refers to the provision of support to allow people to achieve equal outcomes. For example, wheelchair users have the right to vote but, if the polling stations don't have disabled access, they need extra support in terms of ramps and lifts in order to be able to enact this right. Many of our present cultural systems have been built on a history of inequality, so considering equity is important in making sure people really do have equal opportunities.

The difference between equity and equality is often brilliantly visually distilled in variations of an original diagram by Dr Craig Froehle, like the one below.

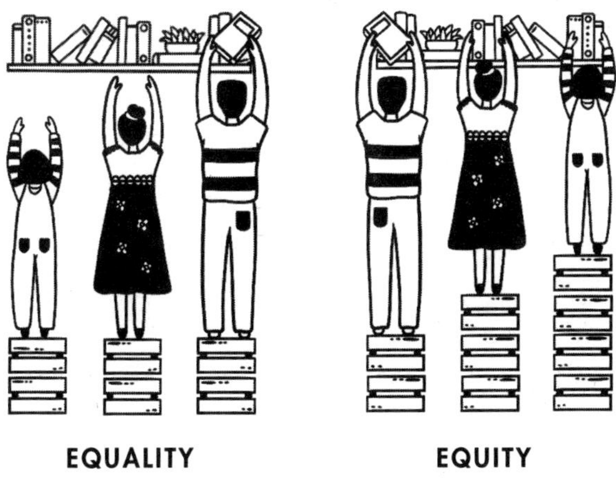

14 DECEMBER

Brevity Is the Soul of Wit

It's great to be well read but many of the canonical classics were written in a time when there were very few other sources of information or entertainment. In our world of streaming services we have plenty to distract us, so it's useful to know a few international classics worth your time that come in under the thirty-seven hours it takes on average to read the 1,440 pages of Leo Tolstoy's masterpiece, *War and Peace*.

- *One Day in the Life of Ivan Denisovich* by Aleksandr Solzhenitsyn: 144 pages
- *The Turn of the Screw* by Henry James: 128 pages
- *Animal Farm* by George Orwell: 144 pages
- *Of Mice and Men* by John Steinbeck: 128 pages
- *We Have Always Lived in the Castle* by Shirley Jackson: 176 pages
- *Orlando* by Virginia Woolf: 272 pages
- *Sula* by Toni Morrison: 208 pages
- *Candide* by Voltaire: 155 pages
- *Twelve Years a Slave* by Solomon Northup: 248 pages
- *The Art of War* by Sun Tzu: 110 pages
- *Things Fall Apart* by Chinua Achebe: 208 pages
- *Picnic at Hanging Rock* by Joan Lindsay: 208 pages
- *Like Water for Chocolate* by Laura Esquivel: 224 pages
- *No One Writes to the Colonel* by Gabriel García Márquez: 80 pages
- *The Birthday Boys* by Beryl Bainbridge: 192 pages

15 DECEMBER

Tom Smith's Cracking Christmas

In the 1840s master confectioner Tom Smith started to sell sweets wrapped in twists of paper in the style of French bonbons stuffed with little love messages. He developed these into the cracker form we know today and patented his snapping cracker in 1847, apparently inspired by the sound of logs crackling in a fire. It was comprised of two strips of paper pasted together, one with a rough edge and one painted with silver fulminate, which cracked when pulled apart.

Over time, Tom and his family added small toys and paper hats to the crackers and their company grew to have two thousand employees by the 1890s. The crackers were sold in beautifully decorated boxes and originally called 'cosaques', after Cossack soldiers, who were famous for firing their guns in the air. The company still operates today and since 1906 has supplied the British royal family with crackers.

16 DECEMBER

Who Invented the Christmas Tree?

The idea of Christmas greenery has its roots in oral tradition and it's hard to establish exactly where it came from. Records from the Middle Ages show that many churches used holly and ivy as symbols of eternal life. Further back, wreaths were used in ancient Rome in celebration of military prowess, and one can't picture Caesar without his lovely laurel (which, according to chronicler Suetonius, also served to hide his baldness). In Celtic tradition there are records of druids using mistletoe during first-century rituals.

But the rockstar of yuletide greenery is the Christmas tree. Queen Victoria's German husband, Prince Albert, is usually credited with making it fashionable festive decor in Britain. It was in fact Charlotte, the wife of George III, who imported the tradition to our shores in 1800, though she had a yew tree rather than a fir. One legend has it that Protestant reformer Martin Luther was the first person to put candles on fir trees, and Lutherans adopted this practice after him. As for the annual tradition of Norway sending an enormous Christmas tree to London's Trafalgar Square, we have James Bond's creator, Ian Fleming, to thank for that. The story goes that, during the Second World War, Fleming took a young Norwegian spy out on the tiles, including a slap-up meal at the Savoy. When they piled into jeeps at the end of the night, Fleming spotted two Christmas trees in the boot, one of which the young spy intended to give to his king (who was being given safe harbour by the British). Fleming persuaded him to place the other in Trafalgar Square, and, in true glamourous-spy style, they toasted their efforts under it that night by sharing a bottle of Norwegian aquavit.

17 DECEMBER

She Has So Much Rizz

Every year, clever-clogs and lexicographers at the Oxford University Press gather to select their Word of the Year. They nominate, debate and champion, and one word is eventually chosen to reflect the mood of the nation that year. Here is a snapshot of recent cultural history, through the medium of the words of the year:

2023: The delightful Gen Z word 'rizz' was this year's winner. A noun, probably derived from the word 'charisma', which is defined as charm, style, attractiveness and the ability to catch a romantic partner. You could use it thus: 'She has so much rizz, all she had to do was look at him.' The hashtag #rizz has nearly 6 billion views on TikTok.

2022: 'Goblin mode' won out as people on social media talked about rejecting social norms and expectations and made their own self-indulgent choices by going 'goblin mode'.

2021: 'Vax' was the unsurprising word of the year during the Covid pandemic.

2020: This year saw no single winner, again due to the unprecedented influence of the pandemic and other huge global news stories. Among the words of the year were 'impeachment', 'bushfire', 'furlough', 'coronavirus', 'lockdown', 'social distancing', 'key workers', 'Black Lives Matter', 'cancel culture', 'moonshot', 'superspreader' and 'net zero'.

2019: 'Climate emergency' was on people's minds, and other words around the environment shot up in usage.

18 DECEMBER

The Geological Name Game

The world has been around for a very, very long time (around 4.6 billion years) and so geologists and historians have cut up these millennia into different chunks to help orientate themselves. The geological time scale is based on stages in the development of the earth's rocks rather than set numbers of years. The biggest unit of time on this scale is the eon, of which there have been four since the birth of our planet. Eons are broken down into eras, which in turn are broken down into periods.

These periods were idiosyncratically named by various scientists from different countries as the study of geology developed. For example, the Cretaceous period was named by a Belgian geologist in 1822 to refer to the chalk beds that were laid down in Europe during that time ('creta' means 'chalk' in Latin); the Jurassic was named by a French geologist in 1829 after the Jura Mountains of France, where he noted distinct rock deposits; and the Silurian and Ordovician were named by British scientists after ancient British tribes (the Silures and Ordovices) who lived in the area where they made their discoveries about particular local geology.

DATE*	PERIOD
2.6	QUATERNARY
	NEOGENE
23	PALAEOGENE
66	CRETACEOUS
145	JURASSIC
201	TRIASSIC
252	PERMIAN
299	CARBONIFEROUS
359	DEVONIAN
419	SILURIAN
444	ORDOVICIAN
485	CAMBRIAN
541	

* millions of years BCE

19 DECEMBER

A Great Sacrifice

At the reconsecration of the Sixth Great Temple of Tenochtitlan, the ancient capital of the Aztec Empire, on this day in 1487, it's said that over four thousand prisoners of war were gruesomely sacrificed by priests to appease the gods. It was a central belief of Aztec culture that the gods had given themselves to sustain the universe, so humans should be sacrificed to repay the debt. The prisoners were taken to the top of a great flight of stairs on the famous pyramid temple, disembowelled, their still-beating hearts held aloft to show the crowds below.

Tenochtitlan was a magnificent city of over 400,000 people, which stands where Mexico City is today. According to legend, it was founded by the Mexica people under instructions from their god Huitzilopochtli, who told them to settle where they saw an eagle eating a snake on a cactus – you can see this scene depicted on the Mexican flag. Situated on the shores of Lake Texcoco, Tenochtitlan was a bit like watery wonder Venice, connected to the mainland by bridges and canals. It also hosted hundreds of 'chinampas', or 'floating gardens', agricultural land made in the lake from islands of woven reeds. Just thirty-four years after this show of religious devotion, the city was conquered by Spanish conquistador Hernán Cortés and his soldiers, aided by local enemies of the Aztecs, leading to the end of their great empire.

20 DECEMBER

Parental Advisory – Grimms' Fairy Tales

Brothers Jacob and Wilhelm Grimm, authors of the most successful children's book ever, didn't actually intend to write for a younger audience. They were scholars and linguists on a quest to preserve traditional German oral storytelling as an important cultural relic, and indeed their book is listed by UNESCO in its Memory of the World register **(see 24 November)**. In the original edition, their tales ranged from the fantastical to more brutal realist stories.

Opposed to the artifice of modern literature, the brothers felt their tales were a purer form of art, explaining: 'Wherever the tales still exist, they continue to live in such a way that nobody ponders whether they are good or bad, poetic or crude. People know them and love them because they have simply absorbed them in a habitual way. And they take pleasure in them without having any reason. This is exactly why the custom of storytelling is so marvellous.' But over the course of several editions published between 1812 and 1857, they excised some stories that were a stark reflection of the tough living conditions of the nineteenth century, such as 'The Children of Famine', in which a mother driven mad with hunger explains to her daughters that she intends to kill them and eat them. The tales we have today lean into innocence, magic and miracles more than the originals – so we no longer read the version in which Rapunzel found herself pregnant after the nightly visits of the prince.

21 DECEMBER

Radioactive Pages

Chemistry power couple Marie and Pierre Curie were on a mission to change the world. In December 1898 they were labouring away in their Paris laboratory. Marie had identified that pitchblende – a uranium-rich mineral – was much more radioactive than pure uranium, and thought that its highly radioactive nature must be due to undiscovered elements. The Curies worked to separate the substances and then traced the element. Earlier in the summer they had identified the element polonium and then on 21 December Pierre excitedly scribbled the word 'radium' in the pages of his notebook: another element had been found. The Curies' new method for isolating these elements was revolutionary for chemistry research, and radium would go on to be used as one of the first radiation treatments for cancer.

Pierre and Marie were scientific superstars and won the Nobel Prize for Physics in 1903, before Marie also won it for chemistry in 1911. Their daughter Irène won it with her own husband in 1935. Sadly Pierre was killed after being run over by a horse and cart in 1906 and Marie died in 1934 from the result of long-term exposure to radiation through her studies. The couple's papers – and even their cookbooks – are drenched with radioactivity and considered too dangerous to handle, so are stored in lead-lined boxes at France's Bibliothèque Nationale in Paris. Given that radium has a half-life of 1,600 years, that's where they'll remain for some time to come.

22 DECEMBER

Wondrous Winter Solstice

In the northern hemisphere, the winter solstice is the twenty-four-hour period with the fewest hours of daylight, when the tilt of the earth on its axis at 23.4 degrees means the sun is at its lowest in the sky.

Now, one could get depressed about the lack of sunlight, but there's a different approach to take, which is to celebrate being enwrapped in winter's deepest darkness, and to savour the moments of stillness as our side of the planet tips towards the light again. One of the discoveries about the Nazca lines – huge geoglyphs drawn in the Peruvian desert thousands of years ago – is that some of them point to the articular point where the sun rises during the winter solstice, and may have some astronomical purpose. But you don't need to be in the desert to celebrate: here's how you can do it at home. Light a yule log or candle to cast light and warmth on your surroundings – in ancient Scandinavia, fires were lit for luck and good fortune. Go for a wintry walk and pay attention to the world around you. Do some planning – now is a great time to look back at your year and think about what you want from the days ahead. Set the alarm and put aside time to find solace in a winter dawn.

23 DECEMBER

Chag Hanukkah Sameach!

The joyful Jewish holiday Hanukkah – also known as the Festival of Lights – commemorates a miracle that occurred on 25 December 165 BCE, when a rebel band of Jews, the Maccabees, reclaimed their temple from the ruler of the Greek Seleucid Empire (stretching from Thrace in Europe to India), Antiochus IV Epiphanes. Antiochus had outlawed Judaism, and set up an altar dedicated to Zeus at the sacred Second Temple in Jerusalem. It took the Maccabees some time, but after years of fighting with guile and cunning, this group of just a few thousand men was able to defeat the might of the Greek army. The reconsecration process required the menorah, or candelabra, in the temple to burn with specially blessed oil for eight days, but they only had one tiny vial of oil left when they lit it. Miraculously that little flask of oil powered the menorah for eight days, ensuring the temple's holiness was reinstated.

Today, Jews across the world celebrate Hanukkah over eight nights, lighting successive branches of a nine-branched menorah, gathering with friends and family to sing, give blessings, play games like dreidel (which involves a wooden spinning top), eating delicious food fried in oil, like potato latkes or doughnut-like sufganiyot, and exchanging 'Hanukkah gelt' – money in the form of chocolate, or real coins.

24 DECEMBER

How Does He Do It?

How on earth does Father Christmas deliver presents to the world's 700 million children? He would have to move at over 6 million miles per hour, carry around 300,000 tons of gifts, have a thousandth of a second at each address to park up, deliver, scoff his dram and his mince pie, and be off again, all the while wrangling a pack of flying reindeer. It just doesn't add up. But never fear – science is here to tell us how it can be done.

Einstein's theory of relativity maintains that if Father Christmas were travelling really fast, at the speed of light, space would actually contract and time would slow down, allowing him to complete his apparently impossible task. Vacuum energy can explain why reindeer don't need wings to fly and Santa may use repulsive energy to compensate for the force of gravity. Quantum entanglement – in which aspects of one particle of an entangled pair depend on aspects of the other particle, no matter how far apart they are or what lies between them **(see 4 February)** – could also explain how Claus manages to be in a gazillion places at once.

25 DECEMBER

Not So Merry Christmases

Not everyone feels suffused with holiday spirit at this time of year; for some, enforced fun times with our families can feel nerve-shreddingly difficult, and the pressure to spend and consume can simply make us feel quite sick. Our sensitive writers and artists have always shown us the more complicated sides of life, and here are some bad Christmases through literature to remind us we are not alone.

- In Emily Brontë's *Wuthering Heights*, Heathcliff's Christmas makeover does not go to plan when he takes offence and throws a tureen of hot apple sauce at his love rival.
- There is some very bad gifting going on in Stella Gibbons's *Cold Comfort Farm* when Flora gives Adam a mop.
- But at least it's something. The Marches bemoan their lack of festive joy from the very first line of Louisa May Alcott's *Little Women*: '"Christmas won't be Christmas without any presents," grumbled Jo, lying on the rug.'
- Anne Enright's *The Green Road* contains one of the greatest passages ever written about the madness of doing 'the big shop' on Christmas Eve. Constance manages to spend over €400, and even then she forgets the Brussels.

26 DECEMBER

Boxing Clever

There are so many customs associated with Boxing Day in the twenty-first century: think en-masse icy swims, huge queues for extremely ordinary sales, sporting events and, if you happen to live in Wigan, a city-wide fancy dress party, but why is it called Boxing Day?

Traditionally, the day after Christmas was the day on which servants, tradespeople and the poor were given gifts or money in boxes by their employers. The name may have originated in the Middle Ages, when church collections held in alms boxes were given out just after Christmas in celebration of St Stephen, the first Christian martyr. Stephen was given the task of looking after donations to the destitute in the early days of Christianity because of his trustworthy character. This is why, in the famous carol, the Bohemian Good King Wenceslas looks out 'on the feast of Stephen' and sets out through the snow to give money to the poor.

27 DECEMBER

A Very Sage Star

'Love for the joy of loving, and not for the offerings of someone else's heart.'

Marlene Dietrich (1901–92), actress and singer, possessor of considerable rizz

28 DECEMBER

Majestic Mari Lwyd

Picture the scene: the lights are twinkling on the trees, mulled wine is bubbling away on the stovetop and the opening credits of *Die Hard* have started rolling. It couldn't feel more festively cosy and snug, could it? Well, if you live in Wales, now's the time you might hear a knock at the door, which you would open to find a huge puppet, top-loaded with a horrific horse's skull, festooned in a cloak with streamers and ribbons, challenging you to an improvised verse-off. This is the Mari Lwyd – the Grey Mare – and revellers take her from house to house between Christmas Day and Twelfth Night, exchanging songs, stopping for a drink and bestowing luck for the coming year onto the households that welcome her in. Her origins are shrouded in mystery. Some link her to the nativity story, and the legend goes that she is the pregnant horse hoofed out of the stables when Mary arrived to have Jesus and who then spent days roaming the land to find somewhere to birth her foal.

29 DECEMBER

To Infinity and Beyond?

The concept of infinity is used very specifically in maths, where it is often represented by the lemniscate symbol (from the Latin for 'ribbon'), ∞, also called the 'lazy 8' because it looks like an eight having a lie-down. But philosophers and cosmologists have also been fascinated by the idea of infinity for centuries, particularly when ruminating over whether our own universe is infinite or not.

Our current telescopes and methods and devices of measurement do not allow us to see the end of the universe but they can tell that it's expanding. Because of the impossibility of observing it entirely, scientists are not agreed on whether the universe is infinite or not, and whether it might stretch out flat like an infinite sheet of paper or in fact be a sphere or a finite loop shape (a torus or doughnut) where you would eventually double back on yourself if you kept flying in your spaceship for long enough.

There is still so much we have to learn about the big dark universe out there – other scientists theorise that, even if our universe is finite, perhaps there are an infinite number of universes and we're living in just one version of the multiverse. If there really are an infinite number of universes, then in other ones the exact same conditions would have arisen as in ours and there would be other yous, in other universes, reading this sentence right now. Mind-blowing, right?

30 DECEMBER

Would You Hire Rasputin?

One of the most famous political advisors in history is Grigori Rasputin, a Russian mystic who exerted great power over the last Russian royal family, the Romanovs, because of his seeming ability to help with Prince Alexei's haemophilia. If the tsar had taken a full look at his CV before hiring him, perhaps he would have decided differently.

> **Name**: Grigori Yefimovich Novykh. Alias: 'Rasputin', meaning 'Debauched'.
>
> **DOB**: 22.01.1869
>
> **Place of Birth**: Pokrovskoye
>
> **Experience**: Khlysty (Flagellants) monastic sect since 1887
>
> **Skills**: Prediction, hypnotism and healing
>
> **Personal Statement**: I'm an extensively travelled family man, married since age nineteen. I believe in simple modesty of dress and appearance, so I take people pointing out the rotting food in my beard as a compliment. As a people person, I am lucky enough to be able to heal women through sexual intercourse, and others by more conventional spiritual means.

After the tsar's other advisors grew outraged by Rasputin's behaviour they poisoned him with cakes and wine loaded with cyanide, then had to shoot him several times and throw him in the frozen river. He finally succumbed on 30 December 1916.

31 DECEMBER

Balls, Bells and Grapes

Different cultures see new year in at different times but it is celebrated on 1 January by many across the world. The first people to see the new year live in Kirimati in Kiribati, next to the International Date Line. This is the arbitrary line on maps that marks where the new day begins. It's not straight and it wobbles quite dramatically to wrap around the island – on a boat in the sea around Kiribati you will be one day behind those on land. It used to run through the country, meaning people in the same community had weekends at different times, but in 1995 it was moved east.

As the new year dawns across the world, here are some of the ways it's celebrated.

Bells: In Buddhist temples in Japan, bells are rung 108 times in a ritual called Joya no Kane, to cast off the old; each chime represents an unhelpful earthly desire being dismissed.

Circles: In the Philippines circles are lucky for new year, so people wear polka dots and eat round fruits.

Grapes: In Spain it's traditional to eat twelve green grapes as the clock strikes to bring luck to every month of the upcoming year.

Balls: Thousands of visitors flock to Times Square in New York City to watch a big orb lower down a flagpole at midnight. 'Time balls' were originally invented in the nineteenth century to indicate the correct time, from a distance, to ships' captains.

Suitcases: In Colombia it's good luck to carry an empty suitcase with you on New Year's Eve to encourage new opportunities.

Acknowledgements

We feel very lucky to be published by the incredible team at Faber, and in particular our wise, endlessly creative and cheer-leading editor, the magnificent Laura Hassan. Kate Ward is an editorial/design titan. Huge thanks also to: Sara Cheraghlou, Sarah Stoll, SDA, Mallory Ladd & all of the sales team, Arabella Watkiss, Kish Rajani, Jeeshiu, Hannah Turner, Sophie Clarke, Silvia Crompton and Sarah Barlow.

To Oli and Jack – husbands of immense patience. We salute you. And to Iris, Joe, Barney, Lola, Leo and Jeanie, thanks for coming along for the ride. Thanks also to Louis Coates and Brixton Public Library where much of this book was written. Any errors are ours alone.

Further Reading

CROSSWORD ANSWERS FROM P.147

3 Across: Tip
4 Across: Diary
5 Across: Dim
6 Across: Mnemosyne
7 Across: Grave

1 Down: Elephant
2 Down: Hippocampus
5 Down: Deja

IMAGE CREDITS

JEESHIU

5, 10, 23, 44, 56, 59, 84–5, 88–9, 128, 166, 176, 178, 193–4, 201, 237, 259, 270, 274, 311, 319–20, 333, 357, 365, 367, 387, 398

SHUTTERSTOCK

3 (Topuria Design), 6 (Alexander_P), 8 (Pinchuk Oleksandra), 17 (Robert Adrian Hillman), 21 (Lucages), 30 (Viktoriia Protsak), 44 (ONYXprj), 51 (Nattle), 57 (Alhovik), 61 (Yesaulov Vadym), 64 (shopplaywood), 83 (Kolonko), 109 (Jimmylurii), 110 (Erbium888), 126 (song_mi), 141 (Dervik), 149 (Suwi19), 156 (Pyty), 161 (animus81), 209 (samina akter), 229 (Morkhatenok), 246 (NB-Art-NB), 283 (Zern Liew), 287 (963 Creation), 305 (aksol), 344 (MoreVector), 378 (Lemonade Serenade), 381 (Zern Liew), 393 (Zhenyakot)

ALAMY STOCK PHOTO

132 (Niday Picture Library), 185 (Carolyn Jenkins)

PUBLIC DOMAIN

20, 43, 103, 255, 267, 321, 389

TEXT CREDITS

'Harlem' by Langston Hughes reprinted by permission of Serpent's Tail publishers.

Fragment of Sappho poem translated by Tim Whitmarsh

'Independence is a heady draft' from *Mom and Me and Mom* by Maya Angelou, reproduced with permission of Little, Brown through PLSclear

Quotation from *An Autobiography* by Agatha Christie reprinted by permission of HarperCollins Publishers Ltd © 1977 Agatha Christie

© Noor Sufi

E. Foley and B. Coates are editors based in London. They are the bestselling authors of *Homework for Grown-Ups*, *Advanced Homework for Grown-Ups*, *Shakespeare for Grown-Ups* and the *Homework for Grown-Ups Quiz Book*, *What Would Boudicca Do?* and *You Goddess!* @FoleyCoates.